THE SPIRITUAL DIMENSION

The Spiritual Dimension offers a new model for the philosophy of religion, bringing together emotional and intellectual aspects of our human experience, and embracing practical as well as theoretical concerns. It shows how a religious worldview is best understood not as an isolated set of doctrines, but as intimately related to spiritual praxis and to the search for self-understanding and moral growth. It argues that the religious quest requires a certain emotional openness, but can be pursued without sacrificing our philosophical integrity. Touching on many important debates in contemporary philosophy and theology, but accessible to general readers, *The Spiritual Dimension* covers a range of central topics in the philosophy of religion, including scientific cosmology and the problem of evil; ethical theory and the objectivity of goodness; psychoanalytic thought, self-discovery and virtue; the multi-layered nature of religious discourse; and the relation between faith and evidence.

JOHN COTTINGHAM is Professor of Philosophy at the University of Reading. His many publications include *Western Philosophy: An Anthology* (Blackwell, 1996), *Philosophy and the Good Life* (Cambridge, 1998), and *On the Meaning of Life* (Routledge, 2003).

'Il Buon Pastore' (fifth century), mosaic in lunette of the Galla Placidia Mausoleum, Ravenna. Reproduced by permission of Longo Editore, Ravenna.

THE SPIRITUAL DIMENSION

Religion, Philosophy, and Human Value

JOHN COTTINGHAM

University of Reading

CAMBRIDGE
UNIVERSITY PRESS

CAMBRIDGE UNIVERSITY PRESS

Cambridge, New York, Melbourne, Madrid, Cape Town, Singapore, São Paulo

Cambridge University Press
The Edinburgh Building, Cambridge CB2 2RU, UK

Published in the United States of America by Cambridge University Press, New York

www.cambridge.org
Information on this title: www.cambridge.org/9780521604970

First published 2005
Reprinted 2006

Printed in the United Kingdom at the University Press, Cambridge

A catalogue record for this book is available from the British Library

Library of Congress Cataloguing in Publication data

ISBN-978-0-521-84377-5 hardback
ISBN-0-521-84377-4 hardback
ISBN-978-0-521-60497-0 paperback
ISBN-0-521-60497-4 paperback

Contents

Preface and acknowledgements

This book aims to engage not just philosophers but those from several other disciplines concerned with religion, including theology and religious studies, as well as that elusive figure the 'general reader'. But perhaps unavoidably, given the background of the writer, it remains a philosophical piece of work; and hence it may be helpful to begin with some brief remarks on the current state of philosophy, especially in relation to religion.

Since it is part of philosophy's *raison d'être* to be preoccupied with what is elsewhere taken for granted, it is no surprise that philosophers devote a lot of attention to reflecting on their own subject – what it is and what it should be. Anglophone philosophy is a far richer and more exciting discipline today than it was forty years ago, when it was largely preoccupied with conceptual analysis. That restricted conception of how to philosophize still has supporters, many producing first-class work, but philosophy has now diversified into a large array of methods and approaches, and, so far from being restricted to questions about 'what do you mean by the term X?', now encompasses a broad range of substantive issues including those concerned with truth, knowledge, justice, right action, consciousness, and rationality. Conceptual precision is still a paramount concern (and a good thing too); but it is now widely seen as a means to an end, not an end in itself.

So there seems little to be said for the judgement, still sometimes heard among contemporary cultural pundits, that analytic philosophy has run aground, stuck in the shallows of scholastic pedantry and the dissection of language. The ship is afloat, and sails a wide sea. Yet for all that, there remains a sense that the philosophical voyage has somehow become tamer, more predictable, than it used to be – more like joining a carefully planned cruise than venturing forth on the uncharted ocean. Humanity has always had a deep need to raise the kinds of 'ultimate' question to which the great religions have in the past tried to supply answers, and one might suppose that philosophy ought still to have some role to play here. It is disquieting therefore to find that a recent collection of state-of-the-art articles on 'The Future for Philosophy' has no room for a chapter concerned with religion, and indeed that it does not contain a single index entry under any of the headings 'God', 'religion', 'faith', or 'spiritual'. Can we really suppose that an accurate survey of the 'important agendas for philosophy's future'[1] has no need to include any reference to this hitherto central area of human thought and practice?

The future of philosophy will no doubt continue to include philosophy of religion, if only for institutional reasons – because it is an entrenched speciality within the philosophical academy. But there does seem to be a genuine possibility that religious thought and practice may increasingly become sidelined, either brusquely dismissed or politely ignored, in the work being done at the 'cutting edge' of philosophy, by those who are seen as shaping the 'mainstream' philosophical agenda. For that agenda is now largely dominated by what Brian Leiter has aptly identified as the 'naturalistic revolution which has swept anglophone philosophy over the last three decades' – a revolution inspired by the vision that philosophers should 'either . . . adopt and emulate the method of successful sciences, or . . . operate in tandem with the sciences, as their abstract and reflective branch.'[2] This scientistic vision is understandable, for there is ample cause to admire the magnificent edifice that is modern science, and few of us do not have reason to be grateful for the benefits, often including life-saving ones, that it has brought to our existence. But it is important to remember that there are vast swathes of human life where understanding and enrichment does not come through the methods of science; these include not just poetry, music, novels, theatre, and all the arts, but the entire domain of human emotions and human relationships as they are experienced in the inner life of each of us, and in our complex interactions with our fellows.

Religious thought and experience, though it partly connects with the realm of science, has very significant affinities with this other, more personal domain. So if it is not simply to ignore religion entirely, and not just religion but all these other vital areas of human experience, it seems crucial that philosophy should maintain the resources to explore the domain in question. And hence, to set against the 'naturalistic turn'

[1] B. Leiter (ed.), *The Future for Philosophy* (Oxford: Clarendon Press, 2004), Editor's Introduction, pp. 2–3.
[2] Leiter, *The Future for Philosophy*, pp. 2–3.

that has been so influential in the last three decades, it needs (not necessarily in hostility, but as a balance or counterweight)[3] to develop a 'humane turn'. Building on the work of some outstandingly insightful writers in the anglophone philosophical tradition,[4] it needs to address itself unashamedly to questions about human self-understanding and self-discovery that will never be understood via the methods and resources that typify the naturalistic turn. Philosophical thought about religion must not ignore science, but neither should it ape science; for, as Hamlet told Horatio, there are more things in heaven and earth than science dreams of.[5]

Philosophers ought never to be dogmatic, but should 'follow the argument where it leads'; so there is no guarantee in advance that the results of such a 'humane' turn will succeed in vindicating a religious view of life, or show it to provide the kinds of insight and enrichment that are found in the other more personal areas of our human experience just listed, let alone the even deeper kinds of transformative awareness to which religious reflection has traditionally aspired. But if such a hope is even to get off the ground, if the feasibility of a philosophical support for religion is even to be on the agenda, the adoption of a 'humane' approach to the subject seems an essential prerequisite.

Accordingly, and in furtherance of the hope just articulated, this book has as one of its aims the modest attempt to nudge the philosophy of religion just a little way further towards the genre of the 'humane'. The wider aims of the work will, I hope, emerge clearly as the argument develops. In inviting someone on a journey it is not always helpful to describe every turn of the route in advance; but I have tried to offer ample signposting along the way, and an overview of the exact terrain covered by the argument will be provided towards the end.[6] Essentially, the book is

---

[3] Despite this irenic note, it seems to me that there are certain dogmatic forms of naturalism that are open to serious philosophical challenge; see below, Ch. 6, §3.

[4] Among several who might be mentioned, Charles Taylor and Martha Nussbaum come to mind as paradigm cases; see especially Taylor, *Sources of the Self* (Cambridge: Cambridge University Press, 1989), and Nussbaum, *The Fragility of Goodness* (Cambridge: Cambridge University Press, 1986). By mentioning 'anglophone' writers who have particularly influenced my own approach, I do not mean to discount the importance of those from other traditions whose contributions to the understanding of religion have been very significant. Emmanuel Levinas is a prime example here; see his 'God and Philosophy' ['Dieu et la philosophie', 1975], transl. in G. Ward (ed.), *The Postmodern God: A Theological Reader* (Oxford: Blackwell, 1997), pp. 52ff. See also Ch. 7, n. 20, below.

[5] 'There are more things in heaven and earth, Horatio, than are dreamt of in your philosophy.' (William Shakespeare, *Hamlet* [c. 1600], I.v. 166–7.) In the early seventeenth century, 'philosophy' in this sort of context meant something rather closer to what we now call 'science'.

[6] At the start of Ch. 8.

an attempt at integration, at trying to show how a philosophical approach to religion needs to bring together the disparate areas of our human experience, emotional as well as intellectual, practical as well as theoretical, embracing the inner world of self-reflection as well as the outer world of empirical inquiry. Current attitudes to religion among philosophers are highly polarised, some impatient to see it buried, others insisting on its defensibility. But as long as the debate is conducted at the level of abstract argumentation alone, what is really important about our allegiance to, or rejection of, religion is likely to elude us. There is, to be sure, a cognitive core to religious belief, a central set of truth-claims to which the religious adherent is committed; but it can be extremely unproductive to try to evaluate these in isolation. There are rich and complex connections that link religious belief with ethical commitment and individual self-aware-ness, with the attempt to understand the cosmos and the struggle to find meaning in our lives; and only when these connections are revealed, only when we come to have a broader sense of the 'spiritual dimension' within which religion lives and moves, can we begin to see fully what is involved in accepting or rejecting a religious view of reality.

Having indicated something about strategy, let me add a brief word about tactics. The inquiry that follows may well, in its style and content, be too philosophical for some tastes, while at the same time being not philosophical enough for others; all I can plead is that I have earnestly endeavoured to strike an acceptable balance between rigour and readabil-ity. Since the subject-matter also encroaches on theological territory, some parts of the discussion may irritate theologians by over-simplifying, or by spelling out what is excessively familiar to them, while at the same time irking the philosophers by straying from time to time onto matters of faith or personal belief. But I firmly believe that attempts, however inept, to build bridges across these subject-boundaries are essential if our aca-demic culture is not to become even more damagingly fragmented than it already is. The barrier between 'academic' and 'general' readership also seems to me one that needs eroding, particularly when it comes to discussing something as central to human life as religious thought and practice; and for this reason I have tried to write as accessibly as possible, attempting to trim away the array of self-defensive qualifications and hedging that become almost second nature for anyone who has spent many hours in the seminar room. (Where there are important clarifica-tions and distinctions to be made, these have generally been relegated to footnotes, to avoid interrupting the flow.)

The book is based on the Stanton Lectures which I gave at the University of Cambridge in the Easter Terms of 2003 and 2004. Being invited to give a public lecture series of this kind is perhaps the perfect stimulus for producing a book, and I am most grateful to the Electors for the honour they did me in inviting me to give the lectures, and to the audience at Cambridge for the many helpful and invigorating comments and questions that were put to me in the discussion periods following the lectures themselves. I am also very grateful for the kindness and hospitality of the Cambridge Faculty of Divinity during my tenure as Stanton Lecturer, and in particular to Professor Denys Turner, not just for chairing the series, but for his warmth and generosity as my principal host; it is a great pleasure to recall the enjoyable evenings we spent in discussions that illuminated many of the issues covered in this book, as well as much else besides. It is also a pleasure to record my thanks to Mrs Rosalind Paul, the Faculty Administrator, for the kindness and seemingly effortless efficiency with which she dealt with everything to do with the organization of the lectures.

In various places in the book I have drawn on ideas from my previously published work: *On the Meaning of Life* (London: Routledge, 2003); ' "Our Natural Guide": Conscience, "Nature" and Moral Experience', in D. S. Oderberg and T. D. Chappell (eds.), *Human Values* (London: Palgrave, 2005), and 'Spirituality, Science and Morality', in D. Carr and J. Haldane (eds.), *Essays on Spirituality and Education* (London: Routledge, 2003). Earlier versions of some of the chapters or arguments in the book were presented at research seminars at the University of Reading, Rhodes University, Grahamstown, the University of Cape Town, Birkbeck College, London, Heythrop College, London, Trinity College, Dublin, and St John's College, Oxford, and I am most grateful for the helpful criticism and feedback received on those occasions. I have also been fortunate enough to benefit from discussions with many colleagues and friends, including Ward Jones, Eusebius Mckaisar, Andrew Moore, David Oderberg, Peter Hacker, Jim Stone, Philip Stratton-Lake, Samantha Vice, Francis Williamson, Mark Wynn, and many others. I should like to record my special thanks to Myra Cottingham, who read the complete final version and made many invaluable suggestions. I am also very grateful to an anonymous reader for Cambridge University Press for most helpful comments and suggestions on the initial typescript, to Rachel Baynes of Reading University Library, who kindly offered her help in tracing some of the references, and to Hilary Gaskin of Cambridge University Press, who has once again been a most supportive editor.

I should also like to express my gratitude to Barbara Richards and to Derek Joseph, to both of whom I owe a great deal.

Fruitful religious philosophizing is both like and unlike many other kinds of philosophy in so far as it employs rational argumentation but at the same time needs to appeal to more than that – it needs to open the heart as well as to illuminate the mind. For that reason, there are many pitfalls, for one may lose the sympathy of readers in many more ways than simply by failing to make the logic watertight. What is offered here is in no sense intended to be prescriptive or doctrinaire, but simply to reflect the continuing search that I hope at least some readers will be able to identify with – a search conducted in a spirit of intellectual inquiry, but whose motivations and goals go deeper. The book, like several of its predecessors, is dedicated to my immediate family, in love and gratitude.

CHAPTER I

Religion and spirituality: from praxis to belief

Glaube Du! Es schadet nicht. ('Believe! It won't hurt you.')
Ludwig Wittgenstein.[1]

Amor ipse notitia est. ('Love is itself knowledge.')
Gregory the Great.[2]

I FROM ANALYSIS TO EXERCISE

Bernard Williams, perhaps the most distinguished analytic moral philosopher writing at the turn of the twentieth century, once speculated that there might be something about ethical understanding that makes it inherently unsuited to be explored through the methods and techniques of analytic philosophy alone.[3] If that is true, the point may apply *a fortiori* to religion, in so far as religious attitudes, even more than moral ones, often seem to encompass elements that are resistant to logical analysis. Analytic philosophers spend a great deal of their time dealing with propositions and with valid inference from one proposition to another. But as Leszek Kolakowski has reminded us in a recent book

Religion is not a set of propositions, it is the realm of worship wherein understanding, knowledge, the feeling of participation in the ultimate reality and moral commitment [all] appear as a single act, whose subsequent segregation

Lindbeck

1 MS 128 [c. 1944], in *Culture and Value: A Selection from the Posthumous Remains* [*Vermischte Bemerkungen: Eine Auswahl aus dem Nachlaß*, 1994], ed. G. H. von Wright, transl. P. Winch (Oxford: Blackwell, rev. edn., 1998), p. 52.

2 Gregory the Great, *Homelia in Evangelium* 27.4 (*Patrologia Latina*, ed. J. Migne, 76, 1207); cited in Denys Turner, *The Darkness of God* (Cambridge: Cambridge University Press, 1995), p. 222.

3 In an interview on the philosophy of Nietzsche broadcast on the BBC World Service in 1993. The term 'analytic philosophy' is in some respects an unsatisfactory one, since there have been many changes in how the subject is practised since the days of 'conceptual analysis' (see Preface, above); the implied contrast with so-called 'continental' philosophy has also become increasingly problematic. Nevertheless, I shall use the term in this chapter as a convenient shorthand for a certain recognisable way of doing philosophy that remains prevalent in many parts of the anglophone philosophical world.

into separate classes of metaphysical, moral and other assertions might be useful but is bound to distort the sense of the original act of worship.[4]

This 'distortion' as Kolakowski terms it, is particularly apparent in academic philosophical discussions of religious issues. I have witnessed many intricate debates between theistic and atheistic protagonists in the philosophy of religion, but fascinating though these often are, I have seldom seen any of the participants give one inch of ground, as a result of the arguments advanced, let alone be moved by the arguments to modify or abandon their previous religious, or anti-religious, stance. One has a strange feeling that the intellectual analysis, however acute, does not capture what is at stake when someone gives, or refuses, their allegiance to a religious worldview. The focus is somehow wrong.

At first sight this might seem very odd. Isn't the fundamental test that separates theists from atheists how they would answer the question 'Do you or do you not accept the proposition that God exists?' So must not the primary focus always be on this proposition – its precise content and implications, the evidence for its truth, and so on? Well, perhaps not. The propositions are, of course, important (and by the end of this book I hope it will be clear that I am *not* defending the 'non-cognitivist' line that sees beliefs and truth-claims as irrelevant to religious allegiance). But if we want to understand the religious outlook (or its rejection), and if we want to engage in fruitful dialogue about this most crucial aspect of how we view the world, then always putting the primary and initial focus on the propositions may nonetheless be misguided. Jung's attitude seems to me to have been nearer the mark. He is widely and in my view rightly regarded as a strongly religious thinker, preoccupied with religious ideas and their central importance for a flourishing human life; yet he steadfastly refused to be drawn on the '*Do you or do you not . . .?*' question. 'When people say they believe in the existence of God,' he observed, 'it has never impressed me in the least.'[5] (I shall come back to Jung's own particular take on these matters in Chapter 4.)

The approach to be taken in this book is in no sense intended to be disparaging of the analytic tradition (a tradition in which I was myself raised): goals such as those of conceptual clarity and precise argumentation seem to me important elements of any fruitful philosophising.

---

4 Leszek Kolakowski, *Religion* (South Bend: St Augustine's Press, 2001), p. 165.

5 From a letter to H. L. Philp of 1956, in C. G. Jung, *Collected Works*, ed. H. Read et al. (London: Routledge, 1953–79), vol. XVIII, pp. 706–7. Quoted in M. Palmer, *Freud and Jung on Religion* (London: Routledge, 1977), p. 125.

Nevertheless, the *way* many contemporary academic philosophers go about their task – maintaining an astringently dry style modelled on legalistic or scientific prose, scrupulously avoiding literary or other potentially emotive allusions, trying not so much to persuade as to corner their opponent by doggedly closing off any possible escape routes – these techniques, even in the hands of the virtuoso practitioner, often seem somehow to miss the mark, or at least to need supplementing, when we are dealing with the phenomenon of religious allegiance and its significance.

To see why our philosophical discourse about religion may be in need of a certain supplementation or broadening if it is to engage us on more than a narrowly intellectual plane, it may help if we shift the emphasis slightly, moving from the domain of religion to the closely related, but distinct, domain of spirituality. The concept of spirituality is an interesting one, in so far as it does not seem to provoke, straight off, the kind of immediately polarised reaction one finds in the case of religion. This may be partly to do with the vagueness of the term – in popular contemporary usage the label 'spiritual' tends to be invoked by those purveying a heterogeneous range of products and services, from magic crystals, scented candles and astrology, to alternative medicine, tai chi, and meditation courses. Yet at the richer end of the spectrum, we find the term used in connection with activities and attitudes which command widespread appeal, irrespective of metaphysical commitment or doctrinal allegiance. Even the most convinced atheist may be prepared to avow an interest in the 'spiritual' dimension of human existence, if that dimension is taken to cover forms of life that put a premium on certain kinds of intensely focused moral and aesthetic response, or on the search for deeper reflective awareness of the meaning of our lives and of our relationship to others and to the natural world. In general, the label 'spiritual' seems to be used to refer to activities which aim to fill the creative and meditative space left over when science and technology have satisfied our material needs. So construed, both supporters and opponents of religion might agree that the loss of the spiritual dimension would leave our human existence radically impoverished.

There is, I think, a further reason for the widespread agreement on the value of the spiritual domain in this sense, despite the polarisation of outlooks when it comes to acceptance or rejection of religious or supernaturalist claims. Spirituality has long been understood to be a concept that is concerned in the first instance with activities rather than theories, with ways of living rather than doctrines subscribed to, with praxis rather than belief.

In the history of philosophy, the epithet 'spiritual' is most commonly coupled not with the term 'beliefs' but with the term 'exercises'. Perhaps the most famous exemplar is the sixteenth-century *Ejercicios espirituales* ('Spiritual Exercises', c. 1522–41) of St Ignatius Loyola. As its name implies, this is not a doctrinal treatise, nor even a book of sermons, but a structured set of exercises or practices; it is a practical course of activities for the retreatant, to be followed in a prescribed order, carefully divided into days and weeks. The nearest purely philosophical parallel is Descartes' *Meditations*, written over a hundred years later. But although the *Meditations* were perhaps intended by Descartes to be read one-a-day for six days (he had of course been educated by the Jesuits so would have been familiar with the Ignatian way of doing things), this feature of the Cartesian work is in one sense no more than a stylistic conceit: the validity (or otherwise) of the arguments, their persuasiveness and compelling force, float entirely free of any question about the time taken to read them, whether that be a whole term of study or a single day. In Ignatius, by contrast, we are dealing with a practical manual – a training manual – and the structured timings, the organized programmes of readings, contemplation, meditation, prayer, and reflection, interspersed with the daily rhythms of eating and sleeping, are absolutely central, indeed they are the essence of the thing. Ignatius himself opens the work by making an explicit parallel with physical training programmes: 'just as strolling, walking and running are exercises for the body, so "spiritual exercises" is the name given to every way of preparing and disposing one's soul to rid itself of disordered attachments.'[6]

Moving the focus back to a much earlier epoch than the Renaissance, Pierre Hadot, in his remarkable recent study of spiritual exercises in the ancient world, has repeatedly underlined what we might call the practical dimension of the spiritual.[7] There were many Stoic treatises entitled 'On Exercises', and the central notion of *askesis*, found for example in Epictetus, implied not so much 'asceticism' in the modern sense as a practical programme of training, concerned with the 'art of living'.[8] Fundamental to such programmes was learning the technique of *prosoche* – attention, a continuous vigilance and *presence* of the mind (a notion,

6 Ignatius Loyola (1491–1556), *Spiritual Exercises* [*Ejercicios espirituales*, c. 1525], Annotation I; transl. J. Munitz and P. Endean (Harmondsworth: Penguin, 1996), p. 283.

7 Pierre Hadot, *Philosophy as a Way of Life* (Cambridge, Mass.: Blackwell, 1995), ch. 3. Originally published as *Exercises spirituels et philosophie antique* (Paris: Etudes Augustiniennes, 1987).

8 Epictetus, *Discourses* [*Diatribae*, c. 100 CE], III, 12, 1–7; I, 4, 14ff; I, 15, 2. Cited in Hadot, *Philosophy as a Way of Life*, p. 110.

incidentally, that calls to mind certain Buddhist spiritual techniques).[9] Crucial also was the mastery of methods for the ordering of the passions – what has been called the therapy of desire.[10] The general aim of such programmes was not merely intellectual enlightenment, or the imparting of abstract theory, but a transformation of the whole person, including our patterns of emotional response. *Metanoia*, a fundamental conversion or change of heart, is the Greek term; in the Roman Stoic Seneca it appears as a 'shift in one's mentality' (*translatio animi*) or a 'changing' (*mutatio*) of the self. 'I feel, my dear Lucilius', says Seneca, 'that I am being not only reformed but transformed (*non tantum emendari sed transfigurari*).'[11]

This envisaged process of internal transformation, in contrast to the intellectual business of evaluating propositions, seems to me fundamental to understanding not just the nature of spirituality, but also that of religion in general. What holds good for any plausible account of the tradition of spiritual exercises also holds good more generally for any true understanding of the place of religion in human life: we have to acknowledge what might be called the *primacy of praxis*, the vital importance that is placed on the individual's embarking on a path of practical self-transformation, rather than (say) simply engaging in intellectual debate or philosophical analysis. This explains, I think, that strange sense of distortion, of wrong focus, which one has when confronted with many of the classic debates on philosophy of religion in the academic literature – the sense that despite the grandeur and apparent centrality of the issues raised, they do not capture what is at the heart of the religious enterprise.

Yet in case you should think I am suggesting that the philosopher should therefore leave the stage when religion is the subject of discussion, I should hasten to add what may seem a paradox: that this thesis, the thesis of the primacy of praxis in religion, is one that is itself perfectly susceptible of being examined and supported by philosophical argument. And that is what I shall attempt for the remainder of this opening chapter.

2 WHY PRAXIS MUST COME FIRST

To begin with, we should observe that the notion of the primacy, or priority, of praxis is ambiguous. The claim might be simply one of causal or temporal priority – that practical involvement in organized religious

---

9 *Discourses*, IV, 12, 1–21; cf. Hadot, *Philosophy as a Way of Life*, p. 84.
10 Cf. M. Nussbaum (ed.), *The Poetics of Therapy*, Apeiron 23:4 (December 1990).
11 Seneca, *Epistulae morales* [64 CE], VI, 1.

observance generally, in the lives of most individuals, comes at an earlier stage than the theoretical evaluation of doctrines. That seems uncontroversial enough: to quote Kolakowski again, 'people are [typically] initiated into the understanding of a religious language and into worship through participation in the life of a religious community, rather than through rational persuasion.'[12] But I want to suggest something rather stronger than this, namely that it is in the very nature of religious understanding that it characteristically stems from practical involvement rather than from intellectual analysis.

The philosopher Blaise Pascal was a striking advocate of this line of thought. His famous *nuit de feu* or 'night of fire' on 23 November 1654 – the intense religious experience that led to a radical change in his life – generated in him what he describes as feelings of 'heartfelt certainty, peace and joy'. But the God who is the source of these feelings is 'the God of Abraham, Isaac and Jacob', not the God of 'philosophers and scholars'.[13] Commentators have discussed the exact import of these words, but the general point is clear enough: faith, for Pascal, must arise in the context of a living tradition of practical religious observance, rather than from debate and analysis in the seminar room. This is consistent with Pascal's general philosophical stance on the epistemic status of religious claims, which may be described as proto-Kantian: questions about the nature and existence of God are beyond the reach of discursive reason. 'If there is a God,' says Pascal, 'he is infinitely beyond our comprehension . . . and hence we are incapable of knowing either what he is or whether he is'.[14] And since reason cannot settle the matter, we have to make a practical choice, a choice on which our ultimate happiness depends.

Mention of Pascal always conjures up the spectre of his famous (or infamous) 'wager': If God exists, the religious believer can look forward to 'an infinity of happy life'; if there is no God, then nothing has been sacrificed by becoming a believer ('what have you got to lose?' asks Pascal). The upshot is that 'wagering' on the existence of God is a 'sure thing' – a safe bet. Stated thus baldly, the idea of the wager is unlikely to arouse much enthusiasm from either theists or atheists; Voltaire (who was perhaps a bit of both) condemned the introduction of a game of loss and gain as 'indecent and puerile, ill fitting the gravity of the subject.'[15] The

12 Kolakowski, *Religion*, p. 172.
13 Blaise Pascal, *Pensées* [1670], ed. L. Lafuma (Paris: Seuil, 1962), no. 913.
14 *Pensées*, ed. Lafuma, no. 418.
15 *Lettres philosophiques* [1733]. Quoted in Ward Jones, 'Religious Conversion, Self-Deception and Pascal's Wager', *Journal of the History of Philosophy* 36:2 (April 1998), p. 172.

idea of eternal life as an inducement for the believer appears to involve a 'carrot and stick' approach, which fails to respect the autonomy of the human subject – and so it may confirm the suspicions of the critics of religion that allegiance to a superior divine power comes at the cost of radical heteronomy, a loss of our human dignity and independence (I shall be tackling this issue in Chapter 3). But the supporters of religion may be also dissatisfied with the wager, in so far as it seems to misunderstand the nature of salvation: on any plausible understanding of the goodness of God, He cannot be supposed to bribe or threaten human beings with happiness or damnation. Standard Christian doctrine makes it clear, instead, that salvation is offered as the 'free gift of God' (in St Paul's phrase);[16] and that in any case, properly understood, it involves no mere affirmation or placing of a bet, but a radical moral transformation – or, in the image of St John's gospel, a new birth.[17]

Yet Pascal's position is in fact much more subtle than may at first appear. In the first place, though his wager discussion is often called 'the pragmatic argument', he is emphatically not offering an argument for the existence of God (as already noted, he regards the question of the divine existence as outside the realm of rationally accessible knowledge). In the second place, and very importantly, he is not offering an argument designed to produce *immediate* assent or faith in the claims of religion; in this sense, the image of placing a bet, an instantaneous act of putting down the chips, is misleading. Rather, he envisages faith as the *destination* – one to be reached by means of a long road of religious praxis; considerations about happiness are simply introduced as a motive for embarking on that journey.[18] And thirdly and finally, the rewards invoked are not simply those of the next world (though that is, of course, how the wager is initially presented), but instead emerge by the end of his discussion as signal benefits related to this present life.

It is here that the thought of Pascal links up with the ancient tradition of spiritual praxis referred to earlier. The 'therapies for the soul' described in the old systems of Hellenistic philosophy offered to their adherents (to quote again from Pierre Hadot) an instruction not in 'abstract theory', but in the 'art of living'. What was envisaged is

---

16 Romans 6:23.
17 John 3:3 (Jesus to Nicodemus).
18 'Your desired destination is faith but you do not yet know the road.' *Pensées*, no. 418 See further, Ward Jones, 'Religious Conversion'.

not merely on the cognitive level, but on that of the self and of being . . . a progress which causes us to *be* more fully, and makes us better . . . a conversion which raises the individual from an inauthentic condition of life, darkened by unconsciousness and harassed by worry, to . . . inner peace and freedom . . . One was to renounce the false values of wealth, honors, and pleasure, and turn towards the true values of virtue, contemplation, a simple life-style, and the simple happiness of existing.[19]

Similarly, the benefits that Pascal stresses at the culmination of his argument involve precisely such progress in virtue and growth towards contentment. 'What harm will come to you if you make this choice?', he asks. You will renounce the 'tainted pleasures' of 'glory' and 'luxury', but instead 'you will be faithful, honest, humble, grateful, a doer of good works, a good friend, sincere and true.'[20] The carrot here is not so much carrot pie in the sky as the goal of beneficial internal transformation which is the aim of any sound system of spiritual praxis; you have much to gain, says Pascal, and little to lose.

3 THE HEART HAS ITS REASONS

Locating Pascal's advocacy of religious commitment within the ancient tradition of systems of spiritual exercises may go some way towards illuminating the idea of the primacy of praxis, but it still leaves many questions unanswered. There seems no doubt that Pascal, as a devout Christian believer, strongly maintained the *truth* of those claims which his own spiritual journey had led him to accept. Yet if truth-claims are involved, it may be objected, then the emphasis on praxis is highly suspect. For religious praxis, on Pascal's own account, involves a progressive transformation of our emotional attitudes: he explicitly advocates measures for the softening or taming (*abêtir*) of the responses of the aspiring believer.[21] In a typical spiritual exercise, stubborn resistance will

---

19 Hadot, *Philosophy as a Way of Life*, p. 83 and p.104 (cross-referring to Epictetus, *Discourses*, I, 15, 2.)
20 *Pensées*, no. 418.
21 'You want to cure yourself of unbelief, and you ask for remedies: learn from those who were hampered like you and who now wager all they possess. These are people who know the road you would like to follow; they are cured of the malady for which you seek a cure; so follow them and begin as they did – *by acting as if they believed*, by taking holy water, having masses said, and so on. In the natural course of events this in itself will make you believe, this will train you.' Pascal, *Pensées*, no. 418, translated in J. Cottingham (ed.), *Western Philosophy* (Oxford: Blackwell, 1996), pt. V, §6. The connotations of the term *abêtir*, etymologically connected with the training or taming of an animal or beast (*bête*) may initially seem to be particularly disturbing. But see further J. Cottingham *On the Meaning of Life* (London: Routledge, 2003), pp. 92ff.

gradually, or perhaps suddenly and spectacularly, be overcome by a capitulation of will, a flood of remorse, an overwhelming sense of submission, a rush of exaltation, or any of the many heightened emotional states described in the prolific annals of conversion experiences. Pascal himself speaks in the record of his night of fire, on a parchment found sewn into his clothing on his death, of his 'joy, joy, joy, tears of joy'. The poet Rilke in his *Duino Elegies* offers a more extended expression of the same emotional dynamic in an ecstatic prayer that his passionate weeping may sound forth a note of radiant affirmation:

> *Daß von den klargeschlagenen Hämmern des Herzens*
> *keiner versage an weichen, zweifelnden oder*
> *reißenden Saiten.*
> That not one key of the clear struck chords of my heart
> may send out a faint or doubtful note from its strings.[22]

All scepticism or lingering restraint is to be cast aside.

But now (to come to the objection) how can such heightened emotional states be compatible with the judicious evaluation of truth claims? If spiritual praxis precedes intellectual assessment, is there not a serious danger that the former will by its very nature obstruct the latter? At best, it seems possible that it may be a distraction from the process of understanding and evaluating the truth-claims in question; at worst, that it may risk becoming a kind of brainwashing, a softening up process, which leads the devotee to abandon critical rationality in favour of an adoring acquiescence, irrespective of evidence. Like Winston Smith, in Orwell's *Nineteen Eighty-Four*, our course of praxis may end up making us see five fingers when only four are displayed:

He gazed up at the enormous face. Forty years it had taken him to learn what kind of smile was hidden beneath the dark moustache. O cruel, needless misunderstanding! O stubborn, self-willed exile from the loving breast! Two gin-scented tears trickled down the sides of his nose . . .[T]he struggle was finished. He had won the victory over himself. He loved Big Brother.[23]

The worry here is a disturbing one, and it must I think apply to any approach that seems to retreat from a strictly cognitivist account of religious truth, or which appears (as here) to suggest that the route to that truth is anything other than detached rational evaluation. Yet I think

---

22 Rainer Maria Rilke, *Duineser Elegien* [1922], X (transl. J. C.). There is a German text with English translation in J. B. Leishman and S. Spender (eds.), *Rainer Maria Rilke: Duino Elegies* (London: Hogarth Press, 1939; 4th edn. 1968).
23 George Orwell, *Nineteen Eighty-Four* (London: Secker and Warburg, 1949), final paragraph.

the materials for answering the worry, at least in part, may be drawn from
an illuminating exploration, provided by Martha Nussbaum, in a very
different context, of the vital role played by the emotions in human
understanding; in effect, this amounts to a radical critique of the traditional rigid dichotomy between the supposedly antithetical faculties of
reason and the passions. In her justly admired paper 'Love's Knowledge',
Nussbaum deploys an example from Marcel Proust's *A la recherche du
temps perdu*. The hero has just carefully and judiciously examined his
feelings in the most meticulous way, and come to the reasoned conclusion
that he no longer cares for Albertine. But then the housekeeper Françoise
brings him the news that Albertine has left town – just at the moment he
has convinced himself completely and with utter assurance that he no
longer loves her. An immediate, acute, and overwhelming sense of anguish tells him – he was wrong. The authorial voice muses:

> I had been mistaken in thinking that I could see clearly into my own heart. A
> *knowledge* which the shrewdest perceptions of the mind would not have given
> me, had now been brought to me, hard, glittering, strange, like crystallised salt,
> by the abrupt reaction of pain.[24]

Nussbaum uses this striking episode to cast general doubt on a view of
knowledge which has powerful roots in our philosophical tradition.
According to this view, knowledge (for example about oneself, whether
one loves someone) 'can best be attained by a detached, unemotional,
exact intellectual scrutiny of one's condition, conducted in the way a
scientist would conduct a piece of research . . . sorting, analyzing,
classifying.'[25] But the realization achieved by Marcel, the protagonist of
the novel, gives a different result:

> Marcel's account of self-knowledge is no simple rival to the intellectual account.
> It tells us that the intellectual account was *wrong*: wrong about the content of the
> truth about Marcel, wrong about the methods appropriate for gaining this
> knowledge, wrong as well about what sort of experience . . . knowing is. And it
> tells us that to try to grasp love intellectually is a way of not suffering, not loving
> . . . a stratagem of flight.[26]

Pascal once famously observed: *le coeur a ses raisons que la raison ne
connaît point* – the heart has its reasons, which reason does not know at

---

24 M. Proust, *A la recherche du temps perdu* [1913–27], transl. L. Scott Moncrieff (London: Chatto &
    Windus, 1967), vol. III, p. 426. Quoted in Nussbaum, 'Love's Knowledge' [1988], reprinted in
    M. Nussbaum, *Love's Knowledge* (Oxford: Oxford University Press, 1990), p. 265.
25 Nussbaum, *Love's Knowledge*, p. 262.
26 Nussbaum, *Love's Knowledge* pp. 268–9 (emphasis added).

all.[27] Nussbaum's analysis suggests a persuasive variation on this enigmatic theme: there are certain kinds of truth such that to try to grasp them purely intellectually is to avoid them. What I am proposing (and what seems to me to underlie the Pascalian position on faith and praxis) is that religious truth should be seen as falling into just this category.

To anyone brought up on the classic curriculum of canonical texts in the philosophy of religion, the parallel between religious knowledge and the kind of knowledge involved in emotional relationships may seem anathema. How can the objective claims of religion about the nature of the cosmos and our human place within it be put in the same category as the truths relating to the interior world described by the novelist? Well, let us consider in a little more detail Nussbaum's description of knowledge relating to the latter category (this time her literary example is not Proust, but a contemporary love story by Ann Beattie, significantly entitled 'Learning to Fall'). Nussbaum's analysis is worth quoting at length, to bring out what seem to me unmistakeable parallels with religious awareness:

This knowledge . . . unfolds, evolves, in human time. It is no one thing at all, but a complex way of being with another person, *a deliberate yielding to uncontrollable external influences*. There are no necessary and sufficient conditions, and no certainty. To show these idea adequately in a text, we seem to require a text that . . . gives no definitions and *allows the mysterious to remain so*. . .

[Such a text] *enlists us in . . . a trusting and loving activity*. We read it suspending scepticism; we allow ourselves to be touched by the text, by the characters as they converse with us over time. *We could be wrong, but we allow ourselves to believe.* The attitude we have before a philosophical text can look, by contrast, retentive and unloving—asking for reasons, questioning and scrutinizing each claim, wresting clarity from the obscure . . . Before a literary work [of the kind described] we are *humble, open, active yet porous*. Before a philosophical work . . . we are active, controlling, aiming to leave no flank undefended and no mystery undispelled.[28]

Nussbaum herself, I should hasten to add, draws no religious parallel whatever, nor gives even the slightest hint of doing so.[29] But it seems to

---

27 *Pensées*, no. 423. Compare no. 424: *C'est le coeur qui sent Dieu et non la raison. Voilà ce que c'est que la foi* ('It's the heart, not reason, that senses God: that is what faith is').

28 Nussbaum, *Love's Knowledge*, pp. 281 and 282 (emphasis added).

29 Though elsewhere she explores something similar in a religious context: 'We find in [Augustine's] *Confessions* . . . a love of God characterised not by a neat intellectual progression towards contemplative purity but by a sense of longing, incompleteness and passivity.' From 'The Ascent of Love', in G. Matthews (ed.), *The Augustinian Tradition* (Berkeley: University of California Press, 1999), p. 71. The theme of love as involving a kind of knowledge or awareness that is

me hard to reflect on what she says about the need for openness and responsiveness to the message of a powerful work of literature without seeing some link between this and what the architects of the great tradition of spiritual exercises had in mind. It is precisely because the great truths of religion are held to be in part a mystery, beyond the direct comprehension of the human mind, that an attempt to grasp them head on via the tools of logical analysis is, in a certain sense, to evade them. A different strategy, the strategy of involvement, the strategy of praxis, is required by the nature of the material.

Nussbaum's parallel with the reading of a text is suggestive in an additional way, when applied to the mechanisms of spiritual praxis. For of course one crucial element in many traditional spiritual exercises (those of Ignatius, as well as those found in the much older Benedictine tradition) is the reading of a text, indeed of the supposedly supreme text. The *lectio divina* – an open and responsive reading of the Bible – is itself taken, in that tradition, to be a principal vehicle for the operation of divine grace, and hence an appropriate and sure route to that special kind of knowledge which the profound and mysterious nature of the subject-matter requires.

Let us draw the threads together. Pascal's strategy culminates in an invitation to his readers not to respond to mercenary inducements, nor to give abrupt assent to doctrines that are not properly substantiated, but rather to open themselves to a process of transformation, which will allow the operation of divine grace, whose eventual goal is faith.[30] Reflection on Nussbaum's analysis of a certain kind of knowledge enables us to construct, in effect, a double parallel for this process. Just as the proper understanding of a certain sort of text involves a process of yielding, of porousness to the power of the literature; and just as properly understanding one's own emotional responses is often best achieved not by detached impartial scrutiny but by listening to the signals from within; so, in just the same way, the religious adherent may claim that the knowledge of God which is the goal of human life is to be found via the path of spiritual praxis – praxis that brings about an interior change, a receptivity, which is the essential precondition for the operation of grace. To reject the

distinct from, and perhaps more revealing than, detached contemplation or critical analysis can be found in various forms in early Christian literature. Compare Gregory the Great's pronouncement *amor ipse notitia est* – 'love is itself knowledge' (cited in the second epigraph to the present chapter).

30 Here I am greatly indebted to the persuasive interpretations of Ward Jones, 'Religious Conversion, Self-Deception and Pascal's Wager.'

primacy of praxis is, in all three cases, not a recipe for more reliable knowledge, but a flight from knowledge, a way of not loving, a stratagem of escape.[31]

4 TRUST AND THE CORRECTIONS OF REASON

At the stage the argument has now reached, several objections may seem to crowd in. The first (touched on already) is about the epistemic credentials of religious belief: how can religious claims be well supported if their adoption is the result of a procedure that appears to involve the abandonment of critical rationality? Plato famously argued that to be 'fastened by the chain of reasoning',[32] is a necessary condition a belief must submit to if it is to deserve the accolade of knowledge. Perhaps religious believers will be content with something less than knowledge in the strict sense; but typically they will want their commitments to have at least some kind of rational support or grounding. Can we really allow that a 'deliberate yielding to uncontrollable external influences' can be an appropriate means to acquire religious belief?

I shall return to the general question of the epistemic credentials of religious belief in a later chapter.[33] But with regard to the specific problem about 'yielding', I want to suggest here that, perhaps surprisingly, the difficulty turns out to be more apparent than real. As I have argued elsewhere,[34] there is a certain passivity in all cognition – something recognized by philosophers as radically different in their attitudes to religion as Descartes and Hume. For Hume, belief is a passive cognitive

---

31 Though the context is very different, there may be some links between the view advanced here and the position taken by Hegel in his *Phenomenology of Spirit*: 'If the fear of falling into error sets up a mistrust of Science, which in the absence of such scruples gets on with the work itself, and actually cognizes something, it is hard to see why we should not turn round and mistrust this very mistrust. Should we not be concerned as to whether this fear of error is not just the error itself.' (*Phänomenologie des Geistes* [1807], transl. A. V. Miller (Oxford: Oxford University Press, 1977), p. 47.) I owe this citation to Philip Stratton-Lake, who aptly comments: 'The further we stand back from some practice, or phenomenon, the more it will appear absurd and senseless. . . The fear of error may be the error itself, for the desire to avoid mistakes and naivety may itself prevent us from getting at the truth.' Introduction to P. Stratton-Lake (ed.), *Ethical Intuitionism* (Oxford: Clarendon Press, 2002), p. 27.
32 Cf. Plato, *Meno* [c. 380 BCE] 98A: 'Opinions, even if true, run away from a person's mind, and are not worth much unless you tether them by working out a reason . . . And this is why knowledge is more honourable and excellent than true opinion, because fastened by a chain.'
33 See below, Ch. 7, esp. §2.
34 See J. Cottingham, 'Descartes and the Voluntariness of Belief', *Monist* 85:3 (October 2002), pp. 343–60.

mechanism, something that so to speak 'happens to us'.[35] For Descartes, the 'natural light', the faculty that makes us assent to clearly and distinctly perceived truths, gives us no choice but to assent so long as we place ourselves in the appropriate, receptive, position. When we focus appropriately on the proposition 'two plus two equals four', then according to Descartes we *cannot but affirm its truth*. The intellectual illumination generated by the light of understanding immediately and directly produces a powerful mental inclination to believe: *ex magna luce in intellectu sequitur magna propensio in voluntate* ('from a great light in the intellect there follows a great inclination in the will').[36] Yet the strict determination of our belief does not undermine its epistemic status, since opening ourselves to the irresistible natural light allows the operation of a process that does not *bypass* our rationality, but operates in virtue of it. Descartes' natural propensity the *lumen naturale* is precisely the *lux rationis*, the light of reason; and our irresistible assent gives us exactly what we could ideally want – the unshakeable conviction that the conclusions of validly supported arguments are true.

It might be thought that this picture of irresistible light still places the epistemic inquirer in a worryingly *passive* situation. But what I take to be Descartes' own resolution of this difficulty seems to me quite satisfactory: the spontaneous mechanism of assent does not, for Descartes, undermine our human epistemic autonomy, for we remain in charge of the conditions under which it operates. The irresistibility of the natural light lasts only so long as we keep the truths in focus, holding our mental gaze on the propositions in question. Descartes' own course of epistemic praxis, the *Meditations*, is designed to turn us in the right direction, but there is no compulsion about following the route to truth; humans will always retain the ability to decline to embark on the path. And even having embarked on it, they will at any time be able to allow the propositions uncovered to slip out of focus. Light irresistibly causes the pupil of the eye to contract, but you can always avoid looking at the light.[37]

---

35 David Hume, Abstract of *A Treatise of Human Nature* [1739–40], ed. L. A. Selby-Bigge, rev. P. H. Nidditch (Oxford: Clarendon, 1978), p. 657. Cf. Bernard Williams, 'Deciding to believe', in *Problems of the Self* (Cambridge: Cambridge University Press, 214), p. 148.

36 *Meditations* [*Meditationes de prima philosophia*, 1641], AT VII 59: CSM II 41. 'AT' refers to the standard Franco-Latin edition of Descartes by C. Adam and P. Tannery, *Œuvres de Descartes*, (12 vols. rev. edn., Paris: Vrin/CNRS, 1964–76); 'CSM' refers to the English translation by J. Cottingham, R. Stoothoff, and D. Murdoch, *The Philosophical Writings of Descartes*, vols. I and II (Cambridge: Cambridge University Press, 1985), and 'CSMK' to vol. III, *The Correspondence*, by the same translators plus A. Kenny (Cambridge University Press, 1991).

37 For more on this, see Cottingham, 'Descartes and the Voluntariness of Belief'.

So yielding to the irresistible is by no means incompatible either with the possibility of knowledge, or, in the second place, with a considerable degree of epistemic autonomy. The picture just sketched would of course need filling in with much more detail to make it fully persuasive; but even if you accept it, at least one important difficulty remains. There is surely a crucial difference between the kind of mathematical case just alluded to, and the truths envisaged as the destination of the Pascalian route to faith. The claims typically involved in Christian belief of the kind Pascal advocated are on his own admission not of the kind which may be established by philosophical argument or scientific reason: they will include, for example, transcendent mysteries such as the mystery of the Incarnation. They turn out, to use a useful Cartesian distinction, to be the kinds of truth which are apprehended not via the natural light, but via the *supernatural* light.[38] But now the advocate of spiritual praxis seems to have a major problem to confront. If the destination of such religious praxis is assent to truths which cannot be rationally validated, does not the type of argument we have examined open the floodgates to all kinds of weird belief systems? We seem here to come back to a variant of the earlier 'Big Brother' objection. If your course of praxis involves joining a totalitarian party, you may end up assenting to the mysteries of the *Führerprinzip*.

Complex issues are involved here, some of which I shall be returning to later on.[39] But I will bring this opening chapter to a close by making two relatively straightforward observations.

First, nothing in the idea of the primacy of praxis necessarily involves a permanent abandonment of critical rationality. Having deployed Nussbaum's point about the necessary receptivity and porousness in certain kinds of understanding, we may now note her own judicious qualification – that the reasons of the heart often have to be supplemented, or ordered, by further rational deliberation: 'Sometimes the human heart needs reflection as an ally.'[40] And this point may now be applied to the religious case. To embark on the religious quest is not to put one's deliberative faculties into general and permanent paralysis, nor suddenly to suspend one's other values and commitments – one's knowledge of human nature, one's moral sensibilities. True, what is envisaged is a process of transformation, but like all transformations, this can only work against a

38 Descartes, Second Set of Replies to Objections to the *Meditations*: AT VII 148, l. 27: CSM II 106.
39 The worry that the kind of line advocated leads to an epistemically irresponsible position of the kind sometimes stigmatised as 'fideist' will be addressed in Chapter 7.
40 Nussbaum, *Love's Knowledge*, p. 283.

background of what is held constant. To put it in slightly more concrete terms, the kind of transforming power that their Christian advocates discern in the great parables of the gospels (the good Samaritan, the prodigal son, and so on) is going to operate – since this is the only way it can operate – through an activation, and a deepening, of moral intuitions that are already there. And in so far as those intuitions are part of a rational structure of beliefs about the world and the human condition, the results of spiritual praxis will have to work in harmony with them, rather than against them.

The 'floodgates' objection can thus be countered by pointing out that critical moral judgement may be used as a kind of touchstone against which systems of spiritual praxis can be evaluated. The great Kantian thesis of the relative autonomy of moral judgement, its independence from religious premises, thus turns out to be not an obstacle to embarking on a religious path, but on the contrary an essential prerequisite for it (though I shall come back to this, and to the general relationship between morality and religion in Chapter 3). In short, any old system of spiritual praxis will not do, only one whose insights are in harmony with our considered moral reflection. If, as the present chapter has been arguing, religious truth can only be accessed via faith, and faith can only be acquired via a living tradition of religious praxis, then in trusting ourselves to any one path, we need a way of making sure, as far as we can, that our trust is not misplaced. And we can use our intuitions to assess the moral credentials of the systems of praxis on offer (and indeed the moral credibility of those who offer them), as well as the moral fruits of those systems.

The suspicion may remain, however, that once 'inside' a structure of praxis, our outlook may become progressively conditioned by the operating assumptions of that outlook, so that we lose the external perspective from which a more critical evaluation can be made. Here I come to my second, and final point. It is true that at the destination of faith envisaged in the Pascalian route, the judgements of the believer will be, as it were, those of an 'insider', one for whom crucial aspects of the religious outlook have been systematically internalized. But that, in an important sense, is true of all human judgement. From within a given framework, we cannot jump outside to gain some final and definitive assurance that all is going well. But neither can we ensure a detached external stance by remaining outside that framework, for any human stance is necessarily one conditioned by pre-existing frameworks of understanding, structures of belonging and commitment and dependency.[41] If that is a problem, it is a problem for the human condition in general, not for religious frameworks in particular.

The unavoidable nature of our human predicament is that we can only learn through a certain degree of receptivity, by to some extent letting go, by reaching out in trust. This, after all, is how we began to learn anything as children, and this, though we may struggle to resist it, is how we have to be, as adults, if we are to continue growing towards the knowledge and love that are the most precious of human goods. The necessary trust, sadly, may be abused, for there are no guarantees. Just as the individual moral development of a child may go astray, as a result of trust given to those who promised love but delivered only selfishness, so in any other sphere (including that of organized religion) one will find many cases where trust is misplaced. But the primacy of praxis is in some sense a feature of the whole human condition: we learn to be virtuous, said Aristotle, by being trained in virtuous action before we reach the age of rational reflection.[42] We learn how to grow morally by being immersed in a community before we fully understand what morality means.[43] And we learn to trust by trusting. But in human life, there is no other way.[44]

---

41 Compare Rowan Williams' critique of the view that 'the point of reasoning is to get us to an optimal base point of non-commitment, from which we can move outwards to formulate evidentially grounded policies for . . . commitment.' From 'Belief, Unbelief and Religious Education' (London: Lambeth Palace Press Office, 8 March 2004).

42 See Aristotle, *Nicomachean Ethics* [c. 325 BCE], bk. II.

43 For this theme, see Sabina Lovibond, *Ethical Formation,* (Cambridge, Mass.: Harvard University Press, 2002).

44 For a theological application of this principle, compare the following: 'To hear Jesus, and not just his words, we have to stand within the tradition of the Church; we have to put our trust in those to whom our Lord entrusted his mission, his sending. Part of the stillness that is needed for us to hear the words of Jesus is a sense of presence, and it is this that tradition conveys. We become Christians by becoming members of the Church, but *trusting* our forefathers in the faith. If we cannot trust the Church to have understood Jesus, then we have lost Jesus: and the resources of modern scholarship will not help us to find him.' Andrew Louth, *Discerning the Mystery* (Oxford: Clarendon Press, 1983), p. 93.

CHAPTER 2

Religion and science: theodicy in an imperfect universe

Der ganze Erdball kann nicht in größere Not sein als eine *Seele. Der christlicher Glaube – so meine ich – ist die Zuflucht in dieser* höchsten *Not. Wem es, in dieser Not gebeben ist sein Herz su offnen statt es zusammenzuziehen, der nimmt das Heilmittel ins Herz auf.* The whole Earth cannot be in greater distress than *one* soul. Christian faith, so I believe, is refuge in this *ultimate* distress. Someone to whom it is given in such distress to open his heart instead of contracting it, absorbs the remedy into his heart.

Ludwig Wittgenstein.[1]

I RELIGION AND THE STANDARDS OF INFERENCE

I argued in Chapter 1 that religious understanding is not attained from a detached, external standpoint, but arrives as the culmination of a programme of praxis. Here, as in many other human endeavours, we learn through involvement and commitment, through immersion in a living tradition, rather than through abstract debate in the seminar room. But although what I have called the 'primacy of praxis' may be a feature of the human condition in general, there are still some very important distinctions of degree to be drawn between different areas of inquiry. In the area of religious understanding, as with the understanding of certain literary texts dealing with the emotions (and indeed as with the understanding of our own personal involvements and relationships), I have argued that the adoption of a detached critical stance can often function as an evasion, a way of resisting the vulnerability and receptivity on which true insight depends. But there are other areas where it is surely permissible, and indeed essential, to cultivate an attitude of maximum detachment; I do not mean the confused fantasy of a completely Olympian perspective, but rather the more modest but still demanding ideal of the greatest critical

---

1 Ludwig Wittgenstein, *Culture and Value* [*Vermischte Bemerkungen*], MS 128:46 [c. 1944], ed. G. H. von Wright (Oxford: Blackwell, 2nd edn. 1978), p. 52.

distance that is achievable within the constraints of our inevitable human situatedness. The paradigm area where this kind of detachment is *de rigeur* is, of course, natural science. And despite the animadversions of Thomas Kuhn,[2] and despite the latter-day doubts of the postmodernists (to which I shall be returning in a later chapter),[3] I see no reason to deny that the methods of natural science still remain a paradigm of what can properly be termed objective and reliable knowledge. These include careful gathering of evidence, precise mathematical modelling, and systematic empirical testing, all with the goal of providing the fullest and most reliable explanations for everything that occurs in the natural world.

One of the procedures of science is what is sometimes called *abduction* – inference to the best explanation.[4] A scientific hypothesis may reasonably be adopted if it provides the most comprehensive and plausible account available of a given range of observable data. Now religious claims have sometimes been interpreted as inferences to the best explanation in this sense (or something like it). Invoking God, is, for example, taken to be the best way of explaining the order in the world, or the apparent emergence of the cosmos out of nothing at the big bang. Yet once theistic claims are interpreted in this way, they become vulnerable to the possible objection that the inference in question may be *not very plausible*, given certain other observable features of the cosmos. Is the hypothesis of an all-powerful and surpassingly benevolent creator really the best explanation for the existence of the world as we find it – the world that contains so much terrible suffering? Such challenges are, of course, very familiar; but it is this way of formulating them, in terms of the charge that the theist is proposing an *implausible inference*, that I want to focus on.

2 In his influential *The Structure of Scientific Revolutions* (Chicago: University of Chicago Press, 1962), Thomas Kuhn cast doubt on the idea of science as a steady accumulation of objective knowledge based on purely rational methods, arguing that scientific activity takes place within entrenched paradigms whose adoption or eventual abandonment does not come about for strictly logical reasons.

3 The postmodernist challenge (to which I shall be returning in Ch. 6) attempts to cast doubt on the modern ruling conception of science as a paradigmatically rational and objective discourse for determining the truth about the world. As Graham Ward puts it, 'Postmodernism reminds modernity of its own constructed nature; the arbitrariness and instability of its constructions.' G. Ward (ed.), *The Postmodern God: A Theological Reader* (Oxford: Blackwell, 1997), p. xxvi.

4 The term is due to C. S. Peirce; see his *Collected Papers* (Cambridge, Mass.: Harvard University Press, 1958), vol. VII, pp. 89–164. The notion of abductive inference is controversial, since it is not clear that there are in fact any established inferential canons of reasoning for the discovery, as opposed to testing, of scientific hypotheses.

Here is a striking example from the distinguished atheist philosopher Simon Blackburn:

Suppose you found yourself at school or university in a dormitory. Things are not too good. The roof leaks, there are rats about, the food is almost inedible, some students in fact starve to death. There is a closed door, behind which is the management, but the management never comes out. You get to speculate what the management must be like. Can you infer from the dormitory as you find it that the management, first, knows exactly what conditions are like, second, cares intensely for your welfare, and third, possesses unlimited resources for fixing things? *The inference is crazy.* You would be almost certain to infer that either the management doesn't know, doesn't care, or cannot do anything about it. Nor does it make things any better if occasionally you come across a student who declaims that he has become privy to the mind of the management, and is assured that the management indeed knows, cares and has resources and ability to do what it wants. The overwhelming inference is not that the management is like that, but that this student is deluded.[5]

In this nice revamping of Hume's famous critique of religion,[6] Blackburn is arguing that if we start from the observed facts – the balance of evidence in the world around us – then to draw the conclusion that it is created by an omniscient, supremely benevolent, and omnipotent God is a vastly implausible, indeed a crazy, inference.

Crazy may be a bit strong; but let us stick with implausible. It seems to me that if theism is formulated as a supposed inference to the best explanation, then the Hume–Blackburn critique turns out to be more or less unanswerable. One is reminded here of Hume's equally famous critique of arguments for the truth of religion based on miracles: if we *start* from the evidence based on the preponderance of past observation, then since by definition a law of nature is something supported by the whole weight of our uniform previous experience, we already have an argument against miracles that is (in Hume's words) 'as entire as any argument from experience can possibly be imagined.'[7] By this Hume does not of course mean that it is *impossible* that a law of nature should have miraculous exceptions; for he himself insisted that there is no logical or universal necessity about the so-called 'laws' or generalizations of science.[8] His point is rather that the simple balance of probabilities taken on its

5 Simon Blackburn, *Think* (Oxford: Oxford University Press, 1999), ch. 5, p. 170 (emphasis supplied).

6 Cf. David Hume, *Dialogues on Natural Religion* [c. 1755, first published posthumously 1779], pt. x.

7 David Hume, *An Enquiry concerning Human Understanding* [1748], §X.

8 Cf. Hume, *An Enquiry concerning Human Understanding*, §VII.

own must always be against the truth of a reported miracle. For example, since our entire uniform past experience informs us that human beings do not walk on water, if someone claims to have witnessed such an event, it will always be more probable that he or she was mistaken than that the occurrence actually occurred. If we start from the preponderance of previous empirical data, the hypothesis of a miracle can never be a plausible inference to the best explanation.

But while Hume seems to me more or less correct in his assessment of what can plausibly be inferred from the balance of data alone, it is by no means clear that the claims of religion *are* typically advanced as the most plausible inference to be drawn from the empirical facts; moreover, it is by no means clear that the religious adherent needs to advance them as such.

2 ARE RELIGIOUS CLAIMS EXPLANATORY HYPOTHESES?

It is true that there is a certain kind of robust 'no-nonsense' Christianity which makes a point of arguing that religious claims are entirely on a par with scientific explanations. C. S. Lewis (who, significantly, was writing at the time when logical positivism was the ruling creed of the philosophical academy) was fond of doing things this way, and some of his arguments have survived into contemporary popular evangelism such as that found in the literature of the recent apparently very successful 'Alpha' course. Here we are told, for example, that Jesus of Nazareth claimed to be God; and that since, in making this claim he was either (a) mad, or (b) wicked, or (c) God, and since the evidence signally fails to support the first two, the best explanation is that he was indeed God. Well, one could no doubt debate the argument in its own terms – for example by raising the question of whether the initial premise that Jesus claimed to be God is actually supported by the textual evidence, at least from the synoptic gospels.[9] My point, however, is rather different, that such quasi-scientific or knock-down arguments, whether or not they deserve to carry conviction (and my own view is that in general they don't), are quite untypical

9 The Fourth Gospel makes (? reports) the most explicit claims for the divinity of Jesus (compare, for example, John 8:58). Perhaps the most prominent belief recorded in the other gospels is that he was the Christ (that is, the Messiah – a human, not a divine title); cf. Matthew 11:2–6; Mark 8:29, 14:61; Luke 7:18–23, 22:67. The issue of Jesus' claim to and/or acceptance of this and other titles (e.g. 'Lord' (*Kyrios*), 'Son of Man', and 'Son of God') is an immensely complicated one. Among many interesting discussions, see G. Vermes, *Jesus the Jew* [1973] (London: SCM, 1983), pt. II, and N. T. Wright, *The Resurrection of the Son of God* (Minneapolis, Minn.: Fortress Press, 2003), ch. 12.

of the route whereby people are normally drawn to give their allegiance to a religious worldview.

A religious outlook, it seems to me, is never, or at any rate not typically, adopted on the basis of an inference to the best explanation. Even the *a posteriori* arguments of Thomas Aquinas, the so-called Five Ways, which might at first seem to fit this model best, do not in fact conform to it. True, St Thomas reasons from the motion found in the world to a prime mover, and from the chain of causality to an uncaused first cause, but he does not take it that this leads us inferentially to the God of Christianity as the best explanation for the phenomena in question. All that he takes his arguments to support is the existence of an original uncaused, un-moved something, an ultimate X which is labelled 'God' ('and this we call God', or some such phrase, is found at the end of each of the Five Ways).[10] With regard to the characterizations of God that are vital from a religious perspective, his love, his mercy, his providence, these are, in the first place, understood by Aquinas (consistently with his general view of the properties we ascribe to God) not in exactly the same sense as that in which we use these terms of ordinary objects, but only 'analogically';[11] and second, the characteristic way in which these attributes are manifested to humanity in history (for example through the events described in the Bible) is not for Aquinas a matter of explanatory inference at all, but instead falls within the province of faith.[12] In the words of Thomas' famous hymn, where the author is writing from the standpoint of some-one involved in a tradition of worship and praxis rather than as a scientific scrutineer of the evidence, *praestet fides supplementum sensuum defectui* – faith makes up for the deficiencies of the other senses.[13]

10 See Thomas Aquinas, *Summa theologiae* [1266–73], pt. I, qu. 2, art. 3. Aquinas' intentions in the Five Ways are, as Brian Davies aptly puts it in his *Aquinas* (London: Continuum, 2002), 'minimalist' (p. 47).

11 'The word "wise" is not used in the same sense of God and man, and the same is true of all other words, so they cannot be used univocally of God and his creatures.' Aquinas, *Summa theologiae*, pt. Ia, qu. 13, art. 5. For the difficult doctrine of analogical predication in Aquinas, see Davies, *Aquinas*, ch. 8. See also Ch. 5, §4, below.

12 For an illuminating introduction to some of these points, see F. Copleston, *A History of Philosophy* [1950] (New York: Doubleday, 1962), Vol. 2, ch. 32, and Davies, *Aquinas*, ch. 21. As Davies points out, Aquinas' view of the need for faith to support many of the doctrines of Christianity does not, however, imply that the relevant claims, and their relationship to other known truths, cannot be the subject of rational reflection.

13 From the hymn *Pange lingua* [1260]. Aquinas' position on the relation between faith and reason is not what is sometimes called a 'fideist' one, that faith *substitutes* for reason; the two, rather, are complementary. Thomas elsewhere describes an 'ascent' to God, via natural reason, going hand in hand with a 'descent' from God, via revealed truth. *Summa contra Gentiles* [1259–65], transl. A. C. Pegis (Notre Dame, Ill.: Notre Dame University Press, 1975), Bk. IV, ch. 1; see Introduction to Bk. I, p. 39.

So, to come to the problem raised by Blackburn, it is not, I suggest, as if the human inquirer looks around dispassionately at the balance of good and evil in the world and draws the inference 'Yes – the best bet is that an omnipotent benevolent all-knowing creator is responsible.' The religious believer does not detect a jolly, happy world and infer a kindly Father Christmas-type deity as its cause. To the contrary, and this is perhaps the strongest evidence against the inferential interpretation of religious belief, the most profoundly spiritual and passionately religious people in the world's history, the people who produced Moses and the prophets and Jesus and Paul, were a people whose history was conspicuous by the most terrible suffering, the cataclysmic traumas of slavery, wanderings in the desert, a homeland marked by the ever-present threat of war and annihilation, brutal captivity, exile, ruthless suppression and control by a series of imperial subjugators. This is the people who reflected endlessly on *chesed*, the loving kindness of God, who produced the immortal lines *ach tov va'chesed yirdefuniy kol yemey chayai* – 'surely thy goodness and loving kindness shall follow me all the days of my life'.[14] To object that they must have been rather inept in applying the rules of inference to the best explanation is surely to miss the point.

The relationship between observable evidence and religious faith is a difficult one to analyse correctly, but perhaps I have said enough to indicate why I think it is a distortion to construe it in a straightforwardly inferential way. It might appear from the example just given that I am proposing a leap in the other direction, towards a *credo quia absurdum* ('I believe because it is absurd'), or some later Kierkegaardian equivalent.[15] But such approaches seem to me to take us too far towards irrationalism. Given what I have called the primacy of praxis, the route to belief being practical involvement in a tradition of worship, if the destination of such a path was credal allegiance that was utterly unrelated to any evidential phenomena whatsoever, then the decision to become involved would

14 Psalm 23 in the Hebrew Bible (the numeration of which is followed by the Authorized Version and the Book of Common Prayer), or number 22 in the Septuagint and Vulgate versions.
15 The slogan is often attributed to Tertullian, who consequently is often invoked as a champion of irrationalism; but this reputation appears to be distinctly unfair, and the famous slogan is in fact a misquotation. Tertullian actually wrote: 'That the Son of God was crucified: one is not ashamed – because it is shameful (*non pudet, quia pudendum est*); that he died: it is immediately credible – because it is awkward (*credibile prorsus est quia ineptum est*); that he was buried and rose again: it is certain because it is impossible (*certum est, quia impossibile*)'; *De carne Christi* [c. 200 CE], 5, 4. Tertullian's basic argument (hinging on the Aristotelian observation that an extremely improbable element preserved in a historical report may, paradoxically, provide reason to believe it) is in fact designed to support the *probability* of the Incarnation and Resurrection. See Robert D. Sider, 'Credo quia absurdum?', *Classical World* 73 (1980), pp. 417–19. As to

indeed be a leap in the dark, a kind of willed submission to a process of belief inducement that was subject to no reflective correction whatsoever. Yet, as I argued in Chapter 1, there is nothing about the process of submitting oneself trustingly to a process of belief-formation that rules out retaining some critical reflection.

The middle way that I want to propose between quasi-scientific inferentialism on the one hand, and irrationalist hyper-fideism on the other, is that religious claims, while not purporting to be inferentially justified as the best conclusion to be drawn from pre-existing evidence, at least must have some kind of consistency relation with that evidence. This is the very minimum that we should expect (though I shall suggest later on, in Chapter 7, that something quite a bit stronger than this bare minimum may in fact be available). At least, then, the beliefs of the religious adherent must not be rankly incompatible, either logically or probabilistically, with known observable facts.

To make this more precise, one model that could be invoked is the Popperian notion of falsifiability. There is, for Popper, no logical route from data to theory, no certified path of scientific discovery; but there is a logical rule for testing theories once formulated, namely that they must not be contradicted by experience.[16] Could religious claims be like this – not reliably inferable from the data, but required to survive testing against it? From a logical point of view, this must indeed be what is demanded by the consistency requirement I have just proposed. Nevertheless, if we are interested in grasping the relationship between the claims of the religious believer and empirical observation, the Popperian model could be misleading; for as Anthony Flew has pointed out,[17] it is not at all clear that

Kierkegaard's position, though its precise import is disputed by interpreters, it is widely regarded as a precursor of modern defences of the 'leap of faith'. In *Fear and Trembling* [*Frygt og Bæven*, 1843], a meditation on the faith of Abraham in preparing to obey God's ethically repugnant command to sacrifice Isaac on Mount Moriah, Kierkegaard describes faith as 'a paradox inaccessible to thought'; Problema I, transl. in J. Chamberlain and J. Rée (eds.), *The Kierkegaard Reader* (Oxford: Blackwell, 2001), p. 85. In the *Concluding Unscientific Postscript* [*Afsluttende Uvidenskabelig Efterskrift*, 1846], the person of faith is compared to a sailor venturing out on the deep: 'Without risk there is no faith. Faith is precisely the tension between the infinite passion of the individual's inwardness and the objective uncertainty . . . If I wish to preserve myself in faith, I must constantly be intent on holding fast the objective uncertainty, so as to remain out upon the deep, over seventy thousand fathoms of water, still preserving my faith' (transl. D. F. Swenson, repr. in Cottingham, *Western Philosophy*, p. 283). For an acute discussion of Kierkegaard's treatment of the Abraham case, see Stephen Mulhall, *Inheritance and Originality: Wittgenstein, Heidegger, Kierkegaard* (Oxford: Clarendon Press, 2001).

16 Cf. Karl Popper, *Conjectures and Refutations* (London: Routledge, 1963), ch. 1 (following his earlier *Logic of Scientific Discovery* [*Logik der Forschung*, 1935]).

17 Cf. A. Flew, 'Theology and Falsification', in B. Mitchell (ed.), *The Philosophy of Religion* (London: Methuen, 1971).

the religious adherent will normally countenance, let alone trawl for, evidence that might contradict the truth of theism. The religious world-view does not seem to 'stick its neck out' in the way described by Popper: there is no systematic attempt to make it answer to the bar of experiment and observation with a view to abandoning it if found wanting.

A more useful way of presenting the consistency requirement is suggested by the etymology of the term 'theodicy', the ancient project of trying to *defend* the justice of God in the face of the problem of evil; I have in mind a model drawn from the sphere of legal process, rather than that of natural science. A legal defence is not required to provide an account that is the best or most plausible explanation of the facts unearthed by the prosecution, but merely to offer to the jury an account which is *consistent* with those facts. The judicial system does not place on a defendant the onus of giving an account of his or her actions that is the most obvious or common-sense way of accounting for the known evidence; but if it is not inconsistent with any item of presented evidence, and if it is able to show that an innocent construction can legitimately be placed on the defendant's actions or omissions, then in certain circumstances it may reasonably and deservedly carry conviction. The safeguards under our legal system (for example the insistence on proof by the prosecution beyond reasonable doubt) recognize that a chain of wayward circumstances may perfectly well place quite innocent people under suspicion; and a rule of maximum plausibility would be an absurdly demanding one for an innocent person to have to meet – for who after all is to say that plausibility and truth always go hand in hand (or that 'plausibility' is not often merely a name for what most chimes with the prejudices and preconceptions of the listener)?

The religious believer, having committed her allegiance to God (rather, perhaps, as the defence council is committed to doing her best for the defendant) is not required to conduct an impartial assessment of the evidence and show that the hypothesis of God's existence is the most plausible inference to be drawn from the balance of suffering in the world (the notion of plausibility being in any case a distinctly arbitrary one in the present context).[18] What is required, if the theistic commitment is not to be rankly irrational, is the production of a narrative which is consistent with that balance of suffering, and which shows, as it were, that an

---

18 Arbitrariness seems unavoidable here: since notions of 'plausibility' are at home when we are dealing with ordinary explanations of particular phenomena, we have little handle on what is plausibly to be expected in the case of the supposed transcendent creative source of all creation.

innocent construction can be placed on the relevant divine acts or omissions. Without straining the legal analogy too far, this is the kind of response that it seems to me reasonable to require of the theist, and this is the kind of strategy that will be adopted in what follows.

3 THE PROBLEM OF EVIL AND THE NATURE OF MATTER

The 'problem of evil' is undoubtedly the most serious obstacle to belief in a Judaeo-Christian-Islamic type God: a God who is wholly good, all-powerful, and the creator of all things. The existence of so much terrible suffering in the world places a fearful onus of response on those who affirm the existence of such a being. Two main lines of defence for the theist figure in all the textbooks and anthologies: the 'free-will defence' (that the possibility of evil-doing, with its resultant suffering, is a necessary consequence of God's creating free beings),[19] and the 'instrumental' or 'means-to-a-good-end' approach (for example, that a world with suffering is needed for the possibility of moral growth).[20] But neither of these defences seems enough to explain the *pervasiveness* and the *quantity* of suffering to be found: the suffering is far more extensive (think only of the results of earthquakes and hurricanes) than what is the result of bad free acts; and it is far more widespread (consider fatal childhood diseases) than what might be related to the moral improvement of the victims.

19 This approach goes right back to St Augustine; cf. *Confessions* [*Confessiones*, c. 398 CE], VII 3–5, transl. in B. Davies (ed.), *Philosophy of Religion* (Oxford: Oxford University Press, 2000), ch. 54. One of the most comprehensive treatments of the various traditions of Christian theodicy is found in J. Hick, *Evil and the God of Love* (London: Macmillan, 1966; further edns. 1977, 1985).
20 For a modern development of this 'vale of soul-making' idea, see J. Hick 'Soul Making Theodicy' [1981], repr. in M. Peterson et al., *Philosophy of Religion: Selected Readings* (Oxford: Oxford University Press, 1996, 2nd edn. 2001), pt. v, and Richard Swinburne, 'The Problem of Evil', in S. Brown (ed.), *Reason and Religion* (Cornell: Cornell University Press, 1977). A vivid poetic expression of one aspect of this approach is found in Rilke:

> *Wir, Vergeude der Schmerzen*
> *Wie wir sie absehn voraus, in die traurige Dauer,*
> *ob sie nicht enden vielleicht. Sie aber sind ja*
> *unser winterwähriges Laub, unser dunkeles Sinngrün*
> *eine der Zeiten des heimlichen Jahres – nich nur*
> *Zeit – , sind Stelle, Siedelung, Lager, Boden, Wohnort.*

> How we squander our sorrows!
> How we peer anxiously through them, in sombre endurance,
> Worrying if they will end. But, could we know it,
> They are our dark green leaves that give meaning to winter,
> *One* precious time in our heart's year's seasons, yet more still:
> Place for us, settlement, refuge, our soil and dwelling.

From Rainer Maria Rilke, *Duino Elegies* [*Duineser Elegien*, 1922], no. X (transl. J.C.).

So I want to suggest a different approach, one that diverges from the standard defences in focusing on the *material* nature of the cosmos we inhabit.[21] While the ingredients of this approach are not new (the basis for it can be found in several traditional theodicies), they are not, so far as I can see, normally integrated into a distinctive strategy in typical modern discussions of the problem of evil; nor does the literature I am aware of list such a strategy as a distinctive alternative to the free will approach or the instrumental approach.

The starting point is an idea developed by Leibniz (though it has more ancient roots)[22] – that of *metaphysical evil*. Even before any question of 'sin' or defect or suffering, there is, as Leibniz puts it, an 'original imperfection' in the created world.[23] It is logically impossible for a perfect being to create something other than itself that is wholly perfect; for by the principle of the identity of indiscernibles (that if X and Y are exactly identical in all respects they are one and the same thing), a being that was wholly and completely perfect would just be identical with God. It follows as a corollary from this principle that if God and his creation are to be genuinely distinct, they must be 'discernible' – i.e. the creation cannot have all the perfections of God. (To use a somewhat ponderous label, the corollary in question may be called the principle of the 'discernibility of non-identicals'.) The upshot is that if he is to create anything at all, God must necessarily create something less perfect than himself; creation necessarily operates, as a long tradition going back to Augustine has it, by what we may think of as a diminution, or subtraction from the perfect divine essence.[24]

Now the notion of a necessary imperfection in the created cosmos does not of itself necessitate the existence of suffering. Why should not God have created beings that were only *slightly* less perfect than himself, but still immortal and wholly free from pain and distress? Indeed, according to many religious traditions he did create such beings – the angels. Why should God need to go on to create vastly less perfect creatures? As soon as this question is posed ('Why would an infinite creative being not just *stop*?'), an obvious answer suggests itself: infinite creativity is inexhaustible in its outgoing, outgiving power. This corresponds to the ancient notion often called the 'principle of plenitude' – that God's overflowing creative

---

21 I here develop the line taken in my *On the Meaning of Life*, ch. 2.
22 For example in Plotinus, *Enneads* [c. 250 CE], I, 8. Cf. Hick, *Evil and the God of Love*, ch. 3, §2.
23 Gottfried Wilhelm Leibniz, *Theodicy* [*Essais de théodicée*, 1710], Pt. I, §§20–21.
24 Cf. Augustine, *The City of God* [*De civitate Dei*, 413–26 CE], XIV, 13, cited in Hick, *Evil and the God of Love*, ch. III, §4.

power is 'poured forth' in creation.[25] Inexhaustibly active, he goes on and on, beyond the blessed realms of light, until he finally creates matter, the material cosmos that is our home.

The next step is to reflect on what exactly *materiality* involves. Though philosophers have long been preoccupied with concepts like 'physicalism' and 'materialism', they have historically not been very good at identifying the nature of matter (perhaps not very surprisingly, since this is not a task that can easily be performed from the armchair). Descartes thought that matter was passive, inert, extended stuff; Locke thought it was a kind of solid impenetrable dough.[26] But now (though not thanks to philosophy) we know better. With the advent of modern physics, the kind of solidity and permanence that earlier thinkers from Democritus to Descartes attributed to matter has crumbled away: the material world turns out at the micro level to consist of a series of unimaginably fleeting energy-interchanges, with each rapidly decaying particle or sub-particle scarcely qualifying as an enduring thing at all. The whole system, moreover, whether at micro or macro level, seems to be driven by a process of decay, a slide from higher organization to lower, from greater heat to lesser. Everything – galaxies, stars, planets – is on a downward path to eventual extinction. The impermanence, instability, and decay that are inherent characteristics of matter are features we sometimes ignore, partly because our own survival requires environmental conditions of relative local stability, and partly because living organisms create a certain temporary stability within themselves, though only at the cost of drawing on the entropy going on elsewhere. But we humans are still bound up with the material world, formed 'of the dust of the earth' as the Genesis story has it; and with our modern understanding of exactly what that dust is, we can see that human life must necessarily operate in accordance with the downward spiral of all matter.

So far, then, we have:

1. God's creation is necessarily imperfect [from the principles of metaphysical evil and the discernibility of non-identicals];

---

25 'How do we know that God has not produced an infinite number of kinds of creatures, and thus, as it were, poured forth his power in creation?' Descartes, *Conversation with Burman* [1648], AT V 168: CSMK 349; Cf. Spinoza, *Ethics*, pt. I, Appendix. The idea is an ancient one, going back to Plato (see *Timaeus* [c. 360 BCE] 29E), and Plotinus (*Enneads* [250 CE], V, 2, i and V, 4, i). Cf. Hick, *Evil and the God of Love*, p. 21, and pp. 70ff.

26 See Descartes, *Principles of Philosophy* [1644], pt. II, art. 4, and Locke, *An Essay concerning Human Understanding* [1690], bk. II, ch. 4.

2. God's creation, given his infinitely outgoing nature, will include a material universe [from the principle of plenitude];
3. Matter by its nature involves constant entropic decay [finding of modern science];
4. We human beings are formed out of matter [principle shared by the Genesis story and modern evolutionary theory].

Reflection on the implications of (3) and (4) shows that any creatures inhabiting a material planet and themselves made of matter, formed of 'the dust of the earth', will necessarily be *mortal*: just like the sun and the stars, and everything else in the cosmos, their life span will be finite, and in an important sense precarious, depending on a delicate balance of fluctuating forces, subject to change and decay, potential prey to instability and collapse. And therein, of course, lies the key to what we are all aware of anyway: that the human condition is inherently vulnerable, always subject to the possibility of suffering.

Though there are many questions still to be raised, formally speaking, the argument is now at an end. For the pervasive suffering that has been the traditional focus of the 'problem of evil' has now been shown to be not just compatible with standard theistic principles regarding a perfect creator, but actually derivable from those principles.

4 THE DUST OF THE EARTH

Even if the general idea of the necessary fragility of the material cosmos is accepted, it may immediately be asked why an omnipotent and wholly benevolent being could not do something to remedy the resultant suffering. An atheist colleague, confronted with what might be called the 'dust of the earth' argument – that our vulnerability is due to our being formed of the inherently vulnerable and unstable elements of material stuff – once gave me the curt rejoinder: 'God should have used better dust!' But it is not in fact clear that 'better dust' is available, if that phrase means material stuff which is not subject to change and decay. Contemporary essentialist metaphysicians argue plausibly that natural kinds retain their properties in all possible worlds: water is necessarily composed of H_2O (this is a necessary, though an a posteriori, truth),[27] so

27 That all water is H_2O is *necessary* truth (a substance *must* be H_2O to count as water); but it is unlike many familiar types of necessary truth (e.g. 'all bachelors are unmarried') in that it is not known simply by reflecting on the concepts involved, but is arrived at *a posteriori*, via the empirical discoveries of science. Cf. S. Kripke, *Naming and Necessity* (Oxford: Oxford University Press, 1980).

there is no possible world in which this stuff, water, has a different molecular structure.[28] And similarly with hydrogen and oxygen, and so right on down. If this is right, then creation, even by an omnipotent being, is in an important sense constrained: God may be free to create hydrogen, but he is not free to create hydrogen that does not decay into helium under certain conditions, for that is part of the essential nature of hydrogen. So despite how things may superficially appear from the armchair, 'better dust', better material dust, may not after all be a possible option.[29] Perhaps God should not have created a material world at all, given that beings operating within that world would inevitably be subject to all the potential suffering resulting from the necessary impermanence and instability of the material out of which they and their environment are composed. But that is a different complaint – and one which on reflection is unlikely to stick, since most of us would rather have this world existing than not – even with all its attendant risks. What at all events cannot be objected to, if the above argument is right, is the features of our world that are inextricably linked to its material nature.

As I have argued elsewhere,[30] there is a paradox here in that Darwin, so often wheeled in to appear for the prosecution in debates over theodicy,

---

28 But (runs a possible objection) perhaps God could have created instead another substance, not water but '*swater*' – something possessed of all the beneficial properties of water (drinkability etc.) but composed of a different molecular structure ('XYZ' instead of H_2O), such that, for example, it did not drown people. I think we should beware of this kind of speculative 'armchair' metaphysics, which often rests on no more than a half-baked intuition that a certain imaginary scenario 'seems plausible'. In reality, the beneficial properties of water such as drinkability flow from its molecular structure, which is integrally linked, via a host of complex physico-chemical laws, to a vast array of other powers and properties of water itself and of the other substances with which it is disposed to interact. The scenario of 'swater', exactly like water except that it didn't drown people, seems likely to turn out under proper scientific scrutiny to be incoherent – a flimsy fantasy that could not be instantiated in any world remotely like our own. (The issues here are, however, extremely complex, as may be seen from the vast literature generated by Hilary Putnam's 'twin earth' hypothesis, where the compound we call 'water' supposedly has a different atomic structure. See his 'The meaning of "meaning"' [1975], in H. Putnam, *Philosophical Papers, Vol. 2: Mind, Language and Reality* (Cambridge: Cambridge University Press. 1985), pp. 215–71.)

29 How, one may object, can an option not be possible for God (for whom 'all things are possible', Matthew 19:26)? The argument here rests on the assumption that even God's actions necessarily conform to the laws of logic; for example his supreme power does not entail the ability to do such absurd or meaningless things as create a round square. That omnipotence does not encompass the power to violate the laws of logic is the standard view (maintained for example by Aquinas); there is however a dissenting minority of philosophers who hold that God's omnipotence should be regarded as utterly absolute, encompassing even the 'eternal truths' of logic. This is apparently the view taken by Descartes; see his letters to Mersenne of 6 May 1630 and 27 May 1630 (AT I 150, 152: CSMK 24, 25), and cf. Jonathan Bennett, 'Descartes' Theory of Modality', *Philosophical Review* 88 (1979), pp. 639–67, repr. in J. Cottingham (ed.), *Descartes* (Oxford: Oxford University Press, 1998).

30 See J. Cottingham, *On the Meaning of Life*, ch. 2.

actually turns up in the schedule of defence witnesses. It is often pointed out that Darwin made us humans see, for the first time, that we are continuous with the natural world – are not separate from it but inextricably part of it. But if the Darwinian view is correct, then, like the lady who when she dramatically declared 'I accept the Universe!' was curtly told 'Madam, you had better!',[31] so we had better accept our humanity as a natural phenomenon – part and parcel of the created universe. And that means that human life can no longer be seen as some 'special' *sui generis* process, which we can then complain that the deity has not organized better, but rather that it has to be recognised as emerging from the cosmic flux of ever-decaying material energy. Yet in that case, it is not as if illness and pain and death and decay are inexplicable features that one might have expected a benign creator magically to eliminate; rather, our impermanence, like it or not, is our birthright, essential to our very existence as creatures of flesh and blood. These are not, of course, new facts, since in a sense humans have always understood their frailty and mortality; indeed, the biblical writers were clear that the entire fabric of the cosmos is impermanent, and will 'wear out like a garment'.[32] We perceive these features in such starkness, because we can somehow see beyond them, to a possible world where there is no change and decay, but eternal bliss. Perhaps a benevolent God should have confined his creation to that blissful world; but what he could not do, if the above argument is right, is put us in *this* world, the world of matter, and also simultaneously make our existence on this Earth eternal and blissful.

5 DETACHMENT, INTERVENTION, PARTICIPATION

It may seem that the argument so far might acquit a Platonic 'Demiurge', a divine architect doing his best with recalcitrant matter,[33] but will not do much to vindicate an omnipotent creator, who (1) can shape it as he chooses, and who (2) presumably has the power to intervene at any time to prevent the worst consequences of its impermanent nature. I have already indicated that the first point will not stand up very well: omnipotence operates within the sphere of what is logically possible, and

31 The remark is sometimes attributed to Dr Johnson, but according to the *Oxford Dictionary of Quotations* (2nd edn.) it was made by Thomas Carlyle in response to Margaret Fuller.

32 'Lift up your eyes to the heavens, and look at the earth beneath; for the heavens will vanish like smoke, the earth will wear out like a garment.' Isaiah 51:6, Cf. Psalms 102(101):26: 'They shall perish, but thou shalt endure: yea all of them shall wax old like a garment'.

33 This is Plato's conception of the divine role in the *Timaeus* [c. 355 CE]; see F. M. Cornford, *Plato's Cosmology* (London: Routledge, 1937), pp. 37ff.

we cannot determine from the armchair that a material universe could be preserved if stripped of the impermanence and fragility that are its most intimate and pervasive features.

The second point – why doesn't he intervene more? – ultimately rests, it seems to me, on a false dilemma. The available models for the divine relationship to the world are often presented as either the deistic one which Pascal accused Descartes of purveying – the God who merely shoves things into motion and then leaves them to their own devices[34] (a model which seems seriously to erode the attribute of benevolence), or else the idea of a constant supervisor, micro-managing every gust of wind, and drop of rain, and rise in temperature, and bacterial multiplication, in order to produce the results he wants. And of course the latter picture makes his apparent failure to manage things better to eliminate or reduce suffering seem inexplicable. The picture I have presented does, I think, move us away from such a 'managed' world towards the universe we in fact inhabit – one whose energy system operates thermodynamically, by constant inevitable degradations in stability; further, it involves a move away from the fussy micro-manager, towards a conception of a deity who to some extent does indeed let things be. But can we make this move without reverting to the impersonal uncaring God of deism?

Answering this question takes us away from philosophy proper into the domain of theology, where I am not properly qualified to speak, but let me at least make some sketchy suggestions. The sixteenth-century Jewish theologian Isaac Luria (and there are close analogues in Christian thought) envisaged creation as a *withdrawal* by God, a kind of shrinking whereby God, instead of filling all the available space with his supreme and perfect existence, gives way, in order to allow for something *other*, something imperfect, to unfold.[35] (This idea is of course consistent with the point already made about a necessary imperfection in things if anything besides God is to exist.) Something of what this idea of withdrawal involves from the moral point of view is nicely captured, in a very different and entirely secular context, by the present-day French philosopher André Comte-Sponville in his discussion of the virtue of charity:

This kind of love is the rarest of loves, the most precious and miraculous. You take a step back? He takes two steps back. Why? Simply to give you more room, to avoid crowding you, invading you, or crushing you, to give you more space

---

34 This was Pascal's famous complaint: see *Pensées* [c. 1660], no. 1001.
35 The ideas of Isaac Luria (1534–72) are known through the work of his disciples Hayim Vital and Joseph ibn Tabul. For the central idea of *tsimtsum* (withdrawal), see Karen Armstrong, *A History of God* [1993] (London: Vintage, 1999), p. 308.

and freedom and to let you breathe . . . He steps back so as not to impose on you his power, or even his joy or love, so as not to take up all available space, all available being, or all available power. One who forbears in this way is the precise opposite of the *salaud*, the dirty bastard, whom Sartre thinks can be defined as someone possessed by the 'fat fullness of being'.[36]

One is reminded here of Simone Weil's discussion of the self-giving divine nature as one that allows space, that makes room; and this in turn links up with the theology of *kenosis*, the idea of a divine self-emptying, which is found in Paul's letter to the Philippians.[37] Divine creation, it seems, necessarily involves letting go, allowing for the unfolding of the material world.

The impulse *not* to let go, not to withdraw but to hurry back in, is of course one that every parent knows, but it is also clear that any parent who wishes to allow a child independence, self-development, growth, and fulfilment, must vacate the space. The predicament of the parent, if the fundamental Judaeo-Christian insight is correct, is analogous to that of the divine creator. Of course the disanalogy is that when the parent sends the child out into the world, he or she does not have the supreme power to rescue the child from the chaotic, unpredictable nexus of causation that makes up the material universe. But, in one sense, if our argument is right, nor does God. The inherent instability that produces disease, accidents, earthquakes, is something he can only modify by – *per impossibile* – radically altering the essential nature of things; the fragility of our bodies and our environment may be the price to be paid if there is to be a material world at all. Perhaps, it may be objected, God could leave matter as it is, but step in whenever harm threatened. But a world where bacteria self-destructed whenever they risked invading a human organism, where tidal pressures subsided whenever they threatened shipwreck, and so on and on and on in millions of ways every minute of every day – this would not be a material world at all, as we know it, but what Richard Swinburne has aptly called a 'toy world',[38] free of stress perhaps, but flat, two-dimensional, lacking the power and terror and grandeur and danger and vividness and beauty of our material cosmos.

The picture of the world and its divine origin which we end up with is thus in some respects unconventional – or rather, it diverges considerably

36 André Comte-Sponville, *A Short Treatise of the Great Virtues* [*Petit Traité des Grandes Vertus,* 1996] (London: Heinemann, 2002), p. 276.

37 'Christ Jesus . . . though he was in the form of God . . . emptied himself, taking the form of a servant', Philippians 2:7.

38 See R. Swinburne, *The Existence of God* (Oxford: Clarendon, 1979), p. 219; 2nd edn., p. 264.

from the standard conception of God on which philosophical discussions of the problem of evil normally rely. On the view advanced here, omnipotence is construed in a way which involves the power to create certain parts of reality that are outside the sphere of direct managerial control; benevolence is construed as implying a kind of letting be. And the resulting world is a world full of fear and pain, as well as power and wonder. The untameable wildness, the alien quality, of the material world was something the poet Byron captured in his powerful address to the Ocean:

> Roll on, thou deep and dark blue ocean – roll!
> Ten thousand fleets sweep over thee in vain.
> Man marks the earth with ruin; his control
> Stops at the shore, upon thy watery plain.[39]

It is not a tidy, controllable cosmos. Nature, to use another striking poetic image, this time from Gerard Manley Hopkins, is a 'Heraclitean fire', incandescent and perpetually changing: 'million-fueled, nature's bonfire burns on'.[40] But for all that, we still want it to exist. And the theologian can, it seems to me, reasonably conceive that a benevolent God could will it to exist, to let it roll on, until it wears out, like a garment, and time comes to an end. Having made the space, God does not refill it; but on the Christian picture this does not leave us with the other horn of the dilemma, the remote uncaring God, since the Christian God is believed, on faith, to redeem and rescue his creation by entering it, not as a superior being, or as a fussy micro-manager, but on its own terms, utterly unprotected and vulnerable. Only thus is fulfilled the luminous paradox we find articulated in Paul's Second letter to the Corinthians: 'my power is made perfect in weakness'.[41]

6 PROOF, CONSISTENCY, AND FAITH

Let me return very briefly, in closing this chapter, to the notion of theodicy and the image of the law court. The jury cannot convict just because the balance of evidence is against the accused, but only if guilt is established beyond reasonable doubt. Many of course believe that the

---

39 George Gordon, Lord Byron, *Childe Harold's Pilgrimage* [1812–18], canto IV, stanza 179.
40 G. M. Hopkins, 'That nature is a Heraclitean fire and of the comfort of the resurrection' [1888]. From *Poems (1876–1889)*, in W. H. Gardner (ed.), *The Poems and Prose of Gerard Manley Hopkins* (Harmondsworth: Penguin, 1953), no. 49.
41 ἡ γὰρ δύναμις ἐν ἀσθενείᾳ τελεῖται (2 Corinthians 12:9).

amount of suffering in the world does indeed make divine creation so improbable as to put God's non-existence beyond reasonable doubt. But if the defence can produce a narrative which, while it may not appear to many to be the most plausible inference from the facts of the world, is nonetheless consistent with those facts, then their account may stand.

To avoid misunderstanding, I am not saying that the onus of proof is on the atheist to disprove God. That 'onus' question seems a sterile debate, since neither theists nor atheists are in the position of detached observers waiting to be convinced, nor are we dealing here with a law court or a debating chamber, but rather with fundamental choices whose activation (as I shall argue later on, in Chapter 4) often involves responses at a deeply pre-rational level. The believer, through initiation into a community of praxis, has reached a position of faith which is seen as giving meaning to life, and which, in its conception of how we should live, resonates powerfully with some very deep and enduring human intuitions.[42] The position now reached approximates to that described in Immanuel Kant's account of faith: 'I *will* that God exist, and I will not let this be taken from me.'[43] All that is reasonably required now is an account of the suffering world in which we live that is consistent with that faith. And if such an account can be reached – and I have merely outlined one possible avenue here – then the task of theodicy will have been reasonably discharged.

But an important caveat should be entered before we move on. There is always something presumptuous, almost distasteful, about attempts to discuss the problem of evil in an 'academic' context, from the armchair or the study desk. None of the above arguments are meant to constitute anything like a 'solution' of the problem, in the sense that they would enable someone to get it neatly crossed off, on the checklist of 'possible obstacles to theistic belief'. For the question has to do with real human suffering, something that we can only begin to understand properly through personal experience, and something whose qualities and dimensions it is fearfully hard to grasp fully 'from the outside', in areas when our own experience falls short. What is more, religious allegiance for the believer can never be a matter of having sailed into the calm lagoon of

---

42 For more on the connections between religious allegiance and morality see below, Ch. 3, and the latter part of Ch. 7.
43 Immanuel Kant, *Critique of Practical Reason* [*Kritik der Practischen Vernunft*, 1788], pt. I, bk. II, ch. 2, §viii, in *Kant's gesammelte Schriften*, Akademie edition Berlin: Reimer/De Gruyter, 1900–), V: 141 (transl. T. K. Abbott, *Critique of Practical Reason* (London: Longmans, 1873; 6th edn. 1909), p. 241.

faith, all problems and doubts left behind. It is something far more dynamic, even dangerous, charged with the kind of recurring anguish that is conveyed by the poet Hopkins as he recalls

> That night, that year
> Of now done darkness I wretch lay wrestling with (my God!)
> my God.[44]

The horrors of the human condition, of what we do to each other, and what we suffer as denizens of the natural world, are beyond our human power ever fully to encompass with the intellect alone. The world is a terrible place – even if it is also a place of great joy and beauty. But even in a world where the overwhelming majority led lives of comparative joyousness, the ultimate distress of one soul (as our opening epigraph from Wittgenstein reminds us) would be enough to make things fundamentally awry. Quantitative judgements are not the issue here.[45] What the theist has to hold on to (if the reflections in this chapter have been not wholly off the mark) is the idea of vulnerability as inherent in the very idea of a physical universe of the kind we inhabit, even a divinely created one; and what faith has to build on to this (though this will take us beyond the reach of philosophy alone) is the idea that this very vulnerability may be the instrument of redemption and hope.

---

44 Gerard Manley Hopkins, 'Carrion Comfort', in *Poems (1876–1889)*, no. 41. There is an echo here of the strange and disquieting story in Genesis 32:24–31.
45 'Quantitative judgements do not apply': see Evelyn Waugh, *Unconditional Surrender* (London: Chapman and Hall, 1961), Prologue.

CHAPTER 3

Religion and value: the problem of heteronomy

Frate, la nostra volontà quieta
virtù di carità, che fa volerne
sol quel ch'avemo, e d'altro no ci asseta . . .
Anzi è formale ad esto beato esse
tenersi dentro a la divina voglia . . .
E'n la sua volontade è nostra pace
Brother, our Will can find tranquillity
Through that true love which makes us to desire
No more than what we have, nor thirst for more . . .
And blessedness, for any creature, lies
In keeping fast within the will of God . . .
And in His will alone our peace belongs.

Dante Alighieri.[1]

I SUBMISSION TO GOD: AN OBSOLETE IDEAL?

Dante's famous lines follow a long religious tradition in seeing submission to the will of God as representing the deepest fulfilment for the human spirit. The thought is not just that religious devotion provides peacefulness of mind, in the sense of securing some kind of tranquillizing or calming effect; rather, the idea is that God is the source of genuine value, and that orienting ourselves towards that source bestows meaning on our human existence and enables us to find true contentment. In the striking words of Augustine, of which Dante's lines are a clear echo, 'You have made us for Yourself, and our heart is restless until it finds repose in You.'[2]

Yet although this notion is a familiar one, it is not without its difficulties. First, from a metaphysical point of view, one may ask exactly what is

---

1 Dante Alighieri, *The Divine Comedy: Paradise* [*La Divina Comedia: Paradiso* c. 1310], iii, 70–72, 79–80, 85; transl. J. C.

2 Augustine, *Confessions* [*Confessiones*, c. 398], bk. I, ch. 1: 'fecisti nos ad te, et inquietum est cor nostrum donec requiescat in te.'

involved in the idea of God's being the *source* of meaning and value. We all want our lives to have significance and to be of value, but one might think that these are properties which have to be earned, as it were, by our own efforts, rather than being in the gift of an external power, even a divine one. Are significance and goodness the kinds of property that can be *bestowed* on something, just like that? One might suppose, instead, that if something is meaningful or valuable, it must be meaningful or valuable for a *reason* or *reasons*; and if meaning and value are rationally based in this way, if they arise in virtue of features that make it rational for us to judge a life good or significant, then they are properties that cannot be created by fiat, even divine fiat. So, notwithstanding Dante's resonant phrase, it seems that conformity with the will of God cannot merely of itself be enough to confer meaning and value on our lives.

Even if this metaphysical tangle can be sorted out (and I shall return to consider it later on in this chapter), there seems to be a second, moral, problem with the idea of conformity with God's will as the key to a meaningful and valuable life. Even granting that God somehow functions as an external source of meaning and value, one may ask whether it is consistent with our human dignity and autonomy that we should submit ourselves to his will in the manner envisaged by Augustine and Dante. Are we talking of blind obedience, of the kind of 'humble duty' that a subject was in times past thought to owe to an absolute monarch? This does not on reflection seem a very compelling model for a good and meaningful life; on the contrary, it seems more like an abdication or resigning of responsibility into the hands of another. Just as large sections of the human race pride themselves on having come of age politically, of having freed themselves from subservience to monarchs, so one might think a mature religious sensibility can no longer work with the Dante-esque model of submission to the divine will.

It is certainly the case that if one looks at some of the traditional language of prayer one finds an attitude of self-effacement that borders on the servile. The language of the *Book of Common Prayer* for example, takes us into a sixteenth-century world of absolute monarchs, of subjects offering their duty to rulers whose power is taken to be beyond scrutiny or criticism. 'O Almighty God . . . whose power no creature is able to resist, to whom it belongeth justly to punish sinners . . . save and deliver us we humbly beseech thee.' And not merely the petitions, but even the thanksgivings have the same note of abject self-abasement: 'We thine unworthy servants do give thee most humble and hearty thanks.'[3] In the political arena, we would nowadays find such language totally unacceptable – though an exception, apparently palatable to some, is the quaint ritual in which the British constitution still enshrouds itself, as one sees, for example, in the wording of the traditional motion for debate following the Queen's speech that opens a new legislative session of Parliament:

> Most gracious Sovereign: We, Your Majesty's most dutiful and loyal subjects, the Commons of the United Kingdom of Great Britain and Northern Ireland in Parliament assembled, beg leave to offer our humble thanks to Your Majesty for the Gracious Speech which Your Majesty has addressed to both Houses of Parliament.

Droll perhaps, but if taken seriously it might reasonably call forth the rebuke that this is no way for a responsible legislative body to conceive of itself. Their job is not to grovel, but to exercise their autonomous powers of critical judgement.

But what of the religious person's attitude to the will of God? The feminist theologian Daphne Hampson argues in her recent study *After Christianity* that a similarly suspect self-effacement infects the very structure of Judaeo-Christian religion:

> Within the Judaeo-Christian tradition . . . the relationship to God is at least potentially heteronomous, such that the human must be obedient to what he or she conceives to be God's will, rather than obeying his or her own conscience.[4]

And again:

> [The Lord's prayer] opens by addressing God as 'father'; the term used is that by which the head of the family was designated in what was a deeply patriarchal society. Our mind is directed not to ourselves but to God. 'He' is conceived to be in heaven, a reality both other than ours and which transcends ours. 'He' is addressed as one would address a sovereign. Christians pray that 'his' kingdom come, 'his' will be done; not that their will should be realised.[5]

To digress for a moment to consider the specifically feminist tone of this critique, it seems fairly uncontroversial that the language of Christianity bears traces of the patriarchal soil from which it sprung. But is not my

---

3 Both these quotations are from 'Prayers and Thanksgivings upon Several Occasions', in the *Book of Common Prayer* [1662]. 1662 is the date of the finally approved version, though most of the formulations date from the previous century, owing much to Thomas Cranmer (1489–1556).

4 Daphne Hampson, *After Christianity* (London: SCM Press 1996; 2nd edn. 2002), p. 137.

5 Hampson, *After Christianity*, p.129.

concern here, even were I competent to do so, to try to assess the extent to which the masculinism is an inherent part of the underlying religious outlook, or only, as it were, part of its cultural expression. C. S. Lewis was one who quite happily embraced the former view, believing that the masculinity of God is absolutely central to Christianity – though his reasons can sometimes appear a little thin: 'only one wearing the masculine uniform can . . . represent the Lord to the Church; for we are all, corporately and individually, feminine to him'.[6] The idea here seems to be that we need to recognize the active nature of divine creative power in relation to the passiveness or receptivity of creation and the Church; but expressing this thought in terms of the essential *masculinity* of the creator seems to reflect more than a trace of the old Aristotelian biology that takes procreation to involve a toti-potent male seed, with the female component being relegated to that of mere passive receptor. Given that modern micro-biology has long shown such a model to be inaccurate, one might think it makes a somewhat shaky basis for inferring supposedly eternal truths about the nature of divine creativity.

Matters of gender aside, does the addressing of God as a parent put the worshipper into a suspect and heteronomous relationship with the deity in the way Hampson suggests? The analogy of parenthood, it might be said, implies an inherent dependency: the child's relationship to the parent is not that of equal to equal. But as soon as we reflect further, this starts to look like an over-simplification, based, as it were, on a snapshot taken at a particular phase of the child–parent relation. If we look at the phenomenon of parenthood as it actually operates, then to say that X is related to Y as offspring to parent does not imply a fixed and static hierarchy, but points instead to a dynamic relationship that unfolds over time. X begins, to be sure, as an infant, utterly dependent for nutrition and protection on a being of superior wisdom and strength. But as X grows, on any minimally plausible understanding of the obligations of parenthood, it is Y's job to work towards the progressive elimination of the dependency. 'Love is proved in the letting go', says the final line of a fine poem by the other Lewis – C. Day Lewis:

---

6 C. S. Lewis 'Priestesses in the Church' [1948], in *Faith, Christianity and the Church* (London: Harper Collins, 2000), ch. 54, p. 402. Lewis goes on to offer it as an apparently decisive argument against any possible female conceptualisation of God that if *that* were conceivable 'we might just as well pray to "Our Mother which art in Heaven" as to "Our Father".' (ibid.) The shifts in awareness stemming from the gender revolution of the late twentieth century have perhaps rather undermined Lewis's implied *quod est absurdum*.

That hesitant figure, eddying way
Like a winged seed loosened from its parent's stem
Was something I never quite grasp to convey
About nature's give and take, the small, the scorching
Ordeals which fire one's irresolute clay.
I've had worse partings but none that so
Gnaws at my mind still. Perhaps it is roughly
Saying what God alone could perfectly show –
How selfhood begins with a walking away
And love is proved in the letting go.[7]

What this idea implies is not just that a good parent stands back, forbearing to control and dominate, but, more than that, that the very goal of parenthood is to let the child grow to the status of an independent being. The telos, the crown, of the parental relationship is the future hoped-for state when the child itself achieves the status of adulthood, and converses with the parent as an independent being.

2 AUTONOMY AND DEPENDENCY

The paradox of our humanity is that we oscillate between two poles: on the one side our contingency and dependency, and on the other our aspiration to independence and autonomy. The admission of dependency which Hampson so dislikes in the Lord's Prayer is simply a religious expression of something fundamental to what it is to be human. For *pace* the existentialists, we are *not* self-creating beings: our fulfilment hinges on a nature and a context we did not create, and cannot radically change. Today's fashionable talk about 'life-style choices' often seems to gloss over this central truth – indeed the legitimate scope of our choice is taken by some to embrace even the supposed 'self-assignments' of gender and bodily appearance that are made possible by modern plastic surgery. But one does not need to pass judgement one way or the other on these costly attempts at self-recreation with the aid of the surgeon's knife in order to believe that there will always remain (irrespective of gender and appearance) an essential structure to our humanity, not of our making, which has to be accepted, like it or not, if we are to function as human beings in the first place. It is *hubris* to think that we can rewrite these fundamental rules – for example the rules of love and vulnerability that determine what

7 Cecil Day Lewis, 'Walking Away' from *The Gate and Other Poems* (London: Jonathan Cape, 1962).

we can achieve in relationship to our fellow humans. We can try to force things our way, to demand, to insist, to reject, to rant and rail, but ultimately we can only achieve our goals by conforming to the laws of love: give, not take, fellow-feeling not arrogance, patience not grasping, waiting not insisting. These laws are written deep in our nature as moral beings; and the submission to them which is encapsulated in religious expressions such as 'Thy will be done' is not some strange self-abasement before an alien will, but an expression of objective moral realities to which, like it or not, our lives must conform if they are to flourish.

Despite the phrase 'like it or not', it is important to stress that our relationship to these realities is not one of the animal who is forced by bit and spur to conform to what it cannot properly understand. The other pole of our humanity is our reason, our autonomy (in the sense of our free power of decision-making). It is a complete misunderstanding to suppose that the religious stance – 'Thy will be done' – involves a servile submission to an alien power.[8] The Will that is held up as our destiny is the kind of will that a human parent has for a child – a will that envisages not conformity but open-ended growth. A familiar contrast between the kind of moral teleology that applies to a rational as opposed to a non-rational being may serve to bring out the point. The oak tree or the horse glorifies God – in secular terms, moves towards the perfection of its kind – simply by unfolding its determined nature. The full-grown flourishing oak, stretching out its branches and clothed in the vivid green of high summer, achieves all it is, all it can be, just by being a complete and perfect specimen of its kind; and so for the horse, galloping across the prairie in the full exultant prime of its strength and health: nothing more is needed. But the human is unique in that it cannot glorify God, it cannot achieve the perfection of its kind, just by being a healthy specimen of the species.[9] We need, as the religious mode has it, to complete the work of

---

8 Compare the following: 'God has willed that man remain "under the control of his own decisions" [Sirach/Ecclesiasticus 15:14] so that he can seek his Creator spontaneously, and come freely to utter and blissful perfection through loyalty to Him. Hence man's dignity demands that he act according to a knowing and free choice that is personally motivated and prompted from within, not under blind internal impulse nor by mere external pressure.' *Gaudium et spes* (Rome: Pastoral Constitution on the Church in the Modern World, 1965), §16.

9 My line of thought here is heavily indebted to a passage in Thomas Merton: 'A tree gives glory to God by being a tree. For in being what God means it to be it is obeying him. It "consents" so to speak, to His creative love. It is expressing an idea which is in God and which is not distinct from the essence of God, and therefore a tree imitates God by being a tree.' *Seeds of Contemplation* [1961] (Wheathamstead: Anthony Clarke, 1972), p. 23. As developed by Merton, the thought is not just that natural kinds glorify their creator, but that each individual specimen has a unique

creation:[10] our autonomy, our rationality, inescapably require us to do something more with our lives, to grow, to learn, not just physically but intellectually and aesthetically and morally, to orient ourselves progressively and ever more closely towards the true, the beautiful, and the good. None of this is a sacrifice of our autonomy properly understood: rather it is its culmination.

The suggestion that the religious ideal of submission to God's will is compatible with the ideal of autonomy is obviously a controversial one. The term 'autonomy' has a long and complex history which there is no space to explore here, other than to draw attention to one particular ambiguity in use of the term: the autonomous person may be construed as either (a) the entirely 'self-legislating' being, who makes up his own rules by a completely independent act of will, subject to no constraints whatsoever – this may be thought of as the extreme existentialist interpretation; or (b) the being who makes decisions independently of the arbitrary will of another, acting in the full light of reason, free from internal or external interference with her rational processes. It is this second sense that I am employing when I speak here of 'autonomy properly understood'. On this account, to act autonomously is to act rationally and freely; and this seems quite compatible with the religious thought that in making my decisions I have to acknowledge that I live in a world I did not create, which contains other free and rational creatures who are entitled to equal respect with me, and that, whether I like it or

---

role to play: 'the perfection of each created thing is not merely in its conformity to an abstract type but in its own individual identity with itself. This particular tree will give glory to God by spreading out its roots in the earth and raising its branches into the air and the light in a way that no other tree before or after ever did or will do.' The philosophical roots of this idea go back to the notion of *haecceitas* or 'thisness' articulated by the late thirteenth-century Franciscan John Duns Scotus (*Quaestiones in libros metaphysicos*, 7, 13, nos. 9 and 26), which in turn influenced the poet Gerard Manley Hopkins:

> As kingfishers catch fire, dragonflies draw flame;
> As tumbled over rim in roundy wells
> Stones ring; like each tucked string tells, each hung bell's
> Bow swung finds tongue to fling out broad its name;
> Each mortal thing does one thing and the same:
> Deals out that being indoors each one dwells;
> Selves – goes itself; *myself* it speaks and spells,
> Crying: *What I do is me: for that I came.*

From *Poems(1876–1889)*, no. 34, in Gardner (ed.), *Poems and Prose of Gerard Manley Hopkins*, p. 51.

10 For the special 'incomplete' nature of human beings, compare Merton: 'Unlike the animals and the trees, it is not enough for us to be what our nature intends. It is not enough for us to be individual men. For us, holiness is more than humanity' (*Seeds of Contemplation*, p. 24).

not, these facts impose constraints on how I may or may not properly exercise my choice.[11]

Iris Murdoch writes: 'How recognizable, how familiar to us, is the man so beautifully portrayed in the *Grundlegung* who, confronted even with Christ, turns away to consider the judgment of his own conscience and to hear the voice of his own reason . . . this man is with us still, free, independent, lonely, powerful, rational, responsible, brave, the hero of so many novels and books of moral philosophy.'[12] But this noble Kantian vision, properly understood, is not in conflict with the religious vision of our human destiny, but rather is integral to it.[13] The whole history of

11 This is very much in the spirit of Kant's account of autonomous moral choice as governed by the categorical imperative, within what he called the 'kingdom of ends' (the entire community of rational agents who are all to be treated with equal dignity and respect). The other main strand in Kant's account of the autonomy of the moral will has to do with its need to be free from internal interferences: moral imperatives cannot be construed as conditional on whatever contingent desires one happens to have, for 'in these cases the will never determines itself directly by the thought of an action, but only by the motivations which the anticipated effect of the action exercises on the will – *I ought to do something because I want something else.*' (*Groundwork for the Metaphysic of Morals* [*Grundlegung zur Metaphysik der Sitten*, 1785], Akademie edition (Berlin: Reimer/De Gruyter, 1900–), vol. IV, p. 444; transl. T. E. Hill Jr and A. Zweig (Oxford: Oxford University Press, 2003), p. 244.) Because of its dependency on the contingencies of inclination, action of this kind is always for Kant heteronomous. Again, it seems to me that the ideal of autonomous choice to which Kant here aspires is quite consistent with what we find, for example in the Pauline and Augustinian conception of the religious life as freeing the will from the slavery of desire (cf. Romans 7:8–24 and Augustine, *City of God* [*De civitate Dei*, 413–26 CE], ch. 19).

12 Iris Murdoch, *The Sovereignty of the Good* (London: Routledge, 1970), p. 131 (I owe this reference to Sam Vice). Compare Kant on our autonomy, 'the basis of the dignity of human nature and of every rational nature', according to which our will must be considered as *selbstgesetzgebend* ('giving the law to itself'). *Groundwork for the Metaphysic of Morals*, ch. 2; Akademie edition, vol. IV, pp. 436, 431; transl. Hill and Zweig, pp. 236, 232.

13 Why then is Kantian autonomy so often represented as inimical to the religious ideal? Part of the answer may arise from the way Kant often speaks of the will as *self-legislating*: 'whenever the will seeks the law that is to determine it *anywhere else* than in the fitness of its maxims for its *own giving* of universal law, and if therefore it goes outside itself and seeks this law in a property of any of its objects – the result is always heteronomy. In that case the will does not give itself the law; rather, the object gives the law to it, in virtue of its relation to the will' (*Groundwork*, Academie edn. vol. 4, p. 440; Hill and Zweig, p. 241). Certainly the language here, together with Kant's talk of the 'sovereign authority' of the will, may seem to have a very secularising tendency. But it has to be remembered that the context is Kant's insistence that moral action can never be simply a means to the fulfilment of some contingent inclination, or the blind submission to the arbitrary power of another. Nothing here seems intrinsically resistant to being expressed in religious mode: we cannot act rightly by abandoning our (God-given) reason and yielding to the dictates of raw desire, or another's arbitrary power ('blind internal impulse or mere external pressure' – See. n. 8, above).

While (if the above reasoning is correct) the tension between traditional Christian and Kantian conceptions of moral agency may be far less than is often supposed, the respective pictures of the metaphysical foundations of morality do nonetheless turn out to be very different – at any rate if we take the argument of the *Grundlegung* as definitive. This is a point forcefully brought out by Onora O'Neill: 'The Kantian grounding of reason, as of morality, cannot be foundational. Anything that could count as foundations would have to be transcendent, and so alien. Once we

humankind's religious journey is not, as some critics of theism like to portray it, one of submissive deference to alien authority; rather it is the story of progressive moral growth. The ancient story of Abraham and Isaac (despite Kierkegaard's famous interpretation of Abraham's faith as involving a 'suspension of the ethical'),[14] is perhaps best interpreted not so much as an abject subordination of the will as a progression beyond the dark atavistic imperative of human sacrifice to something more morally enlightened – or at least a lesser evil (the substitution of a ram); later there will be an even more enlightened shift, away from blood sacrifice entirely to the moral conduct that alone is acceptable to God: 'I desire mercy not sacrifice'.[15]

The creative power of God need not foreclose a creature's autonomy, provided the latter term is properly understood – not as subscribing to the dangerous fantasy of total independence, as if we could map out our lives from scratch, but rather as the free and unfettered use of our powers of critical reason. Consider an analogy with how we exercise our independent powers of reason in investigating the physical creation. The theistic claim that the source of the physical cosmos is God does not absolve the scientist from responsibility to use her reason to assess what the cosmos is like. ('It says so in Scripture' is never a good reason for adopting a particular scientific hypothesis.) And similarly for the 'moral creation'. If God has laid down an objective moral order, we still have to use our critical rational powers to determine what it is, and how we should act. 'It says so in Scripture' is never a good reason for following a course of action, nor, *pace* her detractors, need the religious adherent ever think this way. 'Thy will be done' is a way of focusing on the objective moral order towards which our lives need to be oriented if they are to have value and meaning. And the prayer is not to lose sight of that order in some blind act of servility but rather to remain in touch with that order, and to ask that it may be fulfilled in our lives.

---

make the Copernican turn [the rejection of transcendent metaphysics and the supposition that objects must conform to our human knowledge, rather than vice versa] we cannot expect any such foundations to be available.' ('Reason and Autonomy in *Grundlegung III*', in *Constructions of Reason* (Cambridge: Cambridge University Press, 1989), pp. 64–5. There is however an interesting question (itself later raised by O'Neill) of how far, in his later *Critique of Practical Reason* (*Kritik der Praktischen Vernunft*, 1788), Kant backtracks from his metaphysically 'independent' vindication of morality and freedom.

14 In *Fear and Trembling* [*Frygt og Bœven*, 1843].

15 Hosea 6:6. Cf. Matthew 9:13.

3 THE METAPHYSICS OF VALUE

In the remaining part of this chapter I want to turn to the metaphysical puzzle to which I alluded at the outset – the puzzle of explicating the sense in which God is thought of by the religious adherent as the source of value and meaning in human life.

A familiar objection to the religious position is that it is repugnant to say that God's commands create value. If God's will is simply the will of a powerful being who controls our lives, then this cannot of itself give us *reason* to conform to his will (that is, a moral reason, as opposed to a merely prudential consideration). If God's commands are *worthy* of our obedience, then this must be because they are good. But this in turn suggests that God's will cannot be the source of value; rather it must reflect value. As Bertrand Russell once put it, 'If you are going to say. . . that God is good, you must then say that right and wrong have some meaning which is independent of God's fiat . . . If you are going to say *that*, you will then have to say that it is not only through God that right and wrong came into being, but that they are in their essence logically anterior to God.'[16]

This reasoning creates a dilemma for the theist who sees morality as rooted in the will of God (a dilemma whose elements go back to the perplexing 'Euthyphro problem' first articulated by Plato).[17] On the one hand, the mere fact that a supreme being (arbitrarily) wills X cannot provide a moral reason for doing X; on the other hand, if the reason we should obey God's commands is they are antecedently right or good, then God no longer appears to be the source of morality. As Daphne Hampson puts it, the will of God ought not to have any call on our allegiance were it to violate what we perceive to be right; yet if on the other hand God is simply 'one with the ethical', then 'God is of no consequence'.[18]

The standard reply to this dilemma (the line taken by Augustine and Aquinas and by several modern defenders of the idea of divinely based morality)[19] is that goodness is inseparable from God's nature. God neither

16 Bertrand Russell, 'Why I am Not a Christian' [1927], in *Why I am Not a Christian and Other Essays* (London: George Allen and Unwin, 1957), ch. 1, p. 8.
17 Plato, *Euthyphro* [c. 390 BCE], 6–10.
18 Hampson, *After Christianity*, p. 137.
19 Compare Aquinas: 'For God alone, [his] essence is his being . . . And so he alone is good through his essence.' *Summa theologiae* [1266–73], pt. Ia, qu. 6, art. 3. See also pt. Ia, qu. 2, art. 3; pt. Ia, qu. 3, art. 4,7; pt. Ia, qu. 6, art. 3. For the way in which Aquinas' position offers a possible solution to the Euthyphro dilemma, see E. Stump, *Aquinas* (London: Routledge, 2002), pp. 90, 127/8. See also R. M. Adams, 'A Modified Divine Command Theory of Ethical Wrongness', in G. Outka and J. P. Reeder (eds.), *Religion and Morality* (Garden City: Anchor, 1973), pp. 318–47.

issues arbitrary commands, nor is he subject to prior moral constraints; rather his commands necessarily reflect his essential nature, as that which is wholly and perfectly good. This need not imply that goodness is 'logically anterior' to God, in Bertrand Russell's phrase: rather, it is thought of as co-existent with God, or as essentially and eternally part of his nature.

This may be theologically unexceptionable (and I shall say something more about its more general appeal in a moment), but it still leaves us with a problem about the sense in which God is the 'source' of morality. Consider a proposition such as 'cruelty is wrong'. We have already seen that this cannot be construed by the theist as an arbitrary command of God; it is better understood as (to use an ancient but useful term) an 'eternal verity', a timeless moral truth or principle held in the mind of God, an inseparable part of the structure of the divine mind. But, someone might object, doesn't this still leave us with an 'is/ought' problem? From the fact that God has these ideas in his mind, it does not seem to follow that they have any normative or evaluative force. We are all familiar with the problems of ethical naturalism, the attempt to equate value or normativity with some feature of the natural world. But isn't there a similar problem with 'ethical *super*naturalism' – the theist's attempt to identify value with some supernatural feature of the mind of God?

The same problem, indeed, seems to go for the eternal truths of logic (and perhaps mathematics). The approach philosophers call 'naturalism' (which broadly speaking attempts to explain everything empirically in terms of the properties of the physical world)[20] has a prima facie problem finding a place for these eternal verities within the architecture of the natural world: the 'mustness' of logical truths, their necessity, and indeed their normativity, does not appear to be derivable from any propositions about what is actually the case.[21] Thus, for example, it seems implausible to explain the laws of logic as empirical truths about how our minds actually work: for we recognize in the laws of logic not just generalizations, however universal, about how we *do* think, but normative principles

---

20 I am of course giving only a very crude characterization here. For more, see J. Cottingham, 'Our Natural Guide: Conscience, "Nature" and Moral Experience', in D. Oderberg and T. Chappell (eds.), *Human Values* (London: Palgrave, 2005).

21 Compare David Hume's analogous argument about causal necessity: 'when we look about us . . . and consider the operation of causes, we are never able, in a single instance, to discover any power or necessary connexion; any quality, which binds the effect to the cause and renders the one an infallible consequence of the other.' *Enquiry concerning Human Understanding* [1748], §7, pt. 1.

to which our thought *ought* to conform.[22] Now, the theist, in contrast to the naturalist, locates the eternal verities of logic within the mind of God; yet although this is to assign them to a realm beyond the domain of mere empirical truth, the same puzzle about their normativity seems to reappear in a different form. For again, if it is just a feature of God that his thought does, as a matter of fact, follow these principles, then it appears there is no more normativity here than there was in the human case.

So it is as if the theist has taken the problematic features of value and necessity, and dumped them (or kicked them upstairs) onto God; but it still remains unexplained how something that *is* the case – even the case about a supernatural being – can yield the required normativity.

The theist, however, can reply along the lines of the traditional approach already referred to – by invoking the essential nature of God. In recognizing the compelling power of values, and of logical principles (their normative, or what is sometimes called their 'magnetic' quality), we humans are plainly recognizing something that goes beyond the observed facts of the natural world. And the theistic outlook now proceeds to interpret these features as signifying the presence, beyond the empirical world, of a transcendent supernatural domain that is by its very nature normative – rational and moral. The two principal categories of the normative, the rational and the good, are features which traditional theology has held to apply to God in virtue of his very nature. God is goodness itself (Aquinas), he is the Logos – ultimate rationality (St John).[23] In short, beyond, or behind, the observable universe – the sequence of events that is simply one contingent happening after another – there is for the theist a domain of eternal value and reason, a domain that impinges on our empirical world, making us respond to something beyond the mere sequence of brute facts.[24] We human creatures (since we are ourselves rational and moral beings, at least in part) are responsive to

---

22 Compare the view set out by Gottlob Frege: logic must be wholly objective – its laws hold independent of contingent facts about human psychology. They are 'fixed and eternal . . . boundary stones set in an eternal foundation, which our thought can overflow, but not dislodge'. *The Basic Laws of Arithmetic* [*Die Grundgesetze der Arithmetik*, vol. I, 1893], transl. M. Furth (Berkeley: University of California Press, 1964), p. 13.

23 See above (n. 19) for references to Aquinas. For the *logos*, see John 1:1. The term has a complex and polyvalent meaning (cf. below, Ch. 5, §4), which embraces notions of 'word', 'significance', and 'reason'; in its Johannine usage it thus becomes a shorthand for the 'dynamic of reason', or 'the creative rationality from which the world has sprung'; see J. Ratzinger, *God and The World* [*Gott und die Welt*, 2000] (San Francisco: Ignatius Press, 2002), pp. 114, 206.

24 The metaphorical talk of a transcendent domain 'beyond' or 'behind' the empirical world of course raises questions about the legitimacy or possibility of such metaphysical claims; this topic will be taken up in Ch. 6.

reason and value, and in being so responsive we participate, however dimly, in the divine nature.

4 GOD AS SOURCE OF MORALITY

Even if one were to be granted the broad outlines of the account just given (an account, clearly, that is more of a statement of the theistic position on normativity than an argument that might be expected to induce the atheistic critic to convert to it), it would still be necessary to clarify what precisely it means for the theist to say that God is the source of value. I began by observing that meaning and value do not seem to be the kinds of things that can be 'bestowed' on our lives – even by a supreme being. Rather, they are properties that depend on, or in the jargon 'supervene on', certain natural features of our lives. So what exactly does the theist claim about God's role here? One bizarre suggestion about this was once made by the distinguished British philosopher John Mackie. Mackie was a strict atheist, and was also a subjectivist about value (he followed the Humean line that goodness is simply a projection of our own inclinations and desires). But in his book *Ethics: Inventing Right and Wrong* he concedes that if there *were* such a thing as objective goodness, then it might provide a good argument for theism. For if objectivism were true, argues Mackie, then there would have to be some objective supervenience relation between a natural empirical property (e.g. an action's alleviating suffering) and the property of its being good:

If we adopted moral objectivism, then we should have to regard the relations of supervenience which connect values and obligations with their natural grounds as synthetic: they would then be in principle something that god may conceivably create; and since they would otherwise be a very odd sort of thing, the admitting of them would be an inductive ground for admitting also a god to create them . . . Moral values, their objectivity and their supervenience would be a continuing miracle . . . a constant intrusion into the natural world.[25]

However, the apparently generous concession that Mackie (perhaps ironically) makes to the theist's case is one which the theist would be ill advised to accept. For it is not at all clear how a relation of supervenience could be 'created', even by a divine being. If we consider the analogous case of beauty, and ask how a human artist could create it, it seems the answer must be that she does it by creating objects (sculptures, paintings)

25 J. Mackie, *The Miracle of Theism* (Oxford: Clarendon, 1982), p. 118.

which have a certain form and rhythm and harmony. No extra 'decree' of supervenience ('Let beauty arise out of these features!') is needed; rather the ordered generation of the appropriate features *eo ipso* creates a thing of beauty. The traditional Genesis account of the creation of the world has God 'seeing' that what he has created is (*already*, as it were) good,[26] not decreeing (whatever that would mean) that goodness or beauty should supervene on what he has done.

There are many analogous cases. To create a healthy creature is not to create a biological organism and then impose some strange supervenience decree which generates health from the created properties; rather it is to create an organism in which all the organs function harmoniously and efficiently, so as to enable ordered growth and reproduction and resistance to disease and so on. And similarly (though this is of course a more controversial example), to create a conscious being is not to create a complete functioning life form and then be required to 'superadd' to it, in John Locke's phrase, a faculty of thinking or consciousness;[27] rather it is, arguably, just to create a life form with a nervous system intricate enough to enable it to respond appropriately to the environment, and monitor its own internal states, in a sufficiently complex and intelligent way.[28]

It might seem that for a theist to make these kinds of down-to-earth response to Mackie's suggestion of divinely created supervenience relations risks moving too far the other way – towards a reductionistic naturalism: if goodness, or health, or beauty, or consciousness are just appropriately organized natural properties, with no divine 'superadditions' needed, does this not make the deity entirely redundant? I shall argue in a moment that such an implication is too swift: theistic metaphysics will still have a certain kind of role to play with respect to value. But in one sense, I think, the move towards focusing on natural properties, and away from Mackie's (ironically proposed) supernaturalism of value, is a move in the right direction; for when we are deciding if something is healthy, or beautiful, or good, any theistic appeal to divine creation will, as it were, do no real work in our deliberations. The whole

26 Genesis 1:10, 12, 21, 25, 31.
27 John Locke, *An Essay concerning Human Understanding* [1690], bk. IV, ch. 3, §6.
28 In saying this is 'controversial', I am referring to the fact that many contemporary philosophers maintain that these abilities, however impeccable, would never be sufficient for consciousness without the further presence of mysterious extra items called 'qualia', the supposed episodes of inner awareness of 'what is it like' to see a red rose, or to smell coffee. The locus classicus for this view is Thomas Nagel's article 'What is it like to be a bat?', in T. Nagel, *Mortal Questions* (Cambridge: Cambridge University Press, 1979), ch. 12.

argument will quite properly focus on the actual natural features in virtue of which the object in question is claimed to be good, not on the metaphysical truth (if it is one) that the object or its properties were divinely created. A transcendent metaphysics of value still leaves the human moralist or the aesthetician with all the work yet to do, just as a transcendent metaphysics regarding the creation of the material universe still leaves the scientist all the work yet to do in establishing what properties the universe actually has.

It does not follow, however, that the theist's assertion of a benevolent creator is, like Wittgenstein's idle cog wheel,[29] left spinning in the void, completely unconnected to the discourse of morality. For if the theistic outlook is correct, there will be a divine teleology at work in the cosmos, and this will make a radical difference (amongst other things) to the meaningfulness we are able to attribute to our human lives, and their *eudaimonia* (or fulfilment). Consider the graphic and somewhat revolting example in the *Hitchhiker's Guide to the Galaxy*, of the cow genetically engineered to be capable of thought and speech, and to enjoy being killed and eaten for the pleasure of the customers in the 'Restaurant at the End of the Universe'. The animal comes up to the table and recommends to the diners that they might like to choose a piece taken from its rump, pointing out that it has been force-feeding itself to increase the tenderness of the meat. When the Earthman, Arthur Dent, expresses his horror at this performance, his intergalactic friends silence him by coolly asking if he would feel any better if the cow *didn't* enjoy being eaten.[30] Now the author's purpose in sketching this grim little episode is of course to point up the dubious ethical status of our everyday behaviour in ordinary terrestrial steakhouses; but behind the obvious moral is also the thought that Arthur Dent's shocked reaction to the willing bovine victim nevertheless still manifests a valid moral scruple – one that his smart intergalactic friends are the worse for lacking. For the cow's *telos* – its striving to achieve the state where it is killed and eaten – has been cynically imposed on it in such a way that its whole existence is merely instrumental to the pleasure of its owners; and this is clearly morally repugnant.

If the theistic view of our human existence were like this, if our lives were merely of instrumental value to some higher being who had shaped

29 Cf. Ludwig Wittgenstein, *Philosophical Investigations* [*Philosophische Untersuchungen*, 1953], I, §271.
30 Douglas Adams, *The Restaurant at the End of the Universe* (London: Pan Books, 1984); the second volume in the *Hitchhiker's Guide to the Galaxy* trilogy.

our nature simply and entirely to suit his own purposes, then it is hard to see how our actions and choices in pursuit of our deepest inclinations could, in these circumstances, have any genuine moral meaning. But the theistic conception is of a good and loving creator who desires that his creatures lead lives that are of value to themselves (as well as to him). And this makes a crucial difference – not to the way in which we go about determining what we should do (for that remains within the province of our own rational deliberations), but rather to the *interpretation* we give to our choices, the *significance* which we see them as possessing.[31] The theist believes, sustained by faith, that the careful use of reason, and the sensitive and reflective response to our deepest inclinations, points us towards a life which is the life that a being of the greatest benevolence, goodness, mercy, and love has desired for us, and has destined us to achieve. This will not mean that the theist has access to some magic formula or short cut in ethics, any more than in physical science; metaphysics is never a substitute for science; faith is never a substitute for hard work. But the theistic belief will nonetheless have the capacity to irradiate the believer's life with hope – the kind of hope that the unfortunate rational cow in Douglas Adams' saga must have been unable, in its more reflective moments, to sustain.

For the flavour of Adams' vignette of the restaurant at the end of the universe is, of course, fundamentally absurdist: in the best tradition of Sartre and Camus, it conveys a stark picture of exactly what is involved in a godless universe.[32] Just as, if Hume's account of science is right, there is no ultimate rationality in the universe,[33] and we as human scientists are no

---

31 Bernard Williams, in supporting the standard modern view (roughly from Nietzsche onwards) that the traditional project of grand theistic metaphysics (see below Ch. 6, §1) has 'irretrievably broken down', nevertheless grants a place for a kind of truth that is not compassed within the robust 'common-sense' species of plain facts. This is the kind of truth involving the *interpretation* of reality (see *Truth and Truthfulness* (Princeton: Princeton University Press, 2002), ch. 1). Yet once this is granted, it is hard to see how a religious metaphysic can automatically be supposed to be untenable; for one plausible way of construing it is as, precisely, an interpretation of reality – of the significance of the existence of the cosmos and of beings such as humans.

32 Compare the conception of human life in a godless universe advanced by Albert Camus in *The Myth of Sisyphus* [*Le Mythe de Sisyphe*, 1943]: our only recourse is the 'refusal to hope and the unyielding evidence of a life without consolation'; transl. J. O'Brian (Harmondsworth: Penguin, 1955), p. 58.

33 Or, at least, if there is any ultimate principle it can never be known: '[T]he utmost effort of human reason is to reduce the principles productive of natural phenomena to a greater simplicity and to resolve the many particular effects into a few general causes . . . But as to the causes of these general causes, we should in vain attempt their discovery . . . These ultimate springs and principles are totally shut up from human curiosity and enquiry.' *Enquiry concerning Human Understanding* [1748], §4, pt. i. For the sceptical or epistemic as opposed to metaphysical interpretation of Hume, see John Wright, *The Sceptical Realism of David Hume* (Cambridge: Cambridge University Press, 1983).

better off than the chicken who forms an induction that whenever the barn door opens it will get fed, only to find one morning that it gets its neck wrung;[34] so, if the universe is an utterly impersonal and random process which throws up planets like Earth with living creatures whose deepest inclinations are determined by a kind of genetic roulette, then we as human moralists are no better off than Adams's cow: we can have no faith that our 'reasons' for action are any more than instrumental calculations relative to drives and goals that subserve either an alien purpose, or, to speak more correctly, no purpose at all. For though many modern biologists follow the lead of Richard Dawkins in speaking as if we are lumbering robots programmed to serve the 'purposes' of our genes,[35] this is of course a convenient shorthand for saying that our human nature is the product of completely random mutation and survival pressure. Such a worldview can perhaps allow for human activities being 'meaningful' in some minimal and reduced sense – roughly that of happening to give satisfaction to the agents, or happening to produce certain desired societal goals; but only the theistic worldview can generate a deeper and more fundamental connection between morality and meaning.

In an entirely godless universe, there would be no divine teleology, no supremely intelligent and benevolent purposes, to underwrite our aspirations to moral goodness. Instead, we would just be members of a species who, at a given epoch of evolution, had a particular collection of characteristics and potentialities. Now perhaps some individuals would have more fun developing some of those capacities (for cruelty, let us say), while others would be happier developing others (for generosity, say). Relative to their desires or inclinations, one could say that some had 'reason' to choose cruel acts (a subjective, or instrumental reason, as it were), while others had 'reason' to choose generous acts. But considering the matter independently of the contingent desires of the creatures in question, there would be, so far as I can see, no satisfactory way of assigning to some features of their possible actions the objective property of providing a reason (let alone a conclusive reason)[36] for the agents to act in a certain way.

---

34 Bertrand Russell's example, in *The Problems of Philosophy* [1912] (Oxford: Oxford University Press, 1967), ch. 6, p. 35.
35 Richard Dawkins, *The Selfish Gene* (Oxford: Oxford University Press, 1976).
36 For this notion, see next section.

5 OBJECTIVITY AND ITS BASIS

This last assertion might be challenged by some modern ethicists who aim to provide an entirely secular account of the metaphysics of (genuine and objective) value.[37] Thus Philip Stratton-Lake (drawing on the work of John McDowell and Tim Scanlon) wholly rejects supernaturalism, but construes the goodness of X as the complex non-natural 'property of having [natural] properties that give us reason to respond in certain positive ways' towards X.[38] This seems to me to be likely to work quite well for non-moral cases (what it is for a raincoat to be good is for it to have natural properties, such as impermeability, that give me reason to give it a preferred place in my suitcase if I am visiting Wales or Ireland). But what of moral properties? Stratton-Lake suggests (in line with his general position) that the wrongness of an act consists in its having (natural) properties that provide us with a reason – but this time a

37 It is a striking fact that recent work in moral philosophy has reacted powerfully against the kinds of subjectivism and projectivism that were dominant in the closing decades of the twentieth century. Examples of such neo-objectivism can be found in Paul Bloomfield's *Moral Reality* (Oxford: Oxford University Press, 2001) and Russ Shafer-Landau's *Moral Realism* (Oxford: Oxford University Press, 2003).

If, in common with modern neo-objectivists, we subscribe to the idea that there are genuine objective values (and reject the deflationary accounts of value offered by various kinds of subjectivism and projectivism as flawed), then the philosophical options for giving account of such values are not too numerous. The jury is still out on the project known as 'ethical naturalism', the attempt to reduce values to natural properties of the empirical world, which continues to generate a vast literature (its most ingenious defender is probably Frank Jackson, *From Metaphysics to Ethics* (Oxford: Clarendon Press, 1998). But if we assume that long-standing doubts about this project (going back to G. E. Moore) turn out in the end to be insurmountable, the only viable alternative would be some form of non-naturalism. Theorists like Shafer-Landau appear content to conceive of such irreducibly non-natural values as 'brute' metaphysical realities (see *Moral Realism*, p. 48) – but this appears to reach a terminus of explanation just a little too soon for comfort. The neo-Aristotelian approach typified by Bloomfield construes moral properties as concerned with human flourishing, and having 'the same ontological status as healthiness' (*Moral Reality*, p. 28); but this appears to require the unacceptably relativistic conclusion that rightness or wrongness depend on the contingencies of species development (compare Bloomfield on how, under different population and survival conditions, sibling rivalry might have turned out to be morally good: p. 39). I shall return to the problem of the 'radical contingency of the ethical' at the end of this chapter. For similar problems with a somewhat different and highly sophisticated form of Aristotelian objectivism, championed by John McDowell, see below, n. 42. If these various approaches to underwriting objectivism fail to deliver a worldview that accommodates the genuine reality of objective values, independent of the contingencies of fluctuating human desire and uncertain historical development, then it seems (against those who appear to rule it out in advance) at least worth considering the possibility that the theistic framework may turn out to offer a way forward.

38 Stratton-Lake, *Ethical Intuitionism*, p. 15, invoking J. McDowell, 'Values and Secondary Properties', in T. Honderich (ed.), *Morality and Objectivity* (London: Routledge, 1985), pp. 110–29, and T. Scanlon, *What we Owe to Each Other* (Cambridge, Mass.: Belknap, 1998), pp. 95ff.

conclusive reason, not do not it: 'To say that [an act] is wrong because it is cruel is to say that it is the cruelness of this act that gives us conclusive reason not to do it.'[39] Yet the 'conclusive' seems to me under-supported; for remember that we are supposed to be talking here of *objective* reasons, not just instrumental reasons, or reasons contingent on the particular desires the agents happen to have.

Let us consider in more detail the proposition that cruelty is wrong, for example that bullying the weak or helpless just for personal gratification is wicked. It is unfortunately true that there are people who gain satisfaction from such behaviour – in the words of John Kekes, there are people whose 'resentment, greed, ambition, selfishness and sense of superiority or inferiority gives meaning to their lives and leads them to inflict grievous unjustified harm on others.' 'Such people', observes Kekes, 'may be successfully engaged in their projects, derive great satisfaction from them, and find their lives . . . very meaningful.'[40] But despite the grizzly subjective satisfactions so described, such actions are wrong, indeed necessarily wrong: cruelty is wrong in all possible worlds. (Those who doubt this are invited to try to construct a coherent scenario of a possible world in which such behaviour is good or right.)

It is important to note that the idea of the validity of such eternal and necessary moral verities is in no way undermined by the fact that we can point to variations in customs and norms from society to society; nor, more crucially, is it impugned by what Bernard Williams has called the 'radical contingency in our current ethical conceptions', namely that 'they might have been different from what they are'.[41] A widespread shift in attitudes to cruelty, for example as happened in Nazi Germany, could never show, even if it became dominant all over the planet, that cruelty is no longer wrong, only that humanity had become massively corrupted (something, unfortunately that is always a dangerous possibility).[42]

---

39 Stratton-Lake, *Ethical Intuitionism*, p. 15. The notion derives from C. D. Broad, who (expounding Joseph Butler) notes that the authority of conscience means that its pronouncements are 'not simply interesting . . . statements of fact, and not simply . . . reasons to be balanced against others, but . . . *conclusive* reasons for or against doing the actions about which it pronounces' (*Five Types of Ethical Theory* [1930], cited in S. Darwall, *The British Moralists and the Internal 'Ought'* (Cambridge: Cambridge University Press, 1995), p. 247. Cf. J. Butler, *Fifteen Sermons* [1726], Sermon II, §8, in D. D. Raphael (ed.), *British Moralists* (Oxford: Clarendon, 1969) §399.

40 John Kekes, *Pluralism in Philosophy: Changing the Subject* (Ithaca: Cornell University Press, 2000), p. 97. Cf. Cottingham, *On the Meaning of Life*, p. 23.

41 Williams, *Truth and Truthfulness*, p. 20.

42 The ever-present possibility of radical corruption in our social fabric seems to me to constitute the main difficulty for John McDowell's form of 'quietist' objectivism about the ethical, notwithstanding the enormous finesse and subtlety with which his account is presented.

If there are eternal and objective ethical truths such as that cruelty is wrong, they cannot be undermined by the 'radical contingency' in the shifting historical development of human ethical attitudes. Yet, and here is the crucial point, one which I take to be a *reductio* of an atheist metaphysics of value, such objective ethical truths *would be* undermined in the absence of the cosmic moral teleology that theism provides.[43] If it is merely the contingencies of our genetic and cultural makeup that have produced our moral aversion to cruelty, then it is hard to see how we have an objective reason (a reason independent of the contingent set of our desires), let alone a 'conclusive' reason, not to be cruel. For the theist, by contrast, there is a domain of eternal and necessary value, a divine reality that infuses all possible worlds; the purposes of God are necessarily good, and the nature of humans, qua created beings, is such that they can only be truly fulfilled by living in conformity with his moral purposes.

The upshot, paradoxically, is that Mackie's talk of moral objectivism implying the 'irruption' of value into the natural world is in a certain sense correct. It is not that goodness or rightness are 'miraculous' properties, or supernaturally decreed supervenience relations. Rather, as we have seen, goodness is like health: the criteria for its attribution to objects and actions have to do entirely with the presence or absence of certain broadly natural features, such as the tendency to alleviate suffering, the promotion of sympathy and fellow feeling, respectful treatment, and the like. But the normative status of the obligations connected with such types of behaviour is, as Kant famously pointed out, not simply instrumental, or hypothetical: we ought to do these things not just because we have contingently evolved to have certain inclinations, not because our society happens contingently to put a premium on certain goals, but rather

McDowell insists that moral properties are real properties (not disguised projections of our own), but, taking his cue from Aristotle, construes the process of social acculturation (or ethical education) as providing a mode of access to this reality: 'immersion in a tradition [is] a respectable mode of access to the real'; and thus 'we can stop supposing that the rationality of virtue needs a foundation outside the formed evaluative outlook of a virtuous person' (*Mind and World* (Cambridge, Mass.: Harvard University Press, 1994), p. 98; *Mind, Value and Reality* (Cambridge, Mass.: Harvard University Press, 1998), p. 174). Whether this idea of a formed evaluative outlook (what McDowell calls 'second nature') lacks proper critical resources, or offers too many hostages to cultural conservativism, has generated a considerable critical literature; for spirited attempts to defend McDowell on this issue, see Lovibond, *Ethical Formation*, ch. 7, and T. Thornton, *John McDowell* (Chesham: Acumen, 2004), p. 91.

43 Or some substitute for it – perhaps some form of the 'rampant Platonism' that John McDowell summarily dismisses as implying that our human responses to value are 'occult' or 'magical' (*Mind and World*, p. 92). However, for the possibility of a 'rampantly' transcendent metaphysical domain, see Ch. 6, §5, below; for its possible interaction with the human world, see Ch. 7, §4, below.

because such behaviour is categorically right. Such behaviour is indeed, in the currently fashionable terminology, behaviour we have conclusive reason to pursue. And ultimately, for the theist, such conclusive objective reasons, riding free of the contingencies of our human development, will be interpreted in a way that makes reference to the moral teleology that permeates the whole cosmos.

It is the idea of a moral teleology, or moral cosmology, that finally underlies the maxim of Dante with which we began, 'in his will is our peace'. And the peace envisaged, to come back full circle to our earlier discussion, is not mere tranquillisation or externally engineered submission to a higher power, but is the peace of an autonomous being whose reason has recognised the truth of the ancient religious idea: to serve goodness is the most perfect freedom.[44]

---

44 The formula is an extremely old one, found in the ancient 'Collect for Peace': 'Deus, auctor pacis et amator, quem nosse vivere, *cui servire regnare est*'; cf. the fine translation of Thomas Cranmer: 'O God, who art the author of peace and lover of concord, in knowledge of whom standeth our eternal life, *whose service is perfect freedom*' (Morning Prayer, *Book of Common Prayer*). In a more literal rendering of the Latin, God is the one 'whom to serve is to reign.' As with so much in Christianity, the thought has Jewish antecedents; cf. §6 (Vau) of Psalm 119(118): 44–5: 'So shall I keep thy law continually, for ever and ever. And I will walk at liberty: for I seek thy precepts.'

CHAPTER 4

Religion and self-discovery: the interior journey

Πρόσεχε σεαυτῷ μῆ γένηται ῥῆμα κρυπτὸν ἐν τῇ καρδὶα σου.
('Give heed to yourself, lest there be a hidden word in your heart').
Basil of Caesarea[1]

I A TRIANGLE OF TENSION

I spoke in Chapter 1 of the vital role played by spiritual praxis in the development of a religious outlook, and also of its importance from a philosophical point of view, in the project of understanding the nature of religion. Practical engagement alone, however, is clearly not a sufficient condition for having a religious allegiance: as discussed in Chapter 2, adherence to a religion involves adopting a worldview that needs to be at least consistent with the character of the universe as we find it – and here again philosophy becomes involved, since examining such consistency relations is in large part a philosophical task. Finally, as explored in Chapter 3, a religious outlook is integrally bound up with certain moral commitments; and (at least in theistic traditions) this immediately raises higher-order philosophical questions of how the domain of morality is related to the transcendent reality which is claimed to be its ultimate source.

From the results so far, it is clear that there is a pretty close relationship between the domain of religion and that of philosophy. This is not, of course, to imply that all religious people have to get involved in philosophical inquiry; but nevertheless the kind of critical reflective analysis that philosophy provides is probably increasingly indispensable for anyone who wishes to hold on to a religious outlook, at least in the highly intellectualised and science-dominated culture of the western world.

---

1 Basil of Caesarea, *In Illud 'Attende tibi ipsi'* [c. 470], in *Patrologia Graeca*, ed. J. Migne (Paris: 1844–55), 31, col. 197ff; the sermon takes as its text the Septuagint version of Deuteronomy 15:9. I owe this reference to Pierre Hadot, *Philosophy as a Way of Life* [*Exercises spirituels et philosophie antique*, 1987] (Cambridge, Mass.: Blackwell, 1995), ch. 4, p. 130.

In addition to the domains of religion and philosophy, a third mode of thinking seems to me clearly implicated in the issues raised so far, namely the domain of psychoanalytic thought. Given the intimate relation between religious observance and spiritual and moral praxis – the training or *askesis* referred to in Chapter 1, with its exercises in self-reflection, self-discovery, self-purification, and the like – it would be very odd for anyone in our contemporary culture to have a view of religion that managed to insulate itself from the ideas of psychoanalysis; for during the past hundred years or so these latter ideas have increasingly infused our understanding of the nature of self-awareness, interior change, and moral development.

What I want therefore to move on to do in the present chapter is to examine certain important aspects of the relationship between these three domains of thought: religious, psychoanalytic, and philosophical. I shall suggest that despite a widespread belief that the three respective outlooks are in serious mutual tension, they can on closer scrutiny be seen to be perfectly compatible, and indeed (I shall end up claiming) actually mutually supportive. As well as connecting up with some of the practical and theoretical issues concerning religious allegiance that have already been broached, the links I shall endeavour to establish will turn out to be important in later chapters, when we come to examine the nature of religious language, and the possible relationship between religious allegiance and the living of a morally sound and integrated life.[2]

It will be helpful to begin with a schematic overview, starting with the relation between psychoanalysis and religion. It is widely supposed that psychoanalytic thought is distinctly hostile to the religious outlook. Though this view is not universally shared, there is a prevailing picture of Freud and his followers as 'driving the last nails in the coffin of Divinity'.[3] In a familiar story about the rise of modernity, Freud is commonly located within a godless trinity of thinkers responsible for undermining religion. First Copernicus dethroned the Earth from its central place under heaven, so that it becomes more difficult to see our planet as the special focus of the Creator's concern. Then Darwin demoted humanity from its unique status, making it harder to see humans as God's special image-bearers, set apart from the animal kingdom. And lastly Freud puts the boot in, arguing that the very idea of God, so far from being the divine image shining in each human soul, is a sign of

2 See below, Ch. 5 and Ch. 7.
3 Victor White, *God and the Unconscious* [1952] (London: Collins, 1960), p. 29.

arrested development – an infantile illusion that humanity needs to outgrow if we are ever to come of age. This, indeed, was how Freud himself presented his views, so it is hardly surprising that psychoanalytic and religious thought are so often seen as antithetical.

What about the relation between philosophy and psychoanalysis? Again, as a generalization, it appears that philosophical thought is on the whole inimical to psychoanalytic ideas. (I am speaking here of the analytic branch of philosophy: among so-called 'continental' philosophers, psychoanalytic modes of thought have been extremely influential.[4]) The analytic academy, by and large, has given Freud a roasting. His theories are accused of being unscientific, over-sweeping, and, by some critics, virtually incoherent: since the defining characteristic of the mind is consciousness (so runs this objection), doesn't the concept of unconscious mentation verge on the absurd?[5] There are admittedly a number of staunch philosophical defenders of Freud to be found,[6] but I think it is fair to say the prevailing reaction of analytic philosophy towards psychoanalytic ideas is either coldly indifferent or markedly hostile.

Finally, the relation between philosophy and religion. Here one may think there is no pattern: some philosophers are theists, others atheists. But, again as a broad generalization, it seems that the dominant position in the modern analytic academy is one of hostility towards religion. The traditional arguments for God's existence are widely supposed not to work, while the arguments against his existence (most notably the problem of evil, discussed in Chapter 2) are taken to be pretty decisive. The general temper of contemporary analytic thought is, moreover, broadly scientistic, or else at least rationalistic, in its methodology and outlook.[7]

---

4 One might, for instance, compare the wealth of references to 'Freud' and to 'psychoanalysis' in the index of the recent *Edinburgh Encyclopedia of Continental Philosophy* (ed. S. Glendinning, Edinburgh: Edinburgh University Press, 1999), with the relative paucity of such references in, for example, *A Companion to Analytic Philosophy* ed. A. P. Martinisch and D. Sosa (Oxford: Blackwell, 2001).

5 For an extended critique unusual in its ferocity, but not untypical in its general approach (albeit coming from someone who was often critical of analytic philosophy), see Ernest Gellner, *The Psychoanalytic Movement* (London: Granada, 1985).

6 The best known is Richard Wollheim; see *The Thread of Life* (Cambridge, Mass.: Harvard University Press, 1984); among the most interesting recent philosophical defenders of Freudian ideas are Sebastian Gardner, *Irrationality and the Philosophy of Psychoanalysis* (Cambridge: Cambridge University Press, 1993), and Jonathan Lear (*Happiness, Death, and the Remainder of Life* (Cambridge, Mass.: Harvard University Press, 2000).

7 Much recent analytic work in the philosophy of mind, for example, sees itself as a branch of the enterprise of cognitive science. The scientistic conception of philosophy's future is of course by no means accepted by all, but even the dissenters are for the most part likely to fit the alternative label

The model to which most or at least a very large number of modern anglophone philosophers aspire is that of the rational, precise, and cautious thinker, with a sceptical (with a small 's') and no-nonsense outlook; and this means that, speaking generally, they tend to have little truck with the idea of the supernatural. In short, atheism appears to be the default position at least in the anglophone philosophical academy.

Although these generalized sketches no doubt paint a very crude and oversimplified picture of our contemporary academic culture, many will, I think, find something recognisable in them (though like all generalizations they can tolerate a good many exceptions without this undermining their truth as generalizations). What we appear to have, then, is a 'triangle of hostility': psychoanalysis opposes religion; religion is opposed by philosophy; and philosophy also opposes psychoanalysis. I want to propose in this chapter that in so far as such antagonisms do in fact obtain, they ought not to; for properly understood, there is no good reason why any of the three respective modes of thought should be taken to be in tension. The psychoanalytic project is, I shall argue, closely related to the religious quest; and an enlightened philosophical outlook can find room to acknowledge the value of both.

2 PSYCHOANALYSIS AND PHILOSOPHY

In order to examine our 'triangle of hostility' in more detail, it will be convenient to start with the relationship between psychoanalysis and philosophy – though here I shall be quite brief, since this is something I have dealt with at length elsewhere.[8] A great deal of the hostility expressed by philosophers towards psychoanalytic thought has come about, I believe, by Freud's own tendency to present himself as the white-coated scientist, barraging his audience with technical jargon and a complex array of quasi-clinical terminology – 'abreaction', 'anaclitic object-choice', 'cathexis', and the like, not to mention baroque and grandiose general theories such as that of the 'pleasure principle' and the 'death instinct' – all of which, not unreasonably, has called forth a demand for precise experimental verification; and when this is not forthcoming, or not fully forthcoming, then the frequent reaction is to condemn the whole system

---

suggested, thinking of themselves *qua* philosophers, as 'rationalistic' in the loose sense (viz. rational, precise, cautious, sceptical, and wary of the 'spooky' claims of the supernaturalists). For more on the naturalistic paradigm, see below, Ch. 6, §3.

8 In *Philosophy and the Good Life* (Cambridge: Cambridge University Press, 1998), ch. 4.

as at worst fraudulent, or at the very least failing to live up to the standards of proper science.

But these criticisms can be avoided if the theories of Freud are presented, as in my view they should be, as hermeneutic tools rather than strictly scientific hypotheses; they are more akin to the insights of the novelist or the playwright than to the results of the laboratory experimenter. By this I don't mean that they do not have a host of careful observational data to support them, but rather that the notions invoked are continuous with a host of pre-theoretical ideas that inform our ordinary understanding of how people operate – ideas that are perfectly valid and illuminating from the point of view of interpreting and understanding our behaviour and that of our fellow-humans, even if they do not meet the criteria of predictive power and repeatability that are required for the testable hypotheses of the scientist. Like many geniuses, Freud's achievement is to succeed in making clear and explicit what in a sense we partly knew all along. Psychoanalytic notions, such as 'repression', 'rationalization', and 'sublimation', and many others, correspond to patterns of human behaviour that have for centuries figured implicitly in the work of novelists, playwrights, and poets; now, thanks to Freud, they are publicly displayed, so to speak, and pretty much taken for granted in our everyday modes of self-understanding – so much so that the vehement philosophical critics of Freud are often found employing them in their very diatribes against psychoanalysis, curiously unaware of all they have come to accept.[9]

The central idea of the Unconscious is of course a complex and controversial one which it would take us too far off our main thread to examine in detail here. But in so far as philosophical opposition has protested that the essence of mental contents is that they are, or can easily be made to be, transparent to the thinker, that opposition is relatively easy to demolish. The so-called doctrine of the *transparency of the mind* is extremely hard to defend, and it is doubtful that any of its supposed originators, including its supposed arch-originator Descartes, ever held it.[10] The doctrine applies, at best, to certain occurrent cognitive and volitional acts; but even Descartes was quick to acknowledge that the *affective* part of our mental life, our awareness of our own emotions and passions, is subject to a pervasive and troubling opacity. Descartes is quite explicit on this point; he describes, for example, a graphic example from

9 See Cottingham, *Philosophy and the Good Life*, p. 112.
10 Cf. *Philosophy and the Good Life*, ch. 3.

his own experience about his troubling tendency to believe he was in love with any woman he saw who suffered from a certain visual defect – namely being cross-eyed – until he was able to recall a childhood episode which had led to an unconscious distortion of his subsequent adult emotions.[11] Bringing to the surface the precise nature of our feelings, and the judgements and choices we make in the light of those feelings, is not a matter of identifying simple items like beliefs and desires, swimming around the transparent tank of consciousness. On the contrary, it often requires serious and systematic work to drag the relevant items into the light; and 'light' is indeed the appropriate metaphor here, since our awareness of our emotional states, and of the nature of the objects to which they are directed, can frequently be distorted by all kinds of dark projections and shadows from the past, shadows whose distorting power can easily elude us because we are unaware of their very existence. None of this need be seen as philosophically problematic: the discoveries of Freud relate to all sorts of phenomena that are of a type with those of ordinary human experience, like the music in the next room, dimly heard but consciously unregistered: phenomena such as the forgotten but partly recoverable memories of childhood, and the elusive, but ultimately encompassable deliverances of dreams.[12] Once we give up the oversimplified 'goldfish bowl' model of mental 'transparency', and acknowledge the complexity and relative opacity of much our mental life, then the view of psychoanalytic thinking as based on an outlandish and unscientific conception of the mind starts to lose much of its plausibility. This need not mean, of course, that the concepts and methods of psychoanalysis should be immune from philosophical scrutiny; but it does suggest that the idea of a radical tension between the two disciplines is misguided, and that philosophy, in the end, may have nothing to fear from psychoanalytic thought, and perhaps even much to learn from it.

---

11 'When I was a child, I loved a girl of my own age who had a slight squint (*une fille de mon âge qui était un peu louche*). The impression made by sight in my brain when I looked at her cross-eyes became so closely connected to the simultaneous impression which aroused in me the passion of love that for a long time afterwards when I saw persons with a squint I felt a special inclination to love them simply because they had that defect; yet I had no idea myself that this was why it was. However, as soon as I reflected on it, and recognized that it was a defect, I ceased to be affected by it. So when we are inclined to love someone without knowing the reason, we may believe that this is because they have some similarity to something in an earlier object of our love, though we may not be able to identify it'. Descartes, letter to Chanut of 6 June 1647 (AT V 57: CSMK 323).

12 *Philosophy and the Good Life*, ch. 4, §4.

3 PSYCHOANALYTIC CRITIQUES OF RELIGION

With this brief preamble on psychoanalysis and philosophy, I now turn to the relationship between psychoanalysis and religion. Freud's fertile and voluminous writings touch on religion at many points, but two of his ideas in particular have probably been most influential in their negative impact on how religion is perceived. The first is the notion of the *omnipotence of thoughts*, as set out in the relatively early work *Totem and Taboo* (1913). Freud there spoke of 'primitive man's immense belief in the power of his wishes';[13] it is characteristic of the primitive or superstitious mind that it tends to defy reality, to radically overestimate the power of the mind to control external events. The original subtitle of *Totem and Taboo* was 'Some Points of Agreement between the Mental Lives of Savages and Neurotics'; Freud's basic insight (which apparently first occurred to him when writing up one of his clinical case studies into obsessional neurosis, the now famous 'Rat Man' case, 1909),[14] was that patients in the grip of neurosis tend to defend themselves by a loosening of their grip on reality. Confronted with frightening psychological pressures that they cannot fully understand or control, individuals tend to retreat into fantasy thinking of a distinctive kind, which attributes a peculiar kind of efficacy to their own mental acts. Thus the patient known as the Rat Man firmly supposed that 'if he thought of someone, he would be sure to meet that very person immediately afterwards, as though by magic . . . If, without any really serious intention, he swore at some stranger, he might be sure that the man would die soon afterwards so that he would feel responsible for his death', and so on.[15]

The phenomenon, once pointed out, has a not unfamiliar ring to it ('I was just thinking of her when she telephoned!'); the fantasy of the 'omnipotence of thoughts' is essentially an extreme form of the superstitious thinking to which all of us except the most austerely rationalistic have probably been prone at one time or another. The point, of course, is that we cannot control reality in this way, but at some level it may serve us as a kind of palliative mechanism to indulge in a more or less conscious

---

13 *Totem and Taboo* [*Totem und Tabu*, 1913], Pt. III; in *The Penguin Freud Library* (London: Penguin Books, 1985), vol. XIII: hereafter '*PFL*'. (Based on J. Strachey (ed.), *Standard Edition of the Complete Psychological Works of Sigmund Freud* (London: Hogarth, 1953–74).

14 The so-called 'Rat Man' case is described in *Notes upon a Case of Obsessional Neurosis* [*Bemergkungen über einen Fall von Zwangsneurose*, 1909], in *PFL* vol. IX.

15 S. Freud, *Totem and Taboo*, ch. 3 ('Animism, Magic, Omnipotence of Thoughts'): in *PFL* vol. XIII, pp. 143–4.

fantasy that there is some effective connection between our own thoughts or actions and what actually comes about. Superstition is born of fear, and in a kind of primitive and pre-rational way it goes some way to alleviating fear: we can't guarantee good fortune, but we can at least touch wood, or keep our fingers crossed.

Applied to religion, Freud's point now becomes seriously damaging. Primitive man is confronted with complex destructive forces he cannot control, and he fantasizes that he can exert some influence through prayers, sacrifices, and the like. The neurotic phenomenon of the 'omnipotence of thoughts' turns out to be strikingly operative here: in the initial 'animistic' phase of human development, on Freud's account, man invests the whole of external reality with magical mentalistic powers modelled on those of his own mind. Then comes the stage of the more developed religions, where these powers are given up and resigned, as it were, to the gods; but 'men do not seriously abandon [their fantasy of the omnipotence of thoughts], since they reserve the power of influencing the gods in a variety of ways according to their wishes'. Only with the onset of the third, scientific phase of human development, do we gradually learn to 'acknowledge [our] smallness, and submit resignedly to death and to the other necessities of nature'.[16] The lesson is plain: religion is part of a pattern of immature apotropaic and displacement mechanisms; healthy living, for the human race in general as for each individual, requires finding a satisfactory way of doing without them.

The second key idea in the psychoanalytic critique of religion is Freud's conception of religion as *illusion*. Though figuring in a slightly later work, *Civilization and its Discontents* (1929), this idea is quite closely connected to Freud's earlier notion of the omnipotence of thoughts. The starting point is human helplessness in the face of 'the majestic, cruel and inexorable powers of nature'. These include both external forces (storms, floods, disease, death) and the internal forces of our own nature (lust, anger, brutality, and so on), which may be just as frightening and threatening. Religion is, consciously or unconsciously, an attempt to mitigate our defencelessness by endeavouring to 'adjure, appease, bribe' or otherwise influence those various powers. Freud famously links all this with mankind's universal longing for a father figure, one who will protect us from suffering, and impose justice on a seemingly chaotic and terrifying universe.[17]

---

16 *Totem and Taboo* (*PFL* vol. XIII, p. 146).
17 *Civilization and its Discontents* [*Das Unbehagen in der Kultur*, 1929], *PFL* vol. XII, p. 195. Jean-Paul Sartre, though he presented himself as a sharp critic of Freudian theory, describes certain

This longing for celestial protection is identified by Freud as something essentially *infantile*. 'The derivation of religious needs form the infant's helplessness and the longing for the father aroused by it seems to me incontrovertible . . . I cannot think of any need in childhood as strong as the need for a father's protection.'[18] The general line, incidentally, is prefigured in David Hume, though in a more matter-of-fact form rather than via the idea of unconscious drives. What prompts humans to suppose there is a God, according to Hume is 'the ordinary affections of human life' such as the dread of misery and the terror of death.'[19] The upshot is the same: religion is an illusion born of helplessness and fear.[20]

4 TWO RESPONSES TO FREUD

I shall now look at two promising ways of defusing this tension between the psychoanalytic and religious outlooks: the first irenic move comes from philosophy, the second from psychoanalysis itself. Take your pick; for they are, I believe, compatible and complementary.

4.1 The philosophical response

The Freudian idea of the omnipotence of thoughts, and the equation of religion with a superstitious attempt to control external reality, needs to be set against the distinction made by Wittgenstein between *faith* and *superstition*. Baptism of a child, if accompanied by the belief that this is an

defence mechanisms whereby humans respond to stress in ways that seem highly reminiscent of Freud: 'When the paths traced out become too difficult, or when we see no path, we can no longer live in so urgent and difficult a world. All the ways are barred. However, we must act. So we try to change the world, that is, to live as if the connection between things and their potentialities were not ruled by deterministic procedures, but by magic.' J.-P. Sartre, *The Emotions: Outline of a Theory* [*Esquisse d'une théorie des emotions*, 1939], transl. B. Frechtmann (Secaucus, N.J.: Citadel Press, 1975), pp. 58–9. Quoted in T. Martin, *Oppression and the Human Condition* (Lanham, Md.: Rowman and Littlefield, 2002), p. 67.

18 *Civilization and its Discontents*, PFL, vol. XII, p. 260.

19 David Hume, *The Natural History of Religion* [1757]. Here and throughout this section I am strongly indebted to Michael Palmer's fascinating study *Freud and Jung on Religion* (London: Routledge, 1997).

20 It is important to note that an 'illusion', in Freudian usage, is not necessarily erroneous. Freud at one point explicitly concedes this, distinguishing 'illusion' from 'delusion' (though his terminology is not always consistent). Cinderella may have the fantasy that a prince will come and marry her – and in a few cases it may actually happen. But Freud argues that it is characteristic of illusions in his sense that they are held without regard for rational justification; further, they characteristically stem from (indeed are generated by) the wishes or needs of the believer. And again the conclusion is all too clear: religion is something we need to grow out of. See Freud, *The Future of an Illusion* [*Die Zukunft einer Illusion*, 1927], PFL vol. 12, p. 213. Cf. Palmer, *Freud and Jung on Religion*, ch. 3.

efficacious procedure for making the child's life more lucky or more successful, is mere superstition – a kind of primitive pseudo-science. If we want to ensure the best opportunities for the child's health and success, we are far better off turning to the methods of science (for example modern medicine). But if the baptism is an act of joyful affirmation and thanksgiving for the new life, it is genuinely religious.[21]

The boundary, despite Wittgenstein's distinction, is doubtless not always clear-cut: there obviously are and have been large numbers of religious adherents who may pray or go to church in the hope of somehow influencing the way their lives, or those of their loved ones, turn out; and if this is done in a way that attributes quasi-magical powers to their petitions or rituals, then it may involve a good measure of superstition, and may thus incur the Freudian charge of failing to accept reality – failing to acknowledge the true weakness of the human condition. But that is not the only way to construe religious practice and language; and here (though without necessarily accepting his general account of religion) one may pick up the point made by D. Z. Phillips, very much in the spirit of Wittgenstein, that religious beliefs cannot be divorced from the situations in human life in which they have their sense.[22] If this is right, then we need to be prepared to subject religious writings to detailed contextual scrutiny before we pontificate on the meaning and function of the propositions found there. And it quickly becomes clear from examining the characteristic sayings of many of the great religious writers that they are extremely hard to interpret as being primitive or superstitious attempts to manipulate reality to make it conform to the wishes of the subject.

Compare, for example, the following passage from a leading twentieth-century theologian, where the tone, so far from betraying the fears or desires of the would-be manipulator, seems on the contrary to manifest a deep awareness of our inescapable human weakness and dependency:

Let us take, for instance, someone who is dissatisfied with his life, who cannot make the good will, errors, guilt and fatalities of his life fit together . . . He cannot see how he is to include God as an entry in the accounting, as one that makes the debit and credit . . . come out right. This person surrenders himself to God . . . he releases his unresolved and uncalculated existence, he lets go in trust and hope.

Here is someone who discovers that he can forgive though he receives no reward from it . . .

---

21 See *Culture and Value* [*Vermischte Bemergkungen*], MS 137 48b [1948], ed. G. H. von Wright (Oxford: Blackwell, 1988), p. 82. For an excellent summary of Wittgenstein's position, see H.-J. Glock, *A Wittgenstein Dictionary* (Oxford: Blackwell, 1996), s.v. 'Religion'.
22 See, for example, Phillips' contribution in J. Runzo (ed.), *Is God Real?* (New York: St Martin's Press, 1993), p. 89.

Here is someone who does his duty where it can apparently only be done with the terrible feeling that he is denying himself and doing something ludicrous which no one will thank him for.

Here is a person who is really good to someone from whom no echo of understanding and thankfulness is heard in return, whose goodness is not even repaid by the feeling of having been selfless, noble and so on . . .

Here is someone who is absolutely lonely; for whom all trustworthy handholds take him into the infinite distance, and who does not run away from this loneliness but treats it with ultimate hope . . .

There is God, and his liberating grace. There we find what . . . Christians call the Holy Spirit of God.[23]

Some of the phrasing here may not appeal to everyone; but irrespective of whether one is in sympathy with the sentiments expressed, they surely illustrate how far adrift we go if we try to assimilate the theistic outlook to a single literalistic template (no matter how widely held) – the super-stitious belief that recalcitrant events can be magically manipulated to make everything come out right. Nor, I think, despite some Kierkegaar-dian 'leap of faith' overtones in the passage, can we dismiss it as a latter-day retreat to extreme fideism, from someone who is irrationally clinging to the vestiges of a religious outlook in the face of the increasing on-slaughts of modern science; on the contrary, the language is recognizably part of a long tradition that goes right back to St Paul, when he described the mindset of the early Christians in the following terms:

in much patience, in afflictions, in necessities, in distresses, in labours . . . in fasting, by pureness, by knowledge, by long-suffering, by kindness, by love unfeigned . . . as deceivers and yet true, as dying and behold we live, as chastened and not killed, as sorrowful yet alway rejoicing, as poor yet making many rich, as having nothing and yet possessing all things.[24]

These are strange, extraordinary words – perhaps incomprehensible to the hyper-rational and scientistic mentality of our own times, as indeed they may well have been to many of the Corinthians to whom they were addressed. (Aristotle would have found the conception of the good thus described to be utterly bizarre: what about success, flourishing, *eudaimonia*, great-souledness, self-pride, dignity, status, noble blood?[25]) But the

23 Karl Rahner, *The Practice of Faith: A Handbook of Contemporary Spirituality* [*Praxis des Glaubens: Geistliches Lesebuch*, 1982] (London: SCM Press, 1985), pp. 69–70.

24 2 Corinthians 6:4ff.

25 For some of the striking contrasts between the standpoints of Aristotelian and of Christian ethics, see J. Cottingham, 'Partiality and the Virtues', in R. Crisp (ed.), *How Should One Live? Essays on the Philosophy of Virtue* (Oxford: Oxford University Press, 1996), pp. 57–76.

point I am making is that if we wish to evaluate the Freudian assessment of the religious outlook, we must look at the language religious people actually use. Interpreting language like that of Paul is of course a highly complex task; but at the very least we can say that a good slice of it does not readily fit the interpretation that sees it simply in terms of a neurotic or superstitious attempt to control reality.[26]

4.2 The psychoanalytic response

So much for the philosophical or linguistic move in our strategy of defusing the Freudian critique – a move based on paying attention to the actual nature of much religious language. I now turn to the second reconciliatory move – one which comes from within the psychoanalytic tradition itself.[27] The tendency of many psychoanalytic thinkers after Freud has been to absorb much of his work on fantasy thinking, but to subject it to a fundamental reappraisal from the evaluative point of view. So far from being a necessary indicator of neurosis or immaturity, the capacity for fantasising turns out, on the analysis of post-Freudians like Donald Winnicott (in his *Playing and Reality*, 1971), to be a fundamental part of natural human creativity. Compare the following assessment by William Meissner:

Man needs to create, to shape and transform his environment, find vehicles for expressing his inner life, or rather the constant commerce between the ongoing worlds of his external experience and his inner psychic reality . . . It is through illusion, then, that the human spirit is nourished . . . The man without imagination, without the capacity for play or for creative illusion, is condemned

---

26 An alternative interpretation of a broadly Freudian kind would be to say that Paul's language reflects a massive attempt at self-deception, or a subconscious attempt at self-compensation in the face of the apparent misfortunes, persecution, and failures encountered in his quest to promote the gospel. Compare Erich Fromm: 'Submission to a powerful authority is one of the avenues by which man escapes from his feeling of aloneness and limitation. In the act of surrender he loses his independence and integrity as an individual, but he gains the feeling of being protected by an awe-inspiring power of which, as it were, he becomes a part.' E. Fromm, *Psychoanalysis and Religion* (New Haven: Yale university Press, 1950), p 35. Similar accounts are commonly offered of the early disciples' belief in the Resurrection – as based on a subconscious refusal to accept the reality that all their hopes had ended in the death and failure of their leader. Such deflationary 'wishful thinking' explanations cannot of course be dismissed out of hand, though it is a matter for legitimate scepticism whether they offer a sufficiently powerful mechanism to explain the dynamism and hope manifested in the lives of the early apostles.

27 Though specialists sometimes restrict the term 'psychoanalytic' to the doctrines of Freud himself or his close followers, I am here using the term in its popular somewhat broader sense, to encompass the movement that began with Freud but branched into many differing schools, including, for example Jungian psychology.

to a sterile world of harsh facts without color or variety, without the continual enrichment of man's creative capacities.[28]

In a rather more complex, but essentially similar vein, the work of Carl Jung stresses the importance of *symbolic thought* for the health of the psyche. The integration of conscious and unconscious elements of the self is a precondition for wholeness, and religious imagery and symbolism performs a vital function here. The struggle for 'individuation' as Jung terms it, the process of achieving internal balance and integration, requires just those modes of thought and expression which the religious archetypes provide. Thus the figure of Christ, for example, can be seen as representing the archetype of the Self, 'the completest expression of that fateful combination we call individuality'.[29]

It would take us too far round to assess the controversial Jungian theory of the archetypes which is presupposed here, nor does the present argument depend on Jung's specific account of the Christ-archetype. The general message to be gleaned for present purposes from the work of psychoanalytic thinkers as diverse as Winnicott and Jung is that Freud's dismissal of the religious impulse as infantile fails to recognise the imaginative and symbolic role of religious modes of thought and expression, and their possible role in the healthy development of the human personality. As Michael Palmer has put it in his thoughtful and informative study of Freud and Jung: 'Religion, far from being neurotic, is revealed as a constant and evolving process in the development of the psychic personality . . . Religious symbols . . . open up a psychic level . . . that is primordial and . . . *of supreme value for the present and future development of the human psyche.*'[30]

Let me add a further observation here, which will turn out to be closely relevant to the exploration of religious language that will be the subject of our next chapter. It seems to me very likely that the failure to recognize the vital role of symbols, for our healthy understanding of ourselves and the reality we inhabit, may be connected with one of the principal sources

---

28 William Meissner, *Psychoanalysis and Religious Experience* (New Haven: Yale University Press, 1984), p. 177. Quoted in Palmer, *Freud and Jung on Religion*, p. 73.

29 From *Aion* [1951], in C. G. Jung, *Collected Works* [hereafter '*CW*'] (rev. edn., London: Routledge, 1967–77), vol. IX (2), p. 183. In similar vein, Jung observes that 'the living and perceptible archetype . . . has been projected onto the man Jesus, and . . . has historically manifested itself in him'; *Psychology and Religion* [1938], *CW* vol. XI, p. 95. These and other significant passages are quoted in Palmer, *Freud and Jung on Religion*, pp. 121, 135, who summarises Jung's thought as asserting that 'what the individual identifies in Christ . . . is the archetype expressing his own need for wholeness and unity' (p. 135).

30 Palmer, *Freud and Jung on Religion*, pp. 110–11 (original emphasis).

of current philosophical misunderstandings of religious language, and consequent philosophical hostility to the religious outlook in general. Seeing scientific thought as the paradigm to which all human cognition should aspire, many philosophers attempt to reduce religious language to a bald set of factual assertions whose literal propositional content is then to be clinically isolated and assessed. The subsequent failure to discern anything in religion that could possibly be worth further attention is highly reminiscent of something familiar to many psychotherapists: the attempts of some patients, particularly highly educated ones, to use intellectual debate about the theoretical claims of psychoanalysis in order to evade the task of guided self-discovery. Far more comfortable to remain at the surface layer of intellectual sparring than to enter the frightening symbolic world of the unconscious where the hidden fears and angers of childhood may gradually become manifest; far safer to debate religious claims as if they were quasi-scientific explanations than to enter a disturbing realm where one's entire self-understanding might be transformed. If the domain of religion is in certain respects more like the domains of art and literature and dreaming than it is like science, if much of its language is more hermeneutic than analytic, more about multi-layered symbolizations of reality than about clinical dissection of phenomena, then (to pick up a point from Chapter 1) to insist on approaching it with complete analytical detachment may be less a sign of intellectual integrity than a stratagem of evasion, a refusal of openness and vulnerability, and hence a flight from acknowledging all the dimensions of our humanity.[31] For religious understanding, as Andrew Louth has nicely put it, involves a

growth in experience [which] is not primarily an increase in knowledge of this or that situation, but rather an escape from what had deceived us and held us captive. It is learning by suffering, suffering in the process of undeception, which is usually painful. . . . [Such] understanding is . . . an exploration of the dimensions of human finitude.[32]

To resume the thread, let us return to the Jung/Winnicott thesis of the importance of religious symbols for the health of the psyche. It could be objected that this more sympathetic strand in psychoanalytic thinking about religion does not provide quite the life-raft for the defender of the religious outlook that might at first appear. Despite all the talk of the valuable role of religious symbols in the integration of the self, do we not

31 See above, Ch. 1, §3.
32 Louth, *Discerning the Mystery*, p. 37.

end up with a kind of psychologizing or subjectivizing of religion – in the words of Michael Palmer, 'a retreat into a self-justifying psychic world, in which the validity of God's image is established by its psychic effect, this effect making it indistinguishable from any other image having the same transforming power.'[33] Jung's own response to this type of criticism was that his role as a psychologist was not to make pronouncements about the existence or non-existence of transcendent realities, but simply to describe the role of certain fundamental and universal images and symbols in human development:

We know that God-images play a great role in psychology, but we cannot prove the [actual] existence of God. As a responsible scientist, I am not going to preach my personal and subjective convictions which I cannot prove . . . To me, personally speaking, the question whether God exists at all or not is futile. I am sufficiently convinced of the effects man has always attributed to a divine being. If I should express a belief beyond that . . . it would show that I am not basing my opinion on facts. When people say they believe in the existence of God, it has never impressed me in the least. Either I know a thing and then I don't need to believe it; or I believe it because I'm not sure that I know it. I am well satisfied with the fact that I know experiences which I cannot avoid calling numinous or divine.[34]

This is an essentially Kantian position: scientific knowledge is confined to the phenomenal world, and any attempt to step outside that world takes us beyond the domain of what can be known or established by reason. It is no part of Jung's project (any more, incidentally, than it is the purpose of this book) to pronounce directly on the standard arguments for God's existence. What the Jungian approach does show, if it is plausible from a psychological point of view, is that religious concepts and images play a crucial role in the development of the human personality and its search for integration. Whether there is an external reality corresponding to those concepts, an 'objective correlative', in T. S. Eliot's phrase,[35] is left beyond the bounds of empirical psychology; what matters is the possibility that opens out of accepting the Freudian idea of the dynamic role of religious notions in the individual psyche without having to take on board Freud's additional assessment of their damaging and neurotic nature.

33 Palmer, *Freud and Jung on Religion*, pp. 187, 196. For a similar reductionist view of Jung's approach, see Fromm, *Psychoanalysis and Religion*, p.20.
34 From a letter of 1956, *CW* vol. XVIII, pp. 706–7. Quoted in Palmer, *Freud and Jung on Religion*, p. 125.
35 A term introduced by T.S. Eliot in his essay 'Hamlet and His Problems' [1919] and defined as the set of objects that will set off a specific emotion in the reader.

A closely analogous point may be made regarding Winnicott's idea of the importance of the creative role of play, mythmaking, and imagination in healthy psychological development. At first sight, despite finding *value* in our religious mythmaking, this view may appear ultimately to support Freud against the *truth* of religion – with God being ultimately relegated to the status of a 'blanky' (security blanket), or teddy bear, or perhaps something more impressive, but still in the end an imaginative creation, like a sculpture, or a figure in a poem. But as with Jung's ideas, the Winnicott approach also suggests that religious activity answers to something deep in our human nature, and is essential for human development. It remains, for the purposes of this part of the discussion, an open question whether there is any 'objective correlative' which is the source toward which our creative human impulses ultimately tend.[36]

5 MORAL IMPROVEMENT, PSYCHOANALYTIC REFLECTION, AND THE RELIGIOUS QUEST

Let me draw together the threads of the argument of this chapter up to this point. Having sketched (in section 1), the 'triangle of hostility' between philosophy, psychoanalysis, and religion, I have briefly indicated (in section 2) a way of defusing the common philosophical hostility to psychoanalytic thought. I then looked (in section 3) at the classic psycho-analytic critique of religion developed by Freud, and explored (in section 4) two principal strategies for defusing the resulting tension between psychoanalytic and religious thought. So far (perhaps) so good. But the results to date, though not unimportant, may seem not to go much further than supporting a bare compatibility – the mere possibility of co-existence between our three domains of thought. I want to end with something stronger: the suggestion that these three areas of human reflection can be seen as intimately intertwined.

At the end of section 2, I observed that philosophy has nothing to fear from psychoanalytic thought, and may even have something to learn from

---

36 One may note in passing here that some theists, including perhaps those with fundamentalist leanings, may object to any notion of religious language being 'creative'. But such qualms seem misplaced: there is quite obviously a human component in the stories of the great religions; any even minimally sophisticated theology must concede that our human language is only an imperfect – and certainly not a literal – representation of the ineffable reality that is God (some of the implications of this will be taken up in our final chapter). In any case, as the 'Jungian' argument of the present section implies, the acknowledgement of humanity's 'creative' role in the development of the great religions need not logically preclude this human activity's being a response to an objective reality that calls it forth.

it. But one may go further and argue that a sound philosophy can hardly subsist without it. This (as may have begun to emerge in section 3) is particularly and obviously applicable to moral philosophy; for in so far as the task here is to establish how humans should best live, a proper understanding of the passions and their role in our choices and decisions is absolutely crucial. And given the pervasive opacity of the passions – the way in which they so often mislead us because they carry a resonance from forgotten early experience of which the subject is typically unaware – any recipe for the good life that fails to find room for systematic self-scrutiny and reflective analysis, in short for a broadly psychoanalytic programme of self-discovery, will be bound to be seriously impoverished.[37]

Moral and psychoanalytic enlightenment thus turn out in practice to be closely connected, and indeed it seems to me highly plausible to suppose – at least for very many if not most human beings – that the first requires the second (I shall pick up this theme and examine it in more detail in Chapter 7). The interdependence of psychoanalytic and religious modes of thinking is even more striking. It is reasonable, as John Hare has argued, to think that the idea of a *moral gap* between how we humans are and what we aspire to be, is central to the religious impulse.[38] In theological terms, this may be expressed in terms of the concept of original sin, or the Fall; more prosaically, we are all aware (to paraphrase a point made by Aristotle, though in a different context) that the very best life we could live would be one that is superior to the ordinary human level.[39] There is a radical difference implied here between the conditions for animal and for human fulfilment. As pointed out in Chapter 3, an animal is fulfilled simply when the biological imperatives of its nature are adequately satisfied.[40] But humans are aware that the satisfied life, the life where

---

37 Compare Victor White: '[Psychoanalysis] is directly concerned with the patient's mental outlook on life, and with patterns and principles of behaviour, with the whole order of values, motives and duties . . . If psychological treatment doesn't issue in the change of a man's mentality, his outlook, his manner of conduct, his attitude to the world and his own place in the world, it surely fails entirely in its own set purpose. And however we may choose to define ethics or for that matter religion, surely we must agree that they are both concerned with precisely these very things.' (*God and the Unconscious*, p. 161.) This seems to me an excellent statement of the continuity of aims between psychoanalysis and ethics (and religion). White stops short of the further claim that sound moral development *requires* psychoanalytic self-scrutiny, though this further step seems easily made, given the plausible additional premise (discussed in our main text) about the opacity of the passions.

38 See J. E. Hare, *The Moral Gap: Kantian Ethics, Human Limits and God's Assistance* (Oxford: Clarendon, 1996), which provides a rich and illuminating exploration of this theme.

39 See Aristotle, *Nicomachean Ethics* [c. 325 BCE], bk. X, chs 6–8.

40 See above, Ch. 3, §2.

our biological wants are satisfactorily or even amply catered for, would still fall far short of meeting our capacities for moral growth and improvement. Humans, in short, face an uncompromising ethical demand to reach beyond their current level of existence towards something higher (the paradoxes in current analytic moral philosophy about the so-called 'problem' of demandingness[41] are but one manifestation of an enduring aspect of the human moral predicament).

Let us assume, for the moment, that it is a moral truth that humans cannot live well if they reject the demand for progressive moral improvement. On a personal and psychological level, the problem of responding to that demand will now immediately become one of achieving integration and wholeness. For as long as there is a psychic split between what I feel like doing and what I am morally called to do, as long as the part of myself that sees the ethical demand as something alien, something harsh and tyrannical that risks interfering with my personal comforts and convenience, then there will be an unresolved tension at the heart of my moral nature. In psychoanalytic terms this split is characteristically described as a compartmentalization or division of the self – the root of all instability, encompassing the full range of disturbance from minor psychic irritation through to entrenched neurosis and even potential catastrophic breakdown. In existential terms, the result will be something variously described as *Angst*, a sense of dread, fear and trembling, nausea. In theological terms, what is involved is the idea of Sin, that inherent sense in each human that it has fallen short of the normative pattern laid down for each of us by the creator.

If the sense of a gap between our ordinary human capacities and what we might best achieve is an ineradicable part of what it is to be a reflective adult human being, then it must be among the most fundamental moral aims for humanity to form some kind of strategy for addressing the problem of that gap. And this is precisely what the psychoanalytic programme, in its broadest sense,[42] sets out to achieve. The psychoanalytic project of self-discovery aims at integration of the demands of

---

41 See for example (from within the utilitarian tradition), Peter Singer, 'Famine, Affluence and Morality', *Philosophy and Public Affairs* (1972), pp. 229–43, and (from the Kantian side) Marcia Baron, *Kantian Ethics Almost Without Apology* (Ithaca, N.Y.: Cornell University Press, 1995), chs. 1 and 2.

42 It is important to note that the psychoanalytic programme, in its 'broadest sense' is not simply emergency therapy for those who are 'disturbed'. Jung's eventual vision, for example, is for a continued discipline of self-discovery that 'is no longer bound to the consulting room' (*Modern Man in Search of a Soul* (London: Routledge, 1933), p. 61). For a further development of this theme, see Cottingham, *Philosophy and the Good Life*, pp. 151–2, and cf. Ch. 7, §7, below.

conscience and morality into a fully adult awareness: the passions that may push us in a direction contrary to those moral demands are neither repressed or denied (for that would be a recipe for instability), nor wantonly indulged (for that would be a recipe for chaos), but rather brought to the surface so that their character, their 'allure', is properly understood. The psychoanalytic project, correctly construed, is a deeply moral project, since it involves nothing less than a radical transformation of the self, a kind of re-birthing or re-education process, where the harsh imperatives of the superego on one side, and the raw urgency of our instinctual impulses on the other, are systematically scrutinized, and brought together into an integrated whole where they lose their threatening and destructive character. So described, the project has an unmistakable similarity to the kind of interior journey that St Augustine describes himself as undertaking in his *Confessions*. The language is different: Augustine in deciding to descend deep into himself, into the 'interior human where truth dwells',[43] sees things in terms of the soul's quest for God. But the idea of a morally driven quest, for individual rebirth and integrity, informs the entire journey.[44]

This Augustinian note is perhaps an appropriate one to have reached in the final section of this chapter, since it is one on which the themes explored by the discourses of moral philosophy, of psychoanalysis and of religion all strikingly converge. The moral restlessness of the human psyche is the central idea of the *Confessions*, and Augustine's search for God via self-reflection is directed towards the allaying of that restlessness. In the words of St Bonaventure, who conducted a similar interior journey very much inspired by the ideas of Augustine – 'the soul is born to perceive the infinite good that is God, and accordingly it must find its

---

43 'Noli foras ire, in teipsum redi; in interiore homine habitat veritas.' ('Go not outside, but return within thyself; in the inward man dwelleth the truth.') *De vera religione* [391 CE], XXXIX 72.

44 Of all recent writers on spirituality, it is perhaps Thomas Merton who shows the strongest implicit awareness of the parallels between the psychoanalytic quest and the religious quest. Compare the following: 'Our desire and our prayer should be summed up in St Augustine's words: *Noverim te, noverim me* ['Let me know you, let me know myself'] . . . In the language of the monastic fathers, all prayer, reading, meditation and all the activities of the monastic life are aimed at *purity of heart*, an unconditional and totally humble surrender to God, a total acceptance of ourselves and of our situation as willed by him. It means the renunciation of all deluded images of ourselves, all exaggerated estimates of our own capacities, in order to obey God's will as it comes to us in the difficult demands of life in its exacting truth. *Purity of heart* is then correlative to a new spiritual identity – the 'self' as recognised in the context of reality willed by God. Purity of heart is the enlightened awareness of the new man, as opposed to the complex and perhaps rather disreputable fantasies of the "old man".' Thomas Merton, *Contemplative Prayer* (London: Darton, Longman and Todd, 1969), ch. II, pp. 83–4.

rest and contentment in Him alone'.[45] As to whether the theistic vehicle in terms of which the Augustinian journey is conceived is a mere quirk of his religious worldview, whether it could simply be jettisoned while leaving intact all that is valuable about the ethical and personal quest, whether, in short, the precious moral core of self-reflection could survive transmission into an entirely secular context – this is a question which raises issues that will have to be postponed till our penultimate chapter, when further essential pieces of the overall argument are in place.

Nevertheless there is one more thing to be said here and now, which bears crucially on the idea of a convergence between the moral and psychological and religious domains. Suppose we were to take seriously Freud's confident predictions, and imagine a world in which the human race had completely 'come of age' – had completely jettisoned the concept of God. Such a thought-experiment turns out to be very interesting, precisely because of its radical impossibility. Some powerful variations on this theme by Karl Rahner deserve quoting at length, to bring this chapter to a close:

The word 'God' exists. This by itself is worth thinking about . . . Even for the atheist, even for those who declare that God is dead, even for them . . . God exists at least as that which they must declare dead, whose ghost they must banish, and whose return they fear. One could not be at peace about him until the word itself no longer existed, that is, until even the question about him would not have to be asked any more. But it is still there, this word, it is present. Does it also have a future? . . . Either the word will disappear without trace and leave no residue, or it will survive, one way or another, a question for everybody.

Consider for a moment these two possibilities. The word 'God' will have disappeared without a trace and without an echo, without leaving any visible gap behind, without being replaced by another word which challenges us in the same way . . . What would it be like . . .? Then man would no longer be brought face to face with the single whole of reality, nor with the single whole of his own existence. For this is exactly what the word 'God' does and it alone, however it might be defined phonetically or in its genesis . . .

Man would forget all about himself in his preoccupation with all the individual details of his world and his existence. *Ex supposito* he would never face the totality of the world and of himself helplessly, silently and anxiously . . . he would remain mired *in* the world and *in* himself, and no longer go through that mysterious process which he *is*. It is a process in which, as it were, the whole of

<hr>

45 *Nata est anima ad percipiendum bonum infinitum, quod Deus est; ideo in eo solo debet quiescere et eo frui.* St Bonaventure, *Commentarii Sententiarum Petri Lombardi* [1248–55], I, iii, 2, in *Opera Omnia* (Collegium S. Bonaventurae: Quarachhi, 1891) vol. I, p. 40. Cf. Augustine, *Confessions* [*Confessiones*, 400 CE], bk. I, ch. I.

the 'system' which he is along with his world, reflects deeply about itself in its unity and totality, freely takes responsibility for itself, and thus transcends and reaches beyond itself to that silent mystery which seems like nothingness, and out of which he now comes to himself and his world, affirming both and taking responsibility for both.

Man would have forgotten the totality and its ground, and at the same time, if we can put it this way, would have forgotten that he had forgotten. What would it be like? We can only say: he would have ceased being a man. He would have regressed to the level of a clever animal . . . Man really exists as man only when he uses the word 'God' at least as a question . . . The absolute death of the word 'God', including even the eradication of its past, would be the signal, no longer heard by anyone, that man himself had died.[46]

Reflection on the fundamental and continuing urge to 'reach forward' beyond our present state suggests (to revert to the Jungian terminology) that what is involved is the kind of 'archetype' that (*pace* Freud's confident predictions) humanity could never entirely abandon. The Augustinian restlessness, if Rahner is right, turns out to be not simply a drive for moral amelioration or individual equilibrium, but something much deeper – the symptom of what one might describe as an enduring and ineradicable existential hunger. Here the psychoanalytic drive for self-awareness and the moral drive towards self-perfectioning are subsumed into a more fundamental search for ultimate meaning in our lives. Nothing in the argument so far, of course, has shown that the discourse of religion points towards the right answer to that search; but at the very least the language of Augustine and his long line of successors offers a powerful way of articulating the question – the question that our nature as human beings will not allow us to sidestep.

---

46 Karl Rahner, *Foundations of Christian Faith* [*Grundkurs des Glaubens*, 1976] (London: Darton, Longman and Todd, 1978), ch. 2, pp. 46–50.

CHAPTER 5

Religion and language: emotion, symbol, and fact

Die Menschen heute glauben, die Wissenschaftler seien da, sie zu belehren, die Dichter & Musiker etc, sie zu erfreuen. Daß diese sie etwas zu lehren haben; *kommt ihnen nicht in den Sinn.*('People nowadays think that the scientists are there to instruct them, the poets and musicians etc. to entertain them. *That the latter have something to teach them* never occurs to them.')

Ludwig Wittgenstein.[1]

I MODES OF DISCOURSE

The previous chapter set out to explore some of the important interrelations between the discourses of philosophy, religion, and psychoanalysis, and ended by suggesting a certain kind of convergence between the goals of psychological maturity, of moral growth, and of religious enlightenment. Among the results to emerge along the way was the idea of the crucial role played by symbols and symbolic thinking in enabling the individual to reach the level of self-awareness required for moral and spiritual health. This leads us very directly to the topic of this present chapter. For one of the obstacles to fruitful philosophical debate between those who subscribe to and those who reject a theistic worldview appears to be the prevalence of systematic misconceptions about the nature of religious language – misunderstandings about the way it is supposed to operate, and what it means to adopt this mode of discourse. As a very rough first shot, it seems to me that many philosophical critics of religion typically construe acceptance of a religious outlook, and readiness to embrace the discourse of religion, mainly in terms of intellectual assent to a set of theses or doctrines. And what the critic then tries to do in examining a religious tradition, is to extract the juice, as it were – the relevant set of theses – from what is taken to be a largely irrelevant

1 Ludwig Wittgenstein, MS of 1939–40, in *Culture and Value*, p. 42.

background 'pulp' or 'mush' of emotive, poetic, narrative, and symbolic elements.

Yet while this kind of austerity may be quite appropriate when we are dealing with science or mathematics, reflection suggests there are many areas of human discourse where this exclusive focus on supposed 'core propositional content' can be a serious obstacle to proper understanding; and religious discourse, I maintain, is one such area. Now it is not my aim anywhere in this book to deny that there is a propositional or cognitive content to religious belief: I am not arguing for the kind of non-cognitivist interpretation of religion that attracted many philosophers and theologians in the latter part of the twentieth century. But I do want to argue that we entirely fail to capture what is involved in someone's adoption or rejection of a religious worldview if we suppose we can extract a pure cognitive juice from the mush of emotional or figurative coloration, and then establish whether or not the subject is prepared to swallow it. An answer to the Yes/No question: 'Do you or do you not believe that P?', where P stands for a statement or series of statements in one of the Creeds, or some other doctrinal summary, often tells us surprisingly little about how far a religious worldview informs someone's outlook. A juice extractor does not, as might at first be supposed, give us the true essence of a fruit; what it often delivers is a not very palatable drink plus a pulpy mess. Someone who has only tasted strawberries via the output of a juicer, and has firmly decided 'this is not for me', may turn out to have a radically impoverished grasp of what it is about the fruit that makes the strawberry lover so enthusiastic.

2 EMOTION AND LAYERS OF MEANING

To explore this question of the meaning of religious language in more detail, I want to start from the concrete rather than the abstract, by looking briefly at a particular example: the Bass recitative from the final act of J. S. Bach's *Matthew Passion* [*Matthäus Passion*, 1729] – a music drama (as we might nowadays call it) that was the result of a particularly fruitful collaboration between Bach and his librettist C. F. Henrici (generally known by his *nom de plume*, 'Picander'). If this were a 'multimedia' book, I could now 'insert' the relevant musical extract, but instead I will have to be content with hoping that readers may be familiar with the passage, or asking them to listen to it when the opportunity arises. The recitative comes in a tiny moment of calm, just after the drama has reached its full tragic climax. The victim has finally expired, and Pilate has allowed the body to be taken down from the cross for burial:

Am Abend, da es kühle war
Ward Adams Fallen offenbar;
Am Abend drücktet ihn der Heiland nieder;
Am Abend kam die Taube wieder
Und trug ein Ölblatt in dem Munde.
O schöne Zeit, O Abendstunde!
Der Friedensschluaß ist nun mit Gott gemacht,
Denn Jesus hat sein Kreuz vollbracht

At evening, time of cool and rest,
Was Adam's fall made manifest;
At evening was our Saviour now brought downward;
At evening did the dove fly homeward,
The leaf of olive gently bearing.
O beauteous time, O hour of evening!
The seal of peace is now with God ensured,
Since Jesus has his cross endured.

It would be quite a task to trace out all the layers of meaning in the passage. The starting point is the calmness of evening, conveyed in a mode entirely outside of verbal description, by the music itself – the long continuous hypnotic line of the pulsing basses and cellos, and the soft plaintive decoration of the violins. We need to be aware of the context: after the frantic fugal counterpoint of the passion narrative – the crowd baying for blood, the soldiers greedily dividing up the garments, we now have a slow, aching peace. It is evening: the struggle is over. *Am Abend da es Kühle war.*

And immediately, the resonances begin to multiply. 'In the evening when it was cool.' This was the time when Adam and Eve 'heard the voice of the Lord God as he was walking in the garden in the *cool of the day*' (Genesis 3:8). We do not have to be fundamentalist or literalistic about the bibilical narrative. The right question is not 'Was there or was there not a geographical location called the garden of Eden?', or 'Was there or was there not an original first man called Adam?'[2] Adam is Everyman,

---

2 Many readers with a background in theology or religious studies may find this a point too obvious to need making, since they will be familiar with a long tradition of figurative readings of the Genesis story, going back at least to Augustine (see *De Genesi ad litteram*, 401–14 CE). Among philosophical critics of religion, however, there are a surprising number who appear tacitly to assume that all religious adherents must subscribe to a naively fundamentalist interpretation of the Bible stories (an assumption, to be fair, that is encouraged by the vociferousness of those believers

finding himself on a planet of surpassing beauty, with the bounty of Nature supplying all he needs to live at peace and contentment. But as evening comes he knows that he has failed: his world is in ruins, just as, in a different though related way, is ours – polluted by war and cruelty and waste. The cool of the evening brings to human beings that chill sense of the gap between what we might have been and what we have become.

The pollution takes hold. And now we are taken straight forward to another powerful scene: when he saw the increasing wickedness on the earth, 'it repented the Lord that he had created mankind' (Genesis 6:6). And Noah, desperate on the dark flood waters, his supplies running out, sends out first the raven, and then the dove. No land is found. But after seven days 'again he sent out the dove from the ark; and *in the evening* the dove came back to him, and there in its beak was a freshly plucked olive leaf; so Noah knew that the waters had subsided from the earth' (Genesis 8:11). There follows the rainbow, a symbol of hope, and a sign of the promise that 'as long as the earth endures, seedtime and harvest shall not cease'.

Not, notice, that the earth will last forever: our world is mortal, finite, as we are – though as long as the cycle of life continues, there is hope. But even as that bright image of the dove with its olive leaf hovers there, Bach's music brings us back to the beat of history: the waste and the violence continues. The bloody corpse is pulled down from its place of torture. Yet we are told that this death, in a way that perhaps cannot be fully grasped by the intellect alone, will somehow be the *Friedensschluss* – the seal of peace between God and humanity. So the evening time, linking Adam's tragic fall and Noah's desperate peril, and the now dead body being taken down from the tree, somehow speaks of the calm of reconciliation and healing.

I have, very crudely and inadequately, indicated just a few of the strands that are woven together in this extraordinary piece of music drama. What is the moral I want to draw? Partly this: that a religious response to the story of the fall and redemption of humankind operates in a very different way from the kinds of response we are familiar with in the philosophy seminar – those based on the clinical and detached evaluation of propositions. One may no doubt distil out from the story a core of metaphysical claims for impassive scrutiny, but the net result may merely

---

who *do* take a fundamentalist line). For more on the role of figurative interpretation in Augustine, and a discussion of the view that 'figurative' and 'literal' should not always be understood antithetically, see C. Kirwan, *Augustine* (London: Routledge, 1989), pp. 12ff.

be the kind of 'disgust' that Wittgenstein noticed when we utter an invented Esperanto word—a word that can only 'play' at being language because it is utterly 'cold' and lacking in associations.[3] In so far as the gospel story carries metaphysical implications, for example about the saviour of mankind and his sacrificial mission, these will not begin to have any real significance for the hearer (and hence will not even be candidates for serious evaluation) unless a *certain mode of receptivity is already in place.* That mode of receptivity, generated so effectively by Bach's musical drama (though others may well have other examples that work better for them) seems to me to have two main components: first, a certain kind of emotional dynamic, and second, a layered structure of mutually resonating symbols and narratives.

3 THE EMOTIONAL DYNAMIC

First, what is the role of emotion, the emotion of the listener, the emotion evoked by the music and poetry, when we hear a piece like the recitative just quoted? Although philosophers in their off-duty hours may consider themselves to be as emotionally responsive as anyone else, when they enter the seminar room they often seem tacitly to adopt a model of meaning which strongly privileges the cognitive or purely intellectual content, sometimes indeed to the point of excluding all other elements from serious consideration. There is a whole vast area of discourse, encompassing emotional resonances, figurative and allusive uses of language, symbolical and metaphorical expression, that is regarded as peripheral to the main fact-stating propositional core that must be present in all significant sentences.

On this view, there are 'the facts', which are expressible in quite unambiguous and literal terms; and any emotional component is seen as a kind of extraneous 'add-on' – of no real interest in terms of the structure and properties of the facts, though it may perhaps say something about the subjective stance of the perceiver, or how he arrived at that stance. The novelist Martin Amis, talking about the difference between his own elaborate writing style and the more straightforward prose of his father, once reportedly observed: 'my father doesn't like my work, because he thinks novels should be mainly composed of sentences like "he put down his drink and left the room".' In somewhat similar vein, many philosophers take truth and meaning to attach primarily to sentences

3 Ludwig Wittgenstein, MS of 1946, in *Culture and Value*, p. 60.

which express these sorts of literal and unambiguous descriptive facts, with emotion and allusion seen as marginal to the main role of language.

Recent work on the emotions, however, has started to correct this simplistic and polarised picture. Robert Stocker has argued that emotional states such as anger and pity can have a vital role in directing and focusing our attention, thus radically affecting the way we perceive things: 'they seek out and collect, even create, sustaining or concordant facts. . . which they then use to justify and sustain that emotion, which then leads to further seeking, collecting, creating and coloring.'[4] The emotions, as Mark Wynn has nicely put it, have a role in 'guiding enquiry by constituting patterns of salience.'[5] What this means, applied to the present example, is that if we are confronted with the statements just examined from the *Matthew Passion*, a clinically detached stance may be precisely the wrong mode of trying to assess the relevant assertions.[6] If the focus of our attention is not coloured by a certain sort of emotion, the very import of the sentences may quite simply be missed. It is, of course, the gift of a supreme composer like Bach to be able, by the use of melody and harmony and rhythm, together with the tone colouring provided by the particular timbre of the soloist's voice and the orchestral accompaniment, to create precisely the right kind of emotional orientation in the listeners, predisposing them, almost from the first chord, to a heightened awareness of the relevant patterns of salience. (Our musical example thus turns out to be no mere incidental illustration, but is intended to function as a kind of metaphor for the way in which I am suggesting that modes of receptivity contribute to meaning.)

One might object that the role of emotion here is merely a heuristic one, pointing us in the right direction, or helping us to keep focused on the right area, but not adding anything to the all-important propositional content. But on the picture we are now starting to unfold, emotion becomes exactly the reverse of an optional extra, whether a preliminary softening up, or a subjective emotive 'add-on' to the true core of factual

---

4 Robert Stocker with Elizabeth Hegeman, *Valuing Emotions* (Cambridge: Cambridge University Press, 1996), p. 94. Cited in Mark Wynn, 'The Relationship of Religion and Ethics: A Comparison of Newman and Contemporary Philosophy of Religion', *Heythrop Journal*, 2005. See also M. Wynn, *Emotional Experience and Religious Understanding: Integrating Perception Conception, and Feeling* (Cambridge: Cambridge University Press, 2005).

5 Wynn, 'The relationship of religion and ethics'.

6 One is reminded here of Martha Nussbaum's claim that there are some truths (for example truths about whether I truly love someone) such that 'to try to grasp [them] intellectually is a way of not suffering, not loving. . . a stratagem of flight.' Nussbaum, *Love's Knowledge*, pp. 268–9. See above, Ch. 1, §3.

meaning. *That* kind of crude two-stage model might be roughly carica-
tured as follows: (a) fact: 'there are particles of sodium chloride on the
sliced tomato' – and (b) emotion: 'oh, by the way, I like them served that
way'. Or (a) 'there is mould on the bread' – and (b) 'oh, by the way, that
generates in me a personal reaction of distaste'. This kind of model
precisely ignores the way in which the whole situation we are dealing
with is reconstituted by the emotional colouring of the supposed facts. Of
the two illustrations just given, the second one is for various reasons rather
more suggestive of the point that needs to be brought out here. Salt may
be regarded as a kind of optional extra for tomatoes, one that perhaps
brings out the flavour, but does not alter their essential constitution. But
mouldy bread is fundamentally altered, in texture and taste and nutri-
tional value, from sound bread; the 'facts' do not remain the same, save
for a minor extra add-on, but rather the presence of the mould brings
about a radical change in what it is that is perceived. Without pushing any
of these approximate analogies too tediously far, we might say that
emotional colouring has the effect not just of supplementing an objective
state of affairs with a subjective reaction, but rather of reconstituting the
state of affairs itself.[7]

One way of putting this result, in very general terms, is to say that our
religious (and moral and aesthetic) experience involves *transformative ways
of perceiving reality*. And this points, incidentally, to something of a
paradigm shift when we look, for example, at some of what have been
considered traditional arguments for God's existence. Every standard
textbook in the philosophy of religion mentions the arguments 'from
religious experience', or 'from moral [or aesthetic] experience', as if what
was involved was a kind of inference *from* one sort of fact – roughly a fact
about a certain kind of subjective occurrence – *to* a conclusion about a
supposed objective correlate or external cause for the relevant experience.
Such inferential arguments may or may not be plausible; but the 'transformative' approach just alluded to suggests a rather different route.
Somewhat as Kant argued that to experience the world causally is not to
perceive a certain correlation and then 'add on' the supplementary idea of

7 Compare Peter Goldie: 'Coming to think of [the world] in [a] new way is not to be understood as
consisting of thinking of it in the old way, plus some added-on phenomenal ingredient – feeling
perhaps; rather, the whole way of experiencing, or being conscious of, the world is new . . . The
difference between thinking of X as Y without feeling and thinking of X as Y with feeling will not
just comprise a different attitude towards the *same* content – a thinking which earlier was without
feeling and now is with feeling. The difference also lies *in* the content, although it might be that
this difference cannot be captured in words.' *The Emotions* (Oxford: Clarendon Press, 2000), pp.
59f., original emphasis. Cited in Wynn, *Emotional Experience and Religious Understanding*.

a necessary connection, but rather that causality is *already*, as it were, one of the categories in terms of which humans must experience the world (the whole distinction between initial data and subsequent human processing being deconstructed or elided);[8] so, in somewhat the same way, to perceive the world religiously is to see certain events, such as the Crucifixion, as *already* infused with a certain moral and emotional and metaphysical meaning. It is not as if the theist and the atheist experience the same facts but interpret them differently; rather, that which is experienced is itself, in each case, of a radically different kind.

The position so far tentatively reached no doubt leaves some important questions unanswered. In particular, while it may be conceded that emotion functions as a kind of perceptual lens, it could still be insisted that there *are* non-emotive ways of perceiving the world. Though we are told that the centurion in charge of the Crucifixion was sufficiently moved to see the events in a radically new way – not just as the standard dispatching of a troublesome insurgent, but as the innocent death of a quasi-divine victim (Matthew 27:54) – one can clearly imagine a hardened imperial solider who would have perceived no such thing. So though the emotional lens may condition what is experienced, it may be a lens that is, so to speak, detachable across individuals, or detachable for any given individual at different times; but in that case not only does the Kantian parallel break down, but the whole link between emotional involvement and 'seeing as' may seem to be robbed of any justificatory or apologetic role it might have appeared to offer for the believer. For if at some level the 'preferred' religious way of experiencing an event is, as it were, optional, then the religious apologist may be faced with the question of whether a more 'scientific' and less involved mode of perception may not after all be preferable – more honest, perhaps, or more equipped to resist the dangers of self-deception or wishful thinking.

Clearly, no one emotional framework for perceiving the world is compulsory or universal. This is a point the atheist may be inclined to stress, but of course it has long been a common theme of religious thought that God always allows the individual a certain autonomy – the space to accept or reject him, to see the world as divinely infused or to see it as no such thing. The orthodox view is that the believer is led by divine grace to faith; but as Aquinas argues, there will always be room for the free agency of the human soul, in either resisting such grace or co-operating

8 Cf. Immanuel Kant, *Critique of Pure Reason* [*Kritik der Reinen Vernunft*, 1781/1787], A 189ff: B 233ff.

with it.[9] Even those, like Descartes, who argue for the *irresistibility* of the supernatural light of faith, still appear to allow room for the possibility that the individual can choose whether or not to direct the mind in such a way as to focus on the truths it reveals. Assent may be unavoidable once there is mental focus (for Descartes, 'a great light in the intellect' is irresistibly followed by 'a mighty inclination of the will'),[10] but human beings have the power to turn away from such illumination, to relax the focus, or to focus elsewhere, often preferring the darkness to the light, as the Fourth Gospel has it.[11]

If the religious worldview is correct, there is a correct way of seeing the world, namely as being 'charged with the grandeur of God', in the remarkable phrase of Gerard Manley Hopkins[12] (and indeed charged with many other non-natural qualities, including moral ones);[13] but no one can be compelled as they look around them to see such a world, and not another world – a random world, for example, or a violent and depressing world, or a world coloured solely by our own human projections, or a world devoid of anything other than temporary and local significance.[14]

---

9 The precise interpretation of the scope of this human freedom is, however, the subject of intricate theological debate. The view of Augustine was that because of original sin the will can only incline towards God in virtue of prior divine redemptive action. Taking his cue from this, John Calvin (1509–64) interprets the doctrine of 'justification through faith' in terms of a gratuitous gift of divine grace to some, the elect, who are predestined to be saved, while others are eternally predestined to destruction (*Institutio Christianae religionis*, 1536, rev. 1559, bks. 3 and 4). For a survey of some of the complexities, see D. Ferguson, 'Predestination', in A. Hastings et al. (eds.), *The Oxford Companion to Christian Thought* (Oxford: Oxford University Press, 2000), pp. 562ff.

10 'Ex magna luce in intellectu sequitur magna propensio in voluntate'; Descartes, *Meditationes* [1641], Fourth Meditation (AT VII 59: CSM II 41).

11 John 3:19. For Descartes' position on the possibility of rejecting the deliverances of the irresistible light by turning away, see Cottingham, 'Descartes and the Voluntariness of Belief', pp. 343–60.

12 Gerard Manley Hopkins, *Poems (1876–1889)*, no. 8.

13 Compare, for example, the following affirmatory vision of the world: 'religious belief emerges as *the* genuine option, an option brought about by the very nature of things; by an ordered cosmos revealing one tiny pocket uniquely capable of sustaining life and growth and thought; by an ordered world of beauty and complexity and variety capable, under favoring conditions, of hosting saints and heroes; by a spot on the map of the universe wherein the otherwise ever-increasing entropic movement toward sameness is opposed by creative moral, aesthetic and intellectual endeavours absent which reality itself would be pointless; by a natural world of sentient creatures, capable of drawing life from their habitats and instantiating, each in its own way, the miracle of creation.' Daniel M. Robinson, 'How Religious Experience "Works".' *Review of Metaphysics*, 224 (June 2003), p. 775.

14 At the other extreme from the view of the world expressed in the previous footnote, compare the dark vision of Arthur Schopenhauer: 'The futility and fruitlessness of the struggle of the whole phenomenon [of life on earth] are more readily grasped in the simple and easily observable life of animals. . . Instead of [any lasting final aim] we see only momentary gratification, fleeting pleasure conditioned by wants, much and long suffering, constant struggle, *bellum omnium* [war among all], everything a hunter and everything hunted, pressure, want, need and anxiety, shrieking and howling; and this goes on in *saecula saeculorum* [world without end], or until once again the crust

All this is compatible with, indeed fits nicely with, the thesis that emotion is partly constitutive of what facts are experienced; but the question now to be faced is whether there is any viable decision procedure for deciding which interpretative framework is to be preferred. If not, then we would seem to have a kind of standoff, with some of us predisposed or perhaps even predestined, possibly at a quite fundamental and pre-rational level, to see the world in a certain light – for example a religious light – while others are equally strongly disposed to see things quite otherwise.

4 THE IMPORTANCE OF LAYERING

Leaving this issue hanging in the air for the moment, I want now to turn to the second component which I mentioned earlier as being involved in the religious mode of receptivity to a piece like the Bach *Matthew Passion*. In addition to the emotional dynamic, which I have suggested is no mere superfluous add-on, but has a crucial role in determining what is experienced, religious language characteristically involves a *layered structure of mutually resonating symbols and narratives*. Hence, proper understanding is not merely a matter of having a transparent grasp of a few isolated truth-claims, but also a matter of responding in the right way – that is to say in a *multi-level way* – to the complex resonances, the multiple harmonics as it were, of the relevant symbols and stories.[15]

Although in recent times there has been some very good philosophical work on metaphorical and symbolic uses of language,[16] many

---

of the planet breaks.' *The World and Will and Representation* [*Die Welt als Wille und Vorstellung*, 1818], bk. II, ch. 28; transl. E. F. J. Payne (New York: Dover, 1966), ii, 354. Cf. B. Magee, *Schopenhauer* (Oxford: Clarendon Press, 1983), ch. 7.

15 I say '*not merely* having a transparent grasp of [the relevant] truth claims', but there is something to be said for a far stronger claim, namely that symbolic meaning entirely transcends the realm of 'transparent' assertion. Compare Pascal's account of the essential role of figurative language in religion, because 'the things of God are inexpressible and cannot be said in any other way' (*Pensées*, no. 272), and also his famous maxim 'the letter kills' (no. 268). However, Pascal's position is perhaps not entirely settled, since he sometimes seems to suggest that literal meaning is compatible with, and even presupposed by, figurative meaning: 'the figure was drawn from the truth, and the truth was recognized from the figure' (no. 826). For these references, and for an excellent discussion of the general question of whether there is a genuine tension between 'aesthetic' and 'cognitive' aspects of language, see D. E. Cooper, *Metaphor* (Oxford: Blackwell, 1986), ch. 1.

16 See for example Janet Martin Soskice, 'Theological Realism', in W. Abraham and S. Holtzer, *The Rationality of Religious Belief* (Oxford: Clarendon Press, 1987). The idea that serious philosophical thought can recognize the importance of symbolic and other non-literal modes of discourse is one that has roots going back at least to the period of German romanticism: Johann Hamann (1730–88) stressed that reality could not be adequately captured except through symbols, while Johann Herder (1744–1803) argued that poetry was the most adequate means of mapping our world. For

philosophers still appear to regard such language as peripheral to the main, the philosophically most central, aspects of human discourse. Again, because of the privileging of the literal and the cognitive, such things as symbols are (rather like the emotive components of language) often tacitly considered as 'add-ons' – elements that may, to use the current vulgarism, 'sex-up' a description by making it more vivid or increasing its impact, but not by adding anything substantial to the content. Thus William Alston, arguing against the irreducibility of metaphor in religious language, claims that while metaphors may involve a 'penumbra' of inexplicit suggestions that cannot be literally paraphrased, any sentence purporting to make a truth-claim must always have a core of propositional content that is 'capable of literal expression, at least in part'.[17] Taking an even harder line, Peter van Inwagen, in an article for the *Oxford Companion to Christian Thought* observes that:

The metaphysician aims at producing sentences that strictly and literally describe reality, and which can, with sufficient effort, be understood by anyone whose intellect is equal to the task. Metaphor may play a heuristic role in metaphysics – as in physics or economics or comparative linguistics – but must be banished from the metaphysician's 'finished product'.[18]

One possible reason why many analytic philosophers sympathetic to theism are suspicious of appeals to symbol and metaphor is that they associate them with a retreat from realism in the philosophy of religion.

---

discussion of these and other interesting cases, see David Brown, 'Symbolism', in A. Hastings, A. Mason, and H. Pyper (eds.), *The Oxford Companion to Christian Thought* (Oxford: Oxford University Press, 2000), pp. 690ff.

17 '[We may concede that] metaphorical statements always have . . . a penumbra of inexplicit suggestions that surround whatever definite propositional content is present [and this penumbra] cannot be captured in a literal restatement. [But] we are not asking whether metaphors can receive exact or exhaustive literal paraphrases. . . Our question is whether there can be a metaphorical statement the propositional content of which cannot be expressed, even in part, in literal terms . . . A statement cannot possess a propositional content unless it is, in principle, possible that a language should contain words that have the meanings required for the literal expression of that content . . . . [Hence] the propositional content of any metaphorical statement issued with a truth claim is, in principle, capable of literal expression, at least in part.' W. P. Alston, *Divine Nature and Human Language* (Ithaca: Cornell University Press, 1989), pp. 26–30.

18 Peter van Inwagen, 'Metaphysics', in Hastings et al. (eds.), *The Oxford Companion to Christian Thought*, p. 427. There are, of course, many species of metaphysics, and the (broadly Aristotelian) kind which P. F. Strawson has identified as 'non-revisionary' in its aims, together with types concerned purely with conceptual analysis and 'conceptual geography', may perhaps conform to such tight restrictions (see below, Ch. 6, §1). But if metaphysics is taken to include claims about putative ultimate and transcendent realities beyond the phenomenal world, the strictures seem too austere, since any use of language to characterize such realities will, ex hypothesi, be stretched beyond its normal context. For more on some of the problems that may arise here, see Ch. 8, §3, below.

That is, they suppose that any departure from literalist construals of theistic language moves us towards the kind of anti-realism that may verge on abandoning traditional theism altogether.[19] Thus William Alston suggests that many modern theologians have become convinced of the failure of traditional proofs for God, and other 'Christian supports for belief in God as an independent reality that we can truly characterise'; and he goes on to observe that

those so convinced are led to think that the only ultimate being we can take seriously, if any, is one that is beyond human cognitive grasp, leaving our humanly characterized God in the status of symbol, mode of appearance, or imaginative construction.[20]

Although Alston does not actually insert the word 'mere' before symbol, the tone seems clearly to imply it. Symbolic expression is a second best, a retreat from the purity of literalism. And associated with this may be the implicit judgement that reliance on the figurative (as opposed to literal) status of religious language paves the way for anti-realism, retreating from the solidity of traditional Christian belief. But both these points seem questionable. First, there need be nothing 'mere' about a symbol or a metaphor: as Janet Martin Soskice has argued, such kinds of language may be among our most powerful conveyors of truth.[21] And in the second place, to say that X requires to be described symbolically, or cannot be grasped through the resources of literal propositional claims, need not at all imply that X does not have a real existence, independent of human beings. On the contrary, if there is an infinite, self-subsistent being behind the phenomenal world, one might well expect it to be beyond the grasp of

19 The label 'anti-realism' covers a range of positions in the philosophy of religion, from the view that God cannot be characterised independently of human thought and discourse, to the denial that God has any kind of objective independent reality. See William Alston, 'Realism and Antirealism' in Hastings et al. (eds.), *The Oxford Companion to Christian Thought.* p. 594.
20 Alston, 'Realism and Antirealism', p. 595.
21 'We speak for the most part metaphorically of God or not at all . . . We need to be cautious with the phrase "merely metaphorical" and its even more slippery associate, "merely metaphorically true". Claims are made true or false by circumstances and not simply by their manner of expression . . . Metaphor is a kind of language use and not a kind of truth.' Janet Martin Soskice, 'Theological Realism', pp. 119, 107. Compare also Andrew Louth: 'Metaphors are not simply embellishments of what could equally easily be stated in plain, literal prose. Metaphors, rather, disclose a way of looking at the world, a way of understanding the world. If we wish to understand the way in which any of the ancients understood their world, we must pay heed to their use of metaphors, we must enter into their metaphorical view of the world. It is a strange world we shall find revealed to us and it will not be easy for us to enter it. It will . . . require enormous effort, but it will be quite a different sort of effort from that demanded of the scientist who seeks to devise experiments which will prise from nature her secrets: it will be an effort not of exact, logical . . . thinking, but of sympathy and *imagination*.' Andrew Louth, *Discerning the Mystery*, p. 19.

our normal literal and scientific language, and thus reasonably suppose that it can be glimpsed, if at all, only via intimations, or symbolic or other figurative modes of discourse.[22]

The theology of Thomas Aquinas provides an interesting possible counter-example here, since his theory of 'analogical predication' is supposed to allow us to make true and literal descriptions of God, based on some intelligible resemblance that created beings bear to their creator. When we say God is a cause, we are, for Aquinas, not speaking figuratively, but truly and literally.[23] For even though the term 'cause' is not applied in exactly the same sense as in ordinary mundane usage, it is not being used in a metaphorical sense either; rather it is based on some strict resemblance that a mundane cause bears to the divine cause. Analogical predication is thus supposed to occupy a kind of intermediate ground between mere equivocal predication (when a term is used of two things in completely different senses), and univocal predication (when it is used of two things in exactly the same sense). In its fine detail, Aquinas' account can be somewhat labyrinthine, but without going into the detail here, it may be doubted whether the theory of analogical predication in the end provides as strong a support as is sometimes supposed for a literalist view of talk about God. In the first place, when discussing Aquinas' view of theistic language, it should in any case be remembered that a great deal of the language traditionally used of God derives not from the philosophy seminar but from sacred scripture, and when dealing with such scriptural language Aquinas not only allowed, but insisted on, the value of allegorical, prophetic, and symbolic interpretations.[24] In the second place, even when wearing his philosophical hat, Thomas himself admits that in calling God 'good' or 'living' or 'wise', based on the analogy with created things that are good or living or wise, we 'fail to represent adequately what God is'.[25] So although the language is not, according to Thomas, metaphorical or figurative, it still appears distinctly stretched or strained in relation to the way it is applied to ordinary imperfect things. The result,

---

22 Compare Richard Swinburne: 'the words which humans have most readily available to them are words whose meaning is learnt from their primary use in connection with fairly down-to-earth human activities. Such words may not be immediately suitable for talk about abstract philosophical concepts, subatomic entities, infinite space and time, or God. They may need to have their meanings stretched, and to be used in odd ways, if they are to be used for talk about such fundamental matters.' *Revelation: From Metaphor to Analogy* (Oxford: Clarendon Press, 1992), p. 50. For more on this issue, see below, Ch. 8.

23 See B. Davies, *Aquinas* (London: Continuum, 2002), pp. 84–7.

24 *Summa theologiae*, pt. Ia IIae, qu. 104, art. 2, ad 2. See below, n. 31.

25 *Summa theologiae*, pt. Ia, qu. 13, art. 2.

in the words of one distinguished Thomist scholar, is that although Aquinas is 'optimistic' when it comes to our ability to speak truly and literally about God, he is also 'decidedly reserved'.[26] This connects with the very 'minimalist' approach Aquinas uses when constructing his famous 'five proofs': just as God's nature cannot be described using terms applied in the same sense as they have in ordinary mundane usage, but only, and then inadequately, by analogy, so the five demonstrations enable Aquinas not to reach an adequate conception of the divine nature, but only to posit an ultimate something 'which we call God'.[27]

Let me insert a brief aside here, namely that one may see a partial parallel between the kind of analogical predication that Aquinas argued for in theology and the use of models and analogies in science. Arguably, the nature of quantum objects is so far beyond anything we are familiar with in the ordinary observable world that we can at best describe them indirectly, in terms of certain effects they are supposed to produce, and also by means of analogies (e.g. that they manifest themselves in ways that are in some ways analogous to waves, and in some respects to particles, etc.). Given that we allow physicists to invoke entities whose nature they can approach only via such indirect means, and which in some cases (e.g. the bizarre entities of string theory) are manifest only by the barest traces in our observable world, it seems hard to deny in advance to the religious adherent any similar right to speak of a divine reality that transcends the resources of directly descriptive language, but which (it is claimed) leaves its trace in the moral and spiritual fabric of our lives. I shall return to this theme in Chapter 7.

But (to resume) if it turns out that literal language fails us for many religious purposes, what reason is there for thinking figurative and other non-literal language will do any better? That this question even needs to

26 See Davies, *Aquinas*, p. 87.
27 Cf. Ch. 2, §2, above. The 'Five Ways' of Aquinas all end with some such phrase as 'and this we call God' (*et hoc dicimus Deum*): they involve an a posteriori inference from some object of mundane experience to something beyond it, which we call God (*Summa theologiae* [1266–73], pt. I, qu. 2, art. 3). This being is held to be in some sense responsible for the motion and causality and goodness and goal-directedness found in the world, and indeed of its mere existence in the first place, but this does not mean that we can understand God to be a cause in quite the same sense that we understand an ordinary mundane object to be a cause: 'It is impossible to predicate anything univocally of God and creatures' (*Summa theologiae* pt. Ia, qu. 13, art. 5). For Thomas's notion of analogical predication, see F. Copleston, *A History of Philosophy* (Westminster, Md.: Newman Press, 1950), vol. II, ch. 35, and B. Davies, *Aquinas*, ch. 8; there is partial criticism of Aquinas' views in Swinburne's, *Revelation: From Metaphor to Analogy*, pp. 150ff. St Thomas also famously argues that humans cannot attain to knowledge of what God is, but only of what he is not (*Summa contra Gentiles*, 33); for discussion of this '*via negativa*', see Copleston, *A History of Philosophy*, vol. II, ch. 35.

be asked says a lot about the way many analytic philosophers have increasingly adopted an austere scientistic model of discourse, which predisposes them to ignore important facts concerning the power of symbolic and other figurative discourse which are often right in the foreground for their 'continental' colleagues (not to mention those working, for example, in literature departments). One such feature is a certain kind of ambiguity – something which the scientistic mentality might see as a drawback, since (as Raymond Geuss has recently pointed out) ambiguity in meaning is 'regarded as a grave defect in propositional forms of investigation and argumentation', and many disciplines 'emphasise the need to adopt the most stringent measure to eliminate [it] as completely as possible'. Yet Geuss reminds us, drawing on the famous work of William Empson, that 'some of the best lyric poetry is characterised by. . . systematic and deep ambiguity, and this gives it a density of texture that is an aesthetic virtue.'[28] It seems to me that the same may very well be true of the best religious discourse; and moreover, that the virtue involved is not merely an 'aesthetic' one (which may suggest something essentially stylistic and extraneous to questions of content), but a virtue that has deep semantic implications.

Part of what gives symbolic language its special semantic power is its *polyvalence*. Symbols work on us not just at the surface level of rational analysis, but by invoking a plethora of complex associations, many of which have the power to tap deep ingrained responses, often below the level of conscious awareness. And the result (as anyone minimally acquainted with psychoanalytic thought will testify) is often not just a subjectively heightened response to something already fully visible, but rather a radically enlarged field of view.

A proper account of the polyvalence of symbolic language, then, would inevitably involve threading our way through that philosophical minefield, the theory of the Unconscious. But without going down that route here,[29] it is possible to provide some kind of schematic account of the 'multi-level' power of symbolic terms, and how essential this is to the way they operate. Let me briefly take as an example one of the best known petitions in all religious language: 'Give us this day our daily bread.' At a literal level, it is a plea for physical sustenance. And notice, incidentally, that by focusing exclusively on this, the literalist critic of religion may

---

28 R. Geuss, 'Poetry and Knowledge', *Arion* 11:1 (Spring/Summer 2003), p. 8. Cf. W. Empson, *Seven Types of Ambiguity* [1930] (Harmondsworth: Penguin, 1995).
29 See Cottingham, *Philosophy and the Good Life*, ch. 4. See also Ch. 4 §4(ii) of the present work.

already be disposed to see the petition in an unfavourable light: does it really do any good to request God to supply bread in this way? If we want food, we surely have to work for it, not pray for it; requests for celestial intervention can only divert attention from the urgent need for humans to take responsibility for providing resources to those many thousands who are seriously undernourished. And so on. Now these practical concerns are of course urgent and important, though in fact even at the literal level, praying for our own need for food to be satisfied does not have to imply any shirking of responsibility for those who go hungry – indeed quite the reverse.[30] But the literal meaning is only the beginning.

As soon as we move beyond literalism, we start to see that the request does not have to be construed as a demand for some supernatural effort-free supply of food, like the magical self-filling basket or inexhaustible pitcher of Grimm's fairy tales. Bread, like most of the goods of life, is something that by its very nature involves co-operation between the labour of humans and the unearned bounty of the natural world: in the words of the ancient Offertory prayer, bread is that 'which Earth has given and human hands have made'. The petition for bread already resonates with a meaning far deeper than a facile request for magical cost-free rations: it symbolically draws our attention to our status as human creatures, both able (through the power of reason and enterprise) to transform the world to our advantage, but also fundamentally dependent for our deepest needs on things we did not create and cannot fully control.

That is perhaps the simplest layer of symbolic meaning. But of course there are many more. The author of the prayer was speaking in part as a Jewish Rabbi; and deeply embedded in the folk-history of his people was a narrative of decisively important feeding – the manna in the desert during the Exodus from Egypt. So bread, that most mundane of everyday foods, was something that was not always available, and whose want had some-how been supplied in a time of direst need. The Jewish escape from starvation had been linked to an escape from slavery, an escape from the perils of the desert into a new start, a new life of freedom. So there is a retrospective symbolism.

---

30 'The presence of those who hunger because they lack bread opens up another profound meaning of this petition. The drama of hunger in the world calls Christians who pray sincerely to exercise responsibility toward their brethren, both in the their personal behaviour and in their solidarity with the human family. This petition of the Lord's Prayer cannot be isolated from the parable of the poor man Lazarus and of the Last Judgement (Luke 16:19–31; Matthew 25:31–46).' *Catechism of the Catholic Church*, (New York: Doubleday, 1995, rev. 1997) [*Latina Catechismi Catholicae Ecclesiae typica editio*, 1992, rev. 1997], §2831.

Third, moving from retrospective to reflexive reference, there is in the mouth of the teacher of the prayer an immediate self-referential symbolism. Bread is the fundamental vehicle for human sustenance, the 'staff of life'; but according to one of the most famous discourses in the Johannine gospel, 'I am the Bread of Life' (John 6:35–58), Christ had identified *himself* as carrying this sustaining role. The bread prayed for thus represents not just a certain number of calories, but symbolises the entry to a level of living that is sustained by this 'spiritual' nourishment (for want of a better term) – something that in this Christological context has many dimensions, but at the very minimum involves the kind of morally focused and enriching life which Jesus aimed to embody – a life of compassion and healing.

Fourth, there is a future, or proleptic symbolism. Within the context of Christianity, the daily bread is also the bread of the Eucharist. The text of the original prayer uses the phrase *artos epiousios* (Luke 11:3; Matthew 6:11); the Greek adjective is a *hapax legomenon* whose meaning has been much disputed, but it has been traditionally interpreted by the Church in a metaphysical sense, as meaning not just quotidian but 'super-essential' bread. So there is a proleptic sacramental resonance, itself linked with the story of the Last Supper, a story yet to unfold when the prayer was first taught; and this resonance in turn links us backwards to the Jewish Passover, a celebration of deliverance, and the Christian Passover, the 'new covenant' which will involve both self-sacrifice (the bread being the body 'given up for you'), and the institution of a perpetual re-enactment of that sacrifice in the form of the people coming together to share words of peace and the breaking of bread.

This is not a work of theology, so it would be inappropriate to go on at greater length, though even a cursory acquaintance with the long tradition of biblical commentary will reveal that the symbolic references so far explored do no more than scratch the surface.[31] But enough has perhaps been said already to indicate something of the phenomenon of multi-layering as it applies in the religious symbolism of such expressions as 'our daily bread'. (Let me add, incidentally, that in drawing attention to this kind of phenomenon, I am taking an approach to language which seems to me at least consistent with recent work from analytic philosophers such

---

31 See for example the most celebrated such commentary on the Gospels, Thomas Aquinas, *Catena Aurea* [1262–67], English transl. ed. J. H. Newman [1841] (London: The Saint Austin Press, 1997), vol. I, pp. 228ff.

as Emma Borg[32] on the nature and meaning of figurative language . This work, if I am not mistaken, clearly recognises the power metaphor has to facilitate the growth and enrichment of our understanding, as an increasing number of associations and links are grasped and internalised.[33])

To avoid misunderstanding: the suggestion is not, of course, that whenever a believer repeats this phrase, all the explored ramifications and resonances are immediately activated in his or her mind. The theory of meaning is not parasitic on, or reducible to empirical psychology (to suppose so is what might be called the 'Lockean' fallacy – that the meaning of a term is to be identified with an 'idea', construed as a psychological object or occurrence activated in the subject's mind).[34] What does seem to me true, however, is that the way such symbolic language operates is such that a religious believer's understanding of what he is saying when he repeats it is liable to be far, far richer than is often realized by the external scrutineer of his words, especially when that scrutineer is working with literalist or uni-level understandings of meaning.[35]

32 Though her purposes are very different from mine, Emma Borg's work on metaphor seems to me to capture nicely this crucial point about multi-layering, when she argues that 'understanding metaphor is a matter of degree'. Borg points out that each metaphorical utterance is distinguished (from a literal utterance) by its being associated with a set of further propositions; 'the larger the number of associate propositions entertained, the more fully the metaphor is understood'. 'An Expedition Abroad: Metaphor, Thought and Reporting', in *Midwest Studies in Philosophy* XXV (2001), ed. P. French and H. Wettstein (Oxford, Blackwell, 2001), pp. 227–48.

33 It is worth noting that the power of metaphor provides but one instance among many of how meaning can operate through a complex network of multiple associations. Compare Martha Nussbaum on 'Sophoclean' versus 'Platonic' understanding (the kind of understanding involved in appreciating the events in a Greek tragedy such as *Antigone*, as against the kind involved in unravelling an abstract philosophical argument): 'We reflect on an incident not by subsuming it under a general rule, not by assimilating its features to the terms of an elegant scientific procedure, but by burrowing down into the depths of the particular, finding images and connections that will permit us to see it more truly, describe it more richly; by combining this burrowing with a horizontal drawing of connections, so that every horizontal link contributes to the depth of our view of the particular, and every new depth creates new horizontal links.' *The Fragility of Goodness*, p. 69.

34 I use the term 'Lockean' simply as a convenient label, which has *some* basis in remarks by Locke, and Locke commentators, though I avoid here any judgement on its ultimate aptness as applied to the actual views of Locke himself. Compare the following: 'Every Man's Reasoning and Knowledge is . . . nothing but Particulars. Every Man's Reasoning and Knowledge is only about the *Ideas* existing in his own Mind'; *Essay concerning Human Understanding* [1690], IV, xvii, 8. Cf. Michael Ayers, *Locke* (London: Routledge, 1991), p. 51: 'Locke's "ideas" are . . . *mental* images in that to have an (occurrent) idea is evidently for Locke to be in a state of consciousness.'

35 There is a difficult issue here about how much the subject, the hearer of a symbolic or metaphorical utterance, contributes to its meaning. Dan Sperber and Deirdre Wilson, whose general approach to metaphorical meaning strikes me as very illuminating, seem to me to go a little too far in the 'Lockean' direction (see previous footnote) when they analyse the content of a metaphorical utterance in terms of 'an indefinite array of weak implicatures whose recovery is triggered by the speaker, but whose content the *speaker helps actively to determine*' ('Loose Talk',

The point can be especially relevant when 'Do you or do you not?' questions are fired off by an external scrutineer in a misguided attempt to 'settle' what it is that the believer subscribes to. Consider for example 'Do you or do you not believe that the Bread is transubstantiated into the Body of Christ?', when asked 'externally' by someone who has heard of this Catholic doctrine about the Mass, and wants to sort out whether Bloggs 'really believes' it. The reason why either answer, positive or negative, will almost certainly be unenlightening is that questions involving this kind of religious language are quite unlike scientific questions of the form 'Do you or do you not believe that gold is soluble in hydrochloric acid?' Someone who is committed to the truth of a doctrine like the transubstantiation is almost certainly so committed because of the role that certain sorts of language about the Eucharist play in her religious praxis, and because her grasp of the language and liturgy of the Eucharist puts her in touch with multiple levels of rich significance, each of which resonates with powerful moral and spiritual aspects of her worldview.[36] Insisting on the question 'But does the substance actually change?' *appears* to cut to the chase, eliminate evasion and ambiguity, and focus on what is 'really' believed. But in the context of a 'cold', no-nonsense question from an external scrutineer who is largely ignorant of the multiple levels of meaning just indicated, the 'yes or no' question functions like the strawberry juicer: the output is an unhelpful mess. For the religious believer, 'signs' such as the bread and wine of the Eucharist[37] can function as, in William Wainwright's phrase, 'a medium for fuller, riper knowing'. Insistence on yes/no answers to literalistically construed questions is a way of mangling what lies at the core of this kind of knowing; it is a denial

---

Proceedings of the Aristotelian Society LXXXVI (1986), p. 170, emphasis supplied). That said, it should be clear that I am strongly supportive of Sperber and Wilson's firm rejection of 'the classical claim that tropes in general, and metaphor in particular, have a purely decorative function', and their claim that 'metaphor has a genuine cognitive content which, particularly with the more creative metaphors, is not paraphrasable without loss.'

36 To reiterate a point made earlier: nothing said here about symbols and the importance of praxis need be taken to imply a retreat from a real and genuine truth claim. Of course, when questions like 'But does the bread *really* change?' are put, the questioner is often insisting on having an answer to what they take to be the damaging question of whether there is any actual physical change – where 'actual' and 'physical' are taken to be more or less equivalent. Yet, as Michael Dummett has persuasively argued, it is a mistake 'to conceive of metaphysical reality after the model of physical reality' ('The Intelligibility of Eucharistic Doctrine', in W. J. Abraham and S. W. Holtzer (eds.), *The Rationality of Religious Belief* (Oxford: Clarendon Press, 1987), p. 247.

37 For the term 'signs' as used of the bread and wine of the Eucharist, see *Catechism of the Catholic Church*, §1333. For an interesting account of Aquinas' view of the sacraments as a kind of sign, see Mark Jordan, 'Theology and Philosophy', in N. Kretzmann and E. Stump (eds.), *The Cambridge Companion to Aquinas* (Cambridge: Cambridge University Press, 1993), ch. 9.

of the unique power such signs have to capture the mystery and complexity of our human experience of the world.[38]

5 MEANING AND JUSTIFICATION

These remarks on the characteristics of religious language, and understandings of its meaning, may or may not be illuminating; but the question remains as to what role if any they play in the justification of a religious outlook. And this brings us back to the issue we earlier left hanging at the end of section 3, about whether there are any rational decision procedures for settling whether any given emotional or symbolic framework of understanding is to be preferred over any other.

How then does 'layering' – the presence of multiple layers or levels of meaning and resonance – help, if at all, towards justification? In the picture presented by Robert Stocker (from which we quoted earlier), a certain structure of emotions can have a role in 'directing and focusing our attention', enabling us to 'seek out and collect, even create, sustaining or concordant facts'.[39] And this, if Stocker is right, is a recursive or reiterable process, since the results unearthed as a result of such focusing and collecting can then be used to 'sustain the relevant emotion', which then leads to 'further seeking, collecting and creating'.

It may not at first sight be easy to grasp exactly what is involved here, but an analogy drawn from the notion of *colouring* (a term which Stocker himself employs from time to time) may help. Suppose, that while working on an archaeological site I am faced with a completely bleached out and indecipherable mosaic – a jumble of hundreds of irregular monochrome triangles and quadrilaterals. Something suggests to me that I can colour in certain blocks of shapes with, say, green and yellow and blue crayons. The colouring so provided immediately creates 'patterns of salience' – certain previously random-seeming line configurations now appear to provide the beginnings of an intelligible context – a background landscape, perhaps, of dry fields dotted with coarse shrubs under a clear blue sky. And now this colouring itself triggers further reactions, which suggest to me further possibilities for colouring the solid objects located within the landscape: the addition of white and grey now makes the scene

---

38 Here I partly follow the phrasing of David Cooper, *Metaphor*, p. 219; the phrase 'medium for a fully and riper knowing' comes from William Wainwright (cited by Cooper, though with some reservations). Cf. Wainwright, *Reason and the Heart* (Ithaca, N.Y.: Cornell University Press, 1995).

39 Section 3, above.

a pastoral one – there is a group of sheep among the shrubs and rocks. And now, with the further addition of a darker reddish brown and a blue strip, the whole mosaic comes alive, the seated figure is a shepherd, robed in classical Roman garb, tending his flock (see frontispiece/jacket illustration to the present volume.) A final colouration discloses a halo, and reveals the shepherd's crook to be cruciform, so that the symbolic significance of the ensemble is now clear: the mosaic depicts the Good Shepherd.[40]

Though the analogy is not an exact one, the basic idea is that layers of meaning may be mutually reinforcing: one colour makes a certain sense of its own, but then in turn focuses attention on a hitherto blank area which is then in turn coloured in and makes its own sense, at the same time reinforcing and confirming the interpretation of the previous segment. The resulting picture is perhaps not the only logically possible interpretation of the mosaic shapes, but it makes such good sense of the whole, with so many inter-resonating patterns of mutually cohesive images, that (to use a somewhat old-fashioned term) the truth of the resulting interpretation becomes a 'moral certainty'.

That this kind of 'moral certainty' can have not just an interpretative but a justificatory force was realized by the philosopher René Descartes, in the following analogy (drawn from a linguistic rather than a pictorial context):

Suppose someone wants to read a letter written in Latin, but *encoded* so that the letters of the alphabet do not have their proper value, and he guesses that the letter B should be read whenever A appears, and C when B appears, i.e. that each letter should be replaced by the one immediately following. If, by using this key, he can make up Latin words from the letters, he will be in no doubt that the true meaning of the letters is contained in these words. It is true that his knowledge is based merely on a conjecture, and it is conceivable that the writer did not replace the original letters with their immediate successors in the alphabet, but with others, thus encoding quite a different message. But this possibility is so unlikely, especially if the message contains many words, that it does not seem credible.[41]

This seems to me in some respects very like what happens when someone is led to adopt a religious worldview. The subject's perception of himself and his place in the world, of his relationships and the meaning of his life, begins slowly and progressively to be transformed. It is not a matter of atomic or piecemeal assessment of individual truth-claims; rather the worldview (to borrow a Quinean idea) meshes with the data

40 *Il Buon Pastore* (fifth century); mosaic in lunette of the Galla Placidia Mausoleum, Ravenna.
41 *Principles of Philosophy* [1644, 2nd edn. 1647], pt. iv, art. 205 (AT VIIIA 328: CSM I 290).

of experience as an entirety.[42] A worldview may be thought of as a kind of net – a complex retiform structure, comprising, amongst other elements, praxis, symbols, narratives, beliefs, and moral commitments.[43] As the net takes shape, the various resonating elements of the structure start to reinforce each other; and once a sufficient number of resonances cohere together, colouring prompting further colourings, or harmonics facilitating further harmonics (depending on which metaphor you prefer), the subject has a growing sense that the constructed framework is secure. It may not (as with any worldview or scientific paradigm) be impregnable or immune from revision; but as it starts to inform and condition such an ever wider area of the subject's experience, it becomes harder and harder to shift.

This chapter has mainly been about meaning and language, not about justification, so in adding these brief closing remarks I am certainly not claiming to have dealt with the many hard justificatory or evidential issues that remain to be faced by the believer. A religious interpretation of reality will still, of course, have many obstacles to overcome – 'Enlightenment' or Kantian worries about the limits of knowledge, contemporary scientistic worries about transgressing the boundaries of so-called 'naturalism', post-modernist worries about the impossibility of grand meta-narratives[44] – issues that will be taken up in the following chapter. But before we decide

---

42 See W. V. O. Quine, 'Two Dogmas of Empiricism', in *From a Logical Point of View* (Cambridge, Mass.: Harvard University Press, 1951; rev. ed., New York: Harper and Row, 1963). The general line taken in the present chapter, namely that understanding operates holistically rather than atomistically, should be uncontroversial, for all that it is sometimes ignored. It has long been a commonplace of literary criticism, for example, that attending to the context in which they occur is necessary for proper interpretation of the passages in a poem or a novel. Interestingly, the Second Vatican Council recognised that this principle applies equally to interpreting the Bible: 'Those who search out the intention of the sacred writers must, among other things, have regard for literary forms . . . But since the Holy Scripture must be read and interpreted according to the same Spirit by whom it was written, no less serious attention must be given to the content and unity of the whole of Scripture, if the meaning of the sacred texts is to be correctly brought to light.' (*Dei Verbum* (Rome: Second Vatican Council Document, 1965), p. 12; cited in Swinburne, *Revelation*, p. 209).

43 Cf. N. T. Wright, *The Resurrection of the Son of God* (Minneapolis, Minn.: Fortress Press, 2003), p. 569.

44 It is a repeated theme of postmodernists (amongst others) that we have to learn to abandon grand meta-narratives, the supposedly final and objective scripts that purport to declare what the ultimate reality of the cosmos is like. As today's deflationary agendas gain currency, the traditional religious worldview is then regularly castigated for clinging to an outmoded and hopelessly over-ambitious aspiration – the aspiration to provide just such suspect 'grand meta-narratives', or the aspiration to offer just such a suspect 'sideways on' perspective to how things really are.

We shall return to some of these issues in the following chapter, but for the present purpose it is enough to note that if such internalistic agendas are accepted, and if as a consequence we agree to take a deflationary view of the traditional grand ambitions of philosophy and science to

whether we can subscribe to the discourse of religion consistently with maintaining the other planks of our philosophical and intellectual outlook, we must first understand the nature of the discourse involved, and the way it relates to our human experience, to the moral and spiritual fabric of our lives. That is a highly laborious process, and of course it might be far easier and more convenient if we could just take out a handful of bald doctrinal claims and subject them to summary evaluation. But unfortunately, or perhaps fortunately, as with so many other areas of philosophy, and so many aspects of our human existence, there are no short cuts.

provide super-narratives, learning instead to make do with internal standards of justification, then there is no good reason to suppose that religious discourse, alone of all forms of human discourse, is somehow disqualified from making the adjustment and cutting itself down to size. One cannot, in short, have it both ways. Either coherence-type justifications, working in terms of what I have described as mutually reinforcing levels of resonance, fall hopelessly short of what is required for genuine justificatory adequacy – in which case the new postmodernist, internalist view is going to have to condemn not just religious accounts of the world, but also physics and chemistry and history and geography and so on ad indefinitum; or else we just have to make do without absolute truth or 'sideways-on' perspectives, and just continue working with the materials to hand and rebuilding our boat as we go along – in which case coherentist justifications of religion put it in no worse a plight than any other area of human understanding.

CHAPTER 6

Religion and the Enlightenment: *modernist and postmodernist obstacles*

Ich mußte also das Wissen aufheben, um zum Glauben Platz zu bekommen
('So I found it necessary to go beyond knowledge in order to make room for faith').

Immanuel Kant.[1]

I THE STIGMA OF METAPHYSICS

In forming a religious outlook (the previous chapter argued) we build up a multi-faceted picture of reality, the elements of which gradually begin to cohere together in a mutually reinforcing way. To change the metaphor, a religious worldview is not an isolated set of doctrines, but a complex retiform structure, a fine-meshed net of praxis and belief and commitment that links together in a coherent fashion many diverse aspects of our human experience. Such a worldview finds expression not just at the narrowly intellectual level, but in a rich array of symbolic and figurative discourse; to use and to understand such discourse is to appreciate that in religion as in many of the most important areas of human life, meaning operates not through bald statements that correlate one-to-one with the facts they purport to describe, but rather through an intricate process of layering, where our understanding is constantly enriched by the interplay of conscious and unconscious resonances and allusions.

Drawing attention to this 'fuller and riper' mode of understanding[2] may irritate those who are professionally committed to reducing all philosophical discourse to an austere, ambiguity-free template modelled on the kinds of language used in natural science; but while there is nothing wrong in itself with such austere language, there seems no sound

---

1 Immanuel Kant, *Critique of Pure Reason* [*Kritik der reinen Vernunft*, 2nd edn., 1787], B xxx.
2 Wainwright, *Reason and the Heart*, cited in Cooper, *Metaphor*, p. 219.

reason to stretch it beyond its natural province. When we are confronting not particles in the void, or molecules in a test tube, but instead realities that have to do with the meaning of our human existence and our struggle for moral and spiritual growth, then the call to purge away all but the uni-level discourse of plain literal assertion seems plainly misguided.

But here we come up against an obstacle. Multi-layered language, the kind we find for example in poetry and in prayer, may be fine for expressing various sorts of human emotion, and indeed also for 'teaching us something' (in Wittgenstein's phrase),[3] if by 'teaching' is meant furnishing a deeper awareness of how we human beings experience the world and each other. But if the 'teaching' refers to something loftier than this – if it purports to give information about a supposed transcendent reality to which our human experience is supposedly responsive, a reality that is the ultimate goal of our human striving – then such 'teaching' plainly goes beyond the normal domain of natural knowledge and enters the problematic realm of metaphysics.

A parallel point applies to the praxis of spirituality – something to which the argument of this book has returned many times as being central to the phenomenon of religious allegiance. If by praxis is simply meant a certain kind of human behaviour – for example liturgical practices, the singing of hymns, the reciting of prayers, the ritualised acts of worship found in nearly all religious traditions – then to say that this is part of the web of religious activity and belief may be no more than a sociological truism: religious people do, as a matter of fact, not just make assertions but also engage in certain special structured activities and performances, both as individuals and as groups. And no doubt the investigation of the language used as part and parcel of that praxis will, if it discards arbitrary scientistic templates, be sensitive to multiple layers of allusion, figuration, and symbolization. But when all this is granted, will there not still be an irreducible 'cognitive content', a residue of implicit or explicit assertions or truth-claims, woven into the religious praxis and the way it finds discursive expression;[4] and will not this content, in so far as it typically

---

3 Ludwig Wittgenstein, MS of 1929, in *Culture and Value*, p. 42; see epigraph to Ch. 5, above.
4 Compare the following: 'Christian prayer cannot be confined, as perhaps other forms of prayer can, to some spiritual or mental activity – meditative or contemplative – which is of value in itself and needs no further justification. Prayer is engagement with the object of our faith, an object which is in some way apprehended or known; and in such cognitive engagement the *mind* is involved. Faith is, to use the traditional phrase, *cum assentione cogitare* to *think* with assent.' Louth, *Discerning the Mystery*, p. 4. However, in case this quotation should make it seem as if Louth's view of these matters is excessively cognitivist or intellectualistic, the following important

makes reference to a supposed supernatural realm, immediately take us beyond the world of purely human experience and into the dubious domain of metaphysics?

But why should such metaphysical freight automatically be thought to be suspect? The short answer is that it is a commonplace of much contemporary thought that we have to learn to give up the grand pretensions of past philosophical and theological systems to access the ultimate truth about how things are. We live (to use an epithet from Jürgen Habermas) in a 'postmetaphysical' age.[5]

Admittedly, a subject called 'metaphysics' has continued to exist for the past fifty years as one of the specialized branches of modern analytic philosophy, but it is striking how scrupulously, for the most part, it has avoided the high-flown aspirations typical of many earlier metaphysical systems. In its earlier 'linguistic phase' (dominant in the middle to latter part of the twentieth century), 'metaphysics' (in so far as the term was used at all) was seen as purely conceptual in character: the aim was to chart the general features of the conceptual landscape, and to investigate and describe the logical structure of those universal categories of thought and language that are common to all the various more specific areas of human discourse.[6] More recently, the subject has come to be conceived in more realist terms, as dealing with the fundamental features of the world, as opposed to simply our language about the world (much work is currently being done, for example, on the structure of time, on the relation between substances and attributes, on the nature of change and

---

continuation of the passage should be noted: 'There is here no division between theology and spirituality, no dissociation between the mind which knows God and the heart which loves him. It is not just that theology and spirituality, though different, are held together; rather *theologia* is the apprehension of God by a man restored to the image and likeness of God, and within this apprehension there can be discerned two sides (though there is something artificial about such discrimination): what we call the intellectual and the affective.' (ibid.)

5 See Jürgen Habermas, 'Transcendence from Within', in *Texte und Contexte* [1991], transl. in *Religion and Rationality* (Cambridge: Polity Press, 2002), ch. 3. See also Habermas's *Postmetaphysical Thinking* [*Nachmetaphysisches Denken*, 1988], transl. Hohengarten (Cambridge: Polity, 1992).

6 Compare Peter Strawson's account of 'descriptivist' (as opposed to 'revisionary') metaphysics, which he sees as following a broadly Aristotelian (as opposed to Platonic) conception of the subject; *Individuals* (London: Methuen, 1959), pp. 9ff. The underlying conception of philosophy as conceptual analysis is one that is shared by a variety of philosophers, including those working under a Wittgensteinian banner, who see their role as having not just a descriptive but a further prescriptive function: by exposing confusions and category mistakes, they aim to point out what it is licit to say, and what is a violation of the proper rules of logical grammar. See, for example, P. S. M. Hacker, 'Metaphysics as the Shadow of Grammar', in *Insight and Illusion: Themes in the Philosophy of Wittgenstein* (Oxford: Oxford University Press, revised edn 1988), ch. 7.

identity).[7] But whether in the 'conceptual' or in the 'realist' mode, most modern academic metaphysics tends to be firmly descriptivist or immanentist in character: it is in general relatively modest in its ambitions, compared with most of the great metaphysical systems of the past.[8] Unlike Aquinas, or Descartes, or Leibniz, it does not any longer aim to invoke ultimate realities that transcend the natural world; it resists trying to tell us about God, or immortality, or to provide any overarching or 'cosmic' account of the meaning of life. I shall call the earlier, traditional, highly ambitious form of metaphysics *grand metaphysics*. If you like (and at the cost of some oversimplification), grand metaphysics is metaphysics in the transcendent rather than the immanent mode. And it is this kind of metaphysics that Habermas is pretty clearly thinking of when he says philosophy now has to operate in a *postmetaphysical* context.

But *why* does it? Anyone who, by some timewarp, had heard the term 'postmetaphysical' back in the period spanning roughly the nineteen-thirties down to the nineteen-sixties might have supposed that what was behind this proclamation of the end of metaphysics was the triumph of logical positivism. But of course that particular triumph rapidly went sour, and the philosophical programme that was supposed to signal the death of metaphysics ended up self-destructing. The attempt to impose strict verifiability as the criterion of meaningfulness collapsed when it became clear that positivism's own darling, natural science, could not pass the proposed test; and if the test were weakened to allow for the somewhat looser relation that typically obtains between a theory and the experience taken to support it, then the discourses of religion and morality and

---

7 For a conspectus of typical current work in these areas, see, for example, the *Oxford Handbook of Metaphysics*, ed. M. J. Loux and D. W. Zimmerman (Oxford: Oxford University Press, 2003). Jonathan Lowe, a prominent representative of the new approach, defines metaphysics as 'a universal discipline', of a non-empirical character' which is 'genuinely concerned with the fundamental structure of reality itself, rather than just with the structure of our thought about reality' (*A Survey of Metaphysics* (Oxford: Oxford University Press, 2002), pp. 5, 11). Lowe's reasons for not restricting metaphysics to the purely semantic or conceptual domain have to do with a carefully argued rejection of any form of idealism: 'our thoughts do not constitute a veil or curtain interposed between us and the things we are endeavouring to think of' (p. 14). The problems addressed by Lowe concern such topics as identity, persistence, change, necessity, possibility, causation, agency, actions and events, space, time, and motion; but it is significant that the term 'God' appears in Lowe's index only four times, and the corresponding passages in the text mention the deity only incidentally and in passing.

8 There are exceptions; for example the emergence of 'analytical Thomism', which in some respects aims to revive the more ambitious goals of an earlier age; see J. Haldane (ed.), *Mind, Metaphysics and Value in the Thomistic and Analytical Traditions* (Notre Dame, Ind.: University of Notre Dame Press, 2002). For an interesting general discussion of the status of contemporary metaphysics, see D. S. Oderberg, 'How to Win Essence Back from Essentialists', *Philosophical Writings* (Autumn, 2001) pp. 27–45.

metaphysics would all come flooding back from exile (since no one could plausibly maintain that the theories in these latter categories do not have at least *some* degree of supporting evidence from observation or experience). Worse still, positivism turned out to be self-refuting, since its radically empiricist central thesis – that the limits of factual verification are the limits of meaningful assertion – turned out to be incapable of verification; it was, in short, itself a metaphysical doctrine.[9]

These debates are now very much water under the bridge. But the question raised by recalling them is this: if the once dominant doctrine of positivism has long since had its heyday, and has now been relegated to the status of a relic in the historiography of modern philosophical thought, why do post-positivist thinkers such as Habermas, together (it must be said) with many subsequent philosophers both analytic and continental, as well as the postmodernist writers who do not quite belong to either camp – why do all these continue to think of our current age as 'postmetaphysical'? Why do all seem to regard traditional 'grand metaphysics' as a lost cause?

2 THE SUPPOSED LEGACY OF THE ENLIGHTENMENT

The long march away from grand metaphysics can plausibly be seen to have its origins in a movement much older and philosophically much more durable than the positivism of the twentieth century, a movement that in many ways defines the emergence of modernity, namely the *Enlightenment.* The label is somewhat imprecise, but it can be taken to denote, roughly, the worldview that came into being with the great scientific revolution of the seventeenth century, and reached its most definitive philosophical expression in the thinking of David Hume and Immanuel Kant in the eighteenth. To tell a familiar story very briefly, the new scientific movement inaugurated by Descartes and Galileo resolutely avoided traditional appeals to divine purposes in physics, and sought for explanations of all the phenomena in the universe in terms of the precise quantifiable language of mathematics.[10] In methodological terms, it

---

9 In answer to this challenge, some defenders of the principle of verification suggested that it should be regarded as a stipulation for the use of the term 'meaningful'; cf. A. J. Ayer, *Language, Truth and Logic* (London: Gollancz, 1936), Introduction to Second Edition (1946).

10 The locus classicus for the 'mathematicization of science' in the early modern period is René Descartes' *Principles of Philosophy* [*Principia philosophiae*, 1644], pt. II, art. 64. Galileo Galilei reached the same conclusion somewhat earlier, observing in 1623 that 'the great book of the universe is written in the language of mathematics'; *Il Saggiatore* ('The Assayer'), in Galileo,

insisted on careful observation, and the testing of hypotheses against experience[11] – something that, together with mathematical modelling, we now think of as the essence of the 'scientific method' (indeed, one of the great achievements of the early-modern period was that it managed for the first time properly to articulate the very notion of 'science', in the modern sense, that we now take for granted).[12]

In specifically philosophical terms, the stance developed by the ruling thinkers of the Enlightenment came to be increasingly hostile to metaphysics. By the middle of the eighteenth century, Hume was famously reviewing the libraries of 'school metaphysics' and offering to 'commit to the flames' as containing 'nothing but sophistry and illusion' any claims of existence that went beyond experience and so exceeded the boundaries of 'matters of fact'.[13] By the end of the century, Kant was exposing the 'paralogisms' and 'antinomies' of pure reason – the contradictions and paradoxes generated by attempts either to prove or disprove matters that lay outside the limits of the phenomenal world described by science. If we invoke 'transcendent' ideas, ideas relating to objects that 'lie outside all possible experience', then, Kant argued, 'we are cut off from any reasons that could establish the possibility of such objects'.[14] We leave the firm

---

Opere, VI, 232. For the rejection of 'final causes' (including appeals to divine purposes) in physics, see Descartes, *Meditations* [*Meditationes de prima philosophia*, 1641], Fourth Meditation, AT VII 55: CSM II 39).

11 The foundations for the so-called 'inductive method' are laid in Francis Bacon's *Novum Organum* [1620], though many other early modern writers stress the importance of empirical testing, including those misleadingly called 'rationalists'; see Descartes, *Discours de la méthode* [1637], pt. vi.

12 The Latin term *scientia*, which was the predecessor of our 'science', meant, in the Middle Ages and Renaissance, simply 'knowledge', but as used in most philosophical authors its connotations diverged widely from our modern understanding of the term 'science', connecting instead with the old deductive Aristotelian idea of certain and indubitable demonstration from axioms that were 'prior to and better known than' the conclusions; see Aristotle, *Posterior Analytics* [c. 330 BCE], bk. I. (It should be noted, however, that Aristotle's own methods of inquiry, for example in biology, are certainly not rigidly deductivist; cf. J. L. Ackrill, *Aristotle the Philosopher* (Oxford: Oxford University Press, 1981), ch. 7.)

13 'It seems to me that the only objects of the abstract sciences or of demonstration are quantity and number, and that all attempts to extend this more perfect species of knowledge beyond these bounds are mere sophistry and illusion . . . All other enquiries of men regard only matter of fact and existence; and these are evidently incapable of demonstration . . . The existence . . . of any being can only be proved by arguments from its cause or its effect; and these arguments are founded entirely on experience . . . When we run over libraries, persuaded of these principles, what havoc must we make? If we take in our hand any volume; of divinity or school metaphysics, for instance; let us ask, *Does it contain any abstract reasoning concerning quantity or number?* No. *Does it contain any experimental reasoning concerning matters of fact and existence?* No. Commit it then to the flames: for it can contain nothing but sophistry and illusion.' David Hume, *An Inquiry concerning Human Understanding* [1748], §XII, pt. iii.

14 Immanuel Kant, *Critique of Pure Reason* [*Kritik der reinen Vernunft*, 1781/1787], A565/B593, transl. N. Kemp Smith (New York: Macmillan, 1929), p. 484.

'island of truth' and launch ourselves onto the 'wide and stormy ocean' of illusion.[15]

This Enlightenment position is widely seen as heralding the effective end of speculative metaphysics in general, and religious metaphysics in particular. By mapping out the 'land of truth', the conditions under which we are able to lay claim to possible knowledge of reality, Hume and Kant are seen as ushering in a new framework for human cognition – a framework into which, like obsolete pieces of computer hardware with the wrong kinds of plug, the traditional theistic claims of religion have, as it were, no place to connect.

I shall be arguing shortly that the implications of the Enlightenment position, when properly understood, are in fact less radically hostile to the claims of religion than is often supposed. But before coming on to evaluate the actual ideas of the Enlightenment thinkers, I want first to say something about one of its apparent modern successors, the contemporary doctrine known as *naturalism*. To lead into this, let me first offer a very brief and general sketch of what one might call the 'default' position of the educated secularist thinker as it has developed in the aftermath of Hume and Kant.

This position may be expressed in terms of a schematic picture of truth and reality, a *Weltbild*, that is hard to characterize precisely, but which exerts an increasingly powerful influence, in a host of rational and pre-rational ways, on how many people feel able to interpret the world around them. A growing number of educated people start to see themselves as adherents of something called 'modern thought' – the new scientific world order which has transformed the planet over the last few centuries, which has freed increasing numbers from many of the spectres of pain and disease that haunted their forbears, which has provided many with un-dreamt of leisure and individual freedom, which has enabled human beings for the first time to begin to understand the forces that operate on the biological and chemical and physical structures that determine the fabric of their lives, and which has for the first time integrated an understanding of the entire terrestrial environment with a clear grasp of its vast cosmic or astronomical setting; and it is increasingly taken for

---

15 '*Das Land der Wahrheit*'. It is an 'island', says Kant, 'surrounded by a wide and stormy ocean, the native home of illusion, where many a fog bank and many a swiftly melting iceberg give the deceptive appearance of farther shores, deluding the adventurous seafarer ever anew with empty hopes and engaging him in enterprises which he can never abandon and yet is unable to carry to completion.' *Critique of Pure Reason*, A235/B294. Cf. Sebastian Gardner, *Kant and the Critique of Pure Reason*, (London: Routledge, 1999), p. 209.

granted (by those who take the position we are discussing) that this huge and hugely successful revolution in understanding is in the process of elbowing out the older religious view of the world. So although it is allowed that religion continues to flourish in many parts of the planet, this tends to be attributed either to ignorance and superstition, on the one hand, or to special historical or political circumstances on the other; and the tendency which is already strikingly observable in North-Western Europe is thought likely to dominate our intellectual culture in the long run: towards a sturdy, scientistic atheism that allows no space for admitting, or even discussing, 'transcendent' entities, supposed realities beyond the totality of natural facts. Let us now look in a little more detail at the philosophical basis of this increasingly confident secularist outlook.

3 NATURALISM AND CONTEMPORARY PHILOSOPHICAL ORTHODOXY

The picture of things just sketched finds current philosophical expression in the doctrine known as *naturalism*, which has become something of a dominant position in modern analytic philosophy. Though it is often not precisely defined, it signals a determination to account for everything there is without any appeal to supernatural (often pejoratively called 'spooky') or other metaphysically charged explanations.[16] Thus, in the sphere of moral philosophy, for example, the programme aims to explain the realm of the normative, including the domain of moral obligation, in broadly empirical terms – as reducible to or derivable from facts about the ordinary natural phenomenal world around us.[17]

We need, however, to distinguish between weak or *methodological* naturalism and strong or *ontological* naturalism. The former (potentially open-minded) doctrine simply involves a determined attempt to find complete explanations for all phenomena without any reference to transcendent realities – and as a research programme this is simply to be judged on how far the explanations it offers (e.g. of mathematical and of moral necessity) are in fact plausible. We just have to wait and see if it can work; and one may add that the jury is very much still out on this in the philosophical academy. (In moral philosophy, for example, a

---

16 I am using 'metaphysical' in the 'grand' sense identified in §1, above – that is, as involving reference to a supposed transcendent reality.
17 See further Cottingham, '"Our natural guide . . .": Conscience, 'nature' and moral experience', in Oderberg and Chappell (eds.), *Human Values; New Essays on Ethics and Natural Law*, pp. 11–31.

considerable, possibly growing, number of contemporary theorists reject naturalism and construe moral properties as *non-natural* – and these dissenters are by no means confined to those sympathetic to religion.[18]) In contrast to methodological naturalism, *ontological naturalism* is the more rigid thesis that the natural, phenomenal world is all there is – a thesis which plainly goes beyond any result that could be established by scientific inquiry, and which therefore requires additional justification (something that, perhaps surprisingly, is not very often offered in the writings of contemporary naturalists).

The bald insistence that the natural universe is, quite simply, all that there is[19] is a claim that itself looks very like a piece of metaphysics, and, one might think, a remarkably dogmatic one at that.[20] The vision is, as it were, of an entirely *closed* and *self-sufficient* universe – one that could in principle be understood entirely 'from the inside'. Yet there are good reasons for thinking that this apotheosis of naturalism is a fantasy.

One of the most celebrated former advocates of the goal of a naturalistic 'theory of everything' or 'TOE', has recently come to acknowledge that, for logical reasons, our understanding within a closed system can never be complete. The Cambridge physicist Stephen Hawking had earlier in his best-selling *A Brief History of Time* looked forward to a complete all-inclusive set of scientific equations that would explain everything in the universe, and indeed the very existence of the universe itself: 'if we discover a complete [and unified] theory [combining quantum physics with general relativity] . . . we shall all . . . be able to take part in the discussion of the question of why it is that we and the universe exist. If we find the answer to that, it would be the ultimate triumph of human reason.' For the grand unified theory 'might be so compelling that it brings about its own existence'.[21] Since then, however, reflection on Kurt Gödel's famous incompleteness proof of 1931 has led Hawking

---

18 For an elegant conspectus of some of the recent arguments and literature, see P. Stratton-Lake's introduction to his edited collection *Ethical Intuitionism*, pp. 7ff. Compare also Ch. 3, §5, above,

19 This is one interpretation of Wittgenstein's opening claim in the *Tractatus*: 'The World is everything that is the case'.

20 Let S be the total set of object and events from the Big Bang onwards, comprising all the interactions of particles, the formations of stars and planets, the resulting development of biological systems, and, eventually, human activities and everything arising from those activities. The thesis that there exists nothing except what is included within S, or that there is no reality not comprised within S, appears to go beyond anything that could be established by scientific or rational inquiry; it could not be established by examination of, or reflection on, S, or any of the items within S (it is in this sense that it may be called a piece of 'metaphysics').

21 Stephen Hawking, *A Brief History of Time* (London: Bantam Press, 1988), p. 192–3.

to recant. In a more sober assessment he acknowledges that we can never be 'angels who view the universe from the outside', but instead that both we and our models are 'part of the universe we are describing'. One might therefore expect any scientific theory we produce to be 'either inconsistent, or incomplete'. So in place of his earlier jocular ambition to know 'the mind of God' (i.e. to provide a complete naturalistic theory of the cosmos), Hawking now writes that he is glad he has changed his mind: 'I'm now glad that our search for understanding will never come to an end.'[22]

In another rather more sophisticated variant of the strong naturalist view, the natural universe is effectively seen, as it were, as *impermeable* – sealed in from any conceivable influence from beyond the totality of the empirically observable cosmos. The claim is characteristically linked to the idea that all our thinking necessarily operates within the conceptual categories that relate to the phenomenal world,[23] and hence that it will make no sense to think of the world as being somehow impinged on from 'outside'.[24] Hence traditional religion comes to be seen as to a greater or lesser degree incoherent. Since it accepts the idea of supernatural inter- vention (as implied, for example, by doctrines like the Incarnation, or divine action in response to prayer), it is committed to the possibility that the natural world can be affected by forces or entities that are wholly 'other'. But the 'impermeability' of the natural world (on the view we are now considering) means that nothing is going to zoom in from outside to punish us if we are bad or save us if we are good or redeem us if we go astray; and what is more there is no way that the resources of our language can even discuss such a notion – it takes us beyond the limits of any possible domain of knowledge.

The more sophisticated version of naturalism takes us back once more to certain central ideas derived from Enlightenment thinking, which I shall be considering in a moment. I shall be arguing that if we go back to

---

22 'Gödel and the End of Physics', at http://www.damtp.cam.ac.uk/strtst/dirac.hawking/.) Cf. John Cornwall, 'Hawking's Quest: A Search Without End', *The Tablet*, 27 March 2004, pp. 4–5.

23 Compare Kant: the conditions of the employment of the categories are such that they 'can never admit of transcendental but always only of empirical employment' (*Critique of Pure Reason*, A 246/B303).

24 In raising doubts about the coherence of the idea of the transcendent 'impinging' on our world, the naturalist seems on stronger ground than she is in simply insisting that the natural world is all there is. The argument, instead, is that even if there were transcendent entities, outside of our space–time continuum, they would *ex hypothesi* be causally sealed off from any possibility of causal interaction with our own world. The issue of causal interaction is taken up in Ch. 7, § 4, below.

the standard Humean and Kantian arguments they do not in fact close the door to religion as firmly as is often believed: so the actual arguments of the Enlightenment thinkers need not be seen as the bogeyman for the religious adherent that they are standardly presented as being. But let me close the present section by entering a brief caveat concerning the direction in which the argument is now leading us, and the terms in which the contemporary debate between religious apologists and their opponents is often conducted.

One problem about the terms of the discussion as it is now developing is the implication that the key to being religious is a belief in a supernatural domain: that the crucial difference between a religious and an anti-religious thinker lies in whether or not they subscribe to the existence of supernatural entities. Now while this is, on one way, clearly true, I think it can be very misleading: it makes it seem as if what explains religious adherence is above all the commitment to a transcendent realm – precisely the kind of realm that its critics dismiss as 'spooky' – and in this way allows the debate to be conducted largely in terms set by the opposition. For although the religious adherent does indeed (at least in mainstream Christianity, Judaism, and Islam) believe in a transcendent deity, to start by focusing on this as if it is the sole key seems to me to reverse the *order of discovery*. As I have argued in earlier chapters,[25] what does the *work* in bringing people to God is not intellectual debates about the transcendent, but the *immanent* aspects of religion – the transformative power of religious ideas and practice in our human lives and experience. Belief in a God who transcends all natural categories of thought comes as a *result* of trust and involvement in a living community of faith, not through analysis of the concept of the supernatural – which is in any case outside the domain of what can be described and analysed using the normal tools of human investigation. In short, for many purposes and contexts, the contemporary appeal of naturalism seems to me best combated more obliquely, by insisting, as I have been doing at several points in the argument so far, on the primacy of praxis.

For since God can never be grasped in wholly naturalistic terms, his nature and existence can never be satisfactorily established using the tools and techniques of naturalistically based philosophy. By the same token, the natural world itself necessarily remains, from a certain perspective, ambiguous, blank, poker-faced; however well scrutinized, the intimations of a reality beyond or behind it will never be experienced unless the heart

25 See especially Ch. 1.

is open and receptive. And to make it so is a task that cannot be accomplished by philosophical analysis or rational argument alone.[26]

4 THE RELIGIOUS COUNTER: AN UNPROMISING POSTMODERNIST REPLY

Let me now return to the earlier ideas of the Enlightenment, and to the supposed philosophical threat posed by Humean and Kantian thought to the continued survival of religion. Quite a number of recent religious apologists have responded to this supposed threat with an understandable, but I think ultimately misguided counter – the strategy of setting their faces against the Enlightenment, as if it were somehow a wrong turn in humanity's journey. My first example is from the third volume in a most impressive trilogy from the distinguished New Testament scholar Tom Wright. Wright's aim in the volume in question, *The Resurrection of the Son of God*, is to show firstly that the earliest origins of the Christian church are best explained, on textual and historical grounds, as stemming from a firm belief among the early disciples in the actual physical resurrection of Jesus of Nazareth; and, secondly, that that belief is itself best explained by the actual historical occurrence of the resurrection.

---

26 A world picture is never entirely abstract and theoretical in its import, and to complete our brief sketch of the received naturalist view one would need to say something about the fact that its contemporary appeal is strongly linked with a certain kind of robust approach to tackling the inevitable difficulties and setbacks of human existence. If we want answers to our problems, so runs the general line, we have to seek them under our own steam, using the resources of reason and science and technology, instead of cowering in fear or hope of supernatural solutions. This 'Cartesian turn', as Michel Foucault has called it (thinking of Descartes' manifesto for the new science as enabling us to become 'masters and possessors of nature'), involves a significant shift towards a belief in human autonomy and independence, and coincides historically with the dramatic increase in human technical and scientific power which the Enlightenment itself produced. According to this view, when humanity was confronted by a natural world whose vast and mysterious forces it seemed to have no hope of fully understanding, let alone controlling, it had pretty much no option but to cower: a rat terrified and powerless in a cage will be observed to take any option to calm itself, even pushing a bar which never, or only capriciously or randomly, delivers relief. But now that science has given us the option of actually doing something to improve the human lot, the rat can leave off pushing the bar, and can start to make the cage more comfortable, or even restructure it, or break out of it altogether. Hence (according to this picture), instead of frantic prayer, or ultimately pointless superstitious rituals, or the slightly more dignified but ultimately not much more productive stance of resigned Stoic acceptance, human beings can now bravely step forward into the light, and work to make a better world. Compare Michel Foucault, Seminar at the Collège de France of 6 January 1982, published as 'Subjectivité et vérité', in *Cités*, ed. Y. C. Zarka (Vendôme: Presses Universitaires de France), vol. II (March 2000), 143ff. For Descartes' modernist manifesto about humans becoming the 'masters and possessors of nature', see *Discourse on the Method* [*Discours de la méthode*, 1637], part vi (AT VI 62: CSM 142–3). See also J. Cottingham, 'Spirituality, Science and Morality', in D. Carr and J. Haldane (eds.), *Essays on Spirituality and Education* (London: Routledge, 2003), pp. 40–54.

I have not the space here (nor remotely the competence) to start evaluating these claims – certainly not the first, which is bolstered by an enormous wealth of careful scholarship. What I want to draw attention to, instead, is Wright's concluding picture of the Enlightenment worldview as something that is itself ripe for being discarded. The 'dreams of the Enlightenment' are starting to be challenged, argues Wright, and he continues by asking:

What if the moratorium on speaking of Jesus' bodily resurrection . . . should itself turn out to be part of [the] intellectual and cultural hegemony [of the Enlightenment] against which much of the world is now doing its best to react. What if the resurrection . . . should turn out to be, in the twenty-first century as in the first, the most socially, culturally, and politically explosive force imaginable, blasting its way though the *sealed tombs and locked doors of modernist epistemology* and the (now) deeply conservative social and political culture which it sustains.[27]

The references to 'modernist epistemology' clearly point to something like the general Humean and Kantian line as we earlier characterized it – the view that the discourse of human reason cannot aspire to transcend the phenomenal world; and by labelling such a view 'modernist' Wright suggests by implication that it may be a mere passing phase in the development of human culture. Modernism, we are invited to suppose, is giving way to a 'postmodernist' or 'post-Enlightenment' counter-revolution, which may re-open the door to religion that has been shoved ever more firmly towards the closed position in the last two or three centuries. A similar thought surfaces, from a very different quarter, in the thinking of the philosopher John Caputo, who in a recent collection entitled *God, the Gift, and Postmodernism* talks of the need to '[push] past the constraints of [the] old, methodically constricted . . . straight and narrow Enlightenment, which found it necessary to cast "reason" and "religion" in mortal opposition', and to 'restore the good name of the impossible, of what the old Enlightenment declared impossible'.[28] In a separate, even

---

27 Wright, *The Resurrection of the Son of God*, p. 713 (emphasis supplied). The earlier volumes in the trilogy are *The New Testament and the People of God* (1992), and *Jesus and the Victory of God* (1996).

28 J. D. Caputo and M. J. Scanlon (eds.), *God, the Gift, and Postmodernism* (Bloomington: Indiana University Press, 1999), Introduction, pp. 2–3. The label 'postmodernism' covers a multitude of ideas and trends. Chiefly, perhaps, it is a matter of style. A recent essay highlights some of the stylistic features typical of the postmodernist movement: 'irony, parody, self-consciousness, fragmentation, playful self-reflexivity and parataxis'; P. Rice and P. Waugh (eds.), *Modern Literary Theory* (New York: Oxford University Press, 1989; 4th edn. 2001), p. 325. One can see all of this in works of art – novels, painting, film – over the past twenty years or more, as well as in the writing of those philosophers (Jacques Derrida being perhaps the most prominent) to whom

more forthright, manifesto, Caputo argues that 'the impossible has too long been declared off limits':

> To the great astonishment of learned despisers of religion everywhere, who have been predicting the death of God . . . religion in all of its manifold varieties has returned. Even to say that is misleading, since religion was reported missing mostly by the intellectuals; no one outside the academy thought that it had gone anywhere at all. Religion has returned even among avant-garde intellectuals who have given it a new legitimacy by discrediting its discreditors, suspecting its suspectors, doubting its doubters, unmasking its unmaskers. The flower of religion is one of the blossoms in our post-modern anthology.[29]

Bold and in some ways engaging though it is, there seem to me at least three reasons why this style of defending religion by attacking the Enlightenment will not do. First, there is a problem in logic about the structure of the argument employed, namely that it comes very close to committing the fallacy logicians call the 'negation of the antecedent'. If the truth of Enlightenment philosophy entails the unacceptability of religious metaphysics, then it simply does not follow that the refutation of Enlightenment philosophy is enough to reinstate religion's acceptability. To give a parallel illustration of the flaw in the logical structure, modern medicine may outlaw the use of magic potions, but should modern medicine turn out to be flawed that will not be enough to re-validate the potions – they may still be suspect for a host of other reasons.

Second, the notion that the values of the Enlightenment represent an arbitrary 'intellectual and cultural hegemony' that is now mercifully collapsing is surely a fantasy. For one thing, outside the cocooned and somewhat precious world of academic fashion, there is absolutely no sign at all of the supposed collapse: to put the point at its crudest, philosophers and theologians travelling to exotic locations to hold forth on the death of the Enlightenment still rely on Enlightenment science and technology to get them there and back. More seriously, the worldview that has given

the epithet 'postmodernist' is commonly applied. But style is often the outward manifestation of a latent philosophical agenda. And the underlying philosophical creed of postmodernism boils down, in effect, to a kind of anti-creed: a mistrust of any claims to universality, objectivity, or finality; a pervasive 'loss of faith' in the 'progressivist and rationalist discourses of Enlightened modernity' (ibid.). Compare, for example, Derrida's sustained critique of the idea that philosophical (or any) discourse can achieve a determinate and final precision or exactness; cf. *Margins of Philosophy* [*Marges de la philosophie*, 1972], transl. A. Bass (Brighton: Harvester, 1982), pp. 247ff; and Jean-François Lyotard's definition of 'postmodernism' as 'incredulity towards metanarratives' (that is, a suspicion of overarching philosophical accounts of truth, reality and the human condition): *The Postmodern Condition* [*La Condition postmoderne*, 1979] transl. G. Bennington and G. Massumi (Manchester: Manchester University Press, 1984), p. xxiv.

29 John Caputo, *Religion* (London: Routledge, 2001), p. 66.

birth to the modern age, though it may be historically associated with all sorts of undesirable socio-political developments (Western economic exploitation of the developing world, misuse of the natural environment, and so on), cannot realistically be described as a 'cultural hegemony', if that is taken to mean that the ultimate explanation of its success lies in the purely causal relationships of power and control as opposed to the normative relations of reason and justification. The testing of hypotheses against scrupulously assessed experimental evidence, the formulation of theories in terms of carefully defined concepts, mathematical precision in measurement and modelling, the insistence on logical rigour in argument, and free and open debate as opposed to deference to authority – these are now an ineradicable part of our modern scientific and philosophical culture, which it would be inconceivable – or at least inconceivably foolish – to abandon. There is no going back; and not just because, as a matter of fact it is likely to be near impossible to try to put the scientific genie back in the bottle, but because the standards just referred to are an inextricable part of our human commitment to rationality itself. If we are talking of a 'hegemony' here, it is the hegemony of reason, something that is no temporary phase of modern history, but the very essence of our humanity. The point, of course, goes back at least as far as Aristotle's ancient definition of the human as a 'rational animal'; and it finds expression in many forms of religious as well as secular thinking. Thus the idea that the rational part of our nature gives us a point of contact with the divine (a fairly widespread one in ancient Greek philosophy)[30] finds strong echoes in mainstream Christian theology: God is himself *logos* – the creative intelligence that is not simply power but Word or Reason; and in finding expression in our lives it demands not just blind

---

30 Compare, for example, the Stoic cosmology, as set out by Diogenes Laertius, drawing together threads from Zeno (the founder of Stoicism) and his successors Cleanthes and Chrysippus: 'The end is to live in harmony with nature, which amounts to living in accordance with virtue; for nature leads us towards virtue. Now living in accordance with virtue is the same as living in accord with our experience of what happens by nature; for our natures are parts of the nature of the whole. So the end comes down to this: to live in agreement with nature, that is, in accord with our own nature and that of the whole, engaging in no activity forbidden by the universal law. *This law is right reason that pervades everything, and is identical to God who directs and disposes everything that exists.* So virtue, and the smooth flow of life, which we see in those who are happy, arises when everything is done according to the harmony of each person's individual spirit with the rational will of the disposer of all things.' Diogenes Laertius, 7, 87–9, in A. Long and D. Sedley (eds.), *The Hellenistic Philosophers* (Cambridge: Cambridge University Press, 1987), 63C (with omissions, emphasis supplied). Zeno of Citium (335–263 BCE) was the founder of the Stoa; his pupil Cleanthes (331–232) was its second head; and Chrysippus (280–207) its third head (and probably the most important for the subsequent development of Stoic thought). Similar accounts of the salient features of Stoic ethics and its relation to Stoic cosmology can be found in several others sources; cf. Cicero's *De Finibus* [45 BCE], III, 73.

obedience, but a natural responsiveness to the light of truth, the truth that 'shall make you free'.[31]

Critics of so-called Enlightenment values often question the idea of a neutral, decontextualised 'rationality', arguing that what is taken to be 'true' or 'in accord with reason' simply reflects the contingencies of history and culture; and this tends to be coupled with the (perfectly fair) observation that philosophy and science are never in the position of being able to pronounce on the soundness of our conceptual scheme from some detached Olympian standpoint outside of that scheme. So those who extol the 'objectivity' and 'rationality' of the Enlightenment framework (these critics conclude) are simply reflecting their own cultural preconceptions as children of the Enlightenment. However, it is one thing to say that none of our evaluations can float entirely free from the particularities of history, and quite another to say that there can be no good reasons for defending a particular tradition or methodology. We may be unable to escape from the boat on which we sail the ocean, but that does not stop us being confident that the improvements in navigation that have been developed over the past two or three centuries do indeed enable us to steer better than the earlier mixture of luck and guesswork. The values of the Enlightenment cannot in good faith be seen as a temporary aberration, or a dubious passing phase, but are part of the long journey of the human mind towards an ever fuller and more accurate understanding of the natural order. Nor need the most earnest defender of religion dissent from this; for from a religious perspective both the instrument of this search (our God-given faculty of reason) and the object of the search (the rationally describable structures making up the world) need not take us away from our search for God, but on the contrary are one way in which our human activities reflect the ultimate rationality of the creator.

The third and final reason to have serious doubts about the postmodernist strategy of 'dissing' the Enlightenment is that it involves a serious misunderstanding of what Enlightenment philosophy actually entails. Thus, in so far as Caputo's aim, for example, is to allow 'religion to get a word in edgewise', and make room for 'faith where knowledge fails',[32] it appears that he may have the wrong target in his sights. Caputo mentions in particular Kant, whom he attacks for putting religion off limits. But it is now time to recall the words of the quotation that forms the epigraph

---

31 John 8:32. For the theme of logos and light, see John 1:1–5. For a discussion of freedom as responsiveness to the light of truth, see Cottingham, 'Descartes and the Voluntariness of Belief', pp. 343–60. See also Ch. 3, §2, above.
32 *God, the Gift and Postmodernism*, p. 4.

for the present chapter: Kant famously said that he went 'beyond know-ledge in order to make room for faith'.[33] Science, on the Kantian view, is confined to describing the phenomenal world; and what lies beyond the horizon of science cannot therefore be proved – *but neither can it be disproved.* It follows from this that what is 'impossible', in the sense of not being a possible object of human knowledge, can nevertheless be a proper object of faith. According to Kant, I cannot prove (or disprove) God; yet because it would be humanly impossible to devote my life to the good if I thought I was striving after 'a conception which at bottom was empty and had no object', it is appropriate for 'the righteous man to say "I will that there be a God . . . I firmly abide by this and will not let this faith be taken from me".'[34] In short, Kant's fideism seems the precursor, not the pro-scriber, of Caputo's. So while Caputo's 'postmodernist' claim is that the demolition of Enlightenment constraints allows religion to reappear on the philosophical scene, the truth seems to be that by confining science to the phenomenal world, the Enlightenment, in the person of Kant, did not after all rule out the possibility of a deep reality lying beneath that world. Like Descartes and Pascal before him, who thought that our human reason could not comprehend infinite being,[35] Kant allowed for a tran-scendent reality outside the phenomenal world, one that we cannot reach by demonstrative inquiry, but one it makes sense to believe in, and for which (Kant went on to insist) our human existence has a profound need.[36]

5 ENLIGHTENMENT AND FAITH

Some clarifications are now in order. Though I began by sketching out a certain view of the Enlightenment that sees it as putting grand metaphys-ics in general and religion in particular outside the 'land of truth', in the

---

33 *Critique of Pure Reason*, B xxx (transl. N. Kemp Smith (London: Macmillan, 1929, p. 29). Kant's term (prefiguring Hegel) is *aufheben*: it is not so much that Kant 'denies' knowledge in order to make room for faith (as Kemp Smith's translation misleadingly has it), as that he goes beyond it to attain something higher.

34 Immanuel Kant, *Critique of Practical Reason* [*Kritik der Praktischen Vernunft*, 1788], pt. I, bk. II, ch. 2, §8.

35 'I do not grasp the infinite, and there are countless attributes of God which I cannot in any way grasp, and perhaps cannot even reach in my thought'; Descartes, Third Meditation (AT VII 46: CSM II 32); cf. Letter to Mersenne of 27 May 1630 (AT I 152: CSMK 25). 'If there is a God, he is infinitely beyond our comprehension, since having neither parts nor limits he bears no relation to us. We are thus incapable of knowing either what he is or if he is.' Pascal, *Pensées*, no. 418.

36 Compare Kant's notion of a 'need of reason' (*Bedürfnis der Vernunft*); *Critique of Practical Reason*, pt. I, bk. II, ch. 2, §8.

light of what has now emerged such a picture turns out to be misleading. Kant's project, in circumscribing the domain of discursive reason and arguing that it cannot transcend the bounds of experience, may sometimes appear not just to lay down the limits of scientific and philosophical knowledge, but to determine the bounds of all possible human thought. But since (as several passages in Kant make clear) religion is a proper object of faith, he can instead plausibly be interpreted as saying that the test that religious language fails to pass is the test for knowability, not the test for meaningful assertability.[37] The upshot is that, in a certain sense, Kant's metaphor of metaphysics as lying outside the 'land of truth' (*das Land der Wahrheit*) is unhelpful. For suppose for a moment that the theists are right in believing there is a God – an eternal creator who transcends the phenomenal world. Then there would surely be a metaphysical reality that such belief reaches towards, a reality that cannot be encompassed by the resources of human knowledge, but which it is nonetheless natural to think of as 'true', or as a true object of faith. One way of putting this might be to say that metaphysical truth may outrun the domain of possible human knowledge.

The point needs to be put with some care, however, since Kant's critical philosophy, as normally and no doubt correctly interpreted, has a thrust which is not limited to purely epistemic issues, but has profound conceptual implications. In the *Prolegomena*, Kant observes that 'our reason, as it were, sees in its surrounding a space for the cognition of things in themselves, though we can never have determinate concepts of them and are limited to appearances only'.[38] And this is aptly glossed as follows by a recent commentator:

we must picture the land of truth not merely as it appears to us from the inside, as having such and such a character and extent, but as adjoining a space which must remain for us a void.[39]

---

37 I take this formulation from Hare, *The Moral Gap*, p. 47.

38 *Prolegomena to any Future Metaphysic that will be able to present itself as a Science* [*Prolegomena zu einer jeden künftigen Metaphysik die als Wissenschaft wird auftreten können*, 1783], §352.

39 Gardner, *Kant and the Critique of Pure Reason*, p. 213. Despite the possibly misleading implications of this phrase, Gardner in fact provides what seems to me an entirely correct assessment of the implications of the Kantian position: 'Kant does not reject claims about non-empirical objects, however cognitively defective, as literally meaningless . . . Kant's objection to transcendent knowledge turns entirely on the gap between thought and knowledge. He is therefore required to tread a line between granting reason the authority that rationalism [i.e. traditional 'grand metaphysics'] claims for it, and endorsing Hume's demand that volumes of metaphysics be consigned to the flames' (Gardner, *Kant and the Critique of Pure Reason*, p. 210). The only caveat I would add here is that Hume's position is perhaps less radical, and closer to Kant's, than the 'flames' passage suggests; see n. 41, below.

Talking of 'space which must remain a void' seems to allow little scope for traditional religious language: the problem seems to be not just about evidence, but about being able coherently to assert anything whatsoever. And that seems not far off the early Wittgensteinian view that 'the limits of language are the limits of my world', and that 'what we cannot speak of we must pass over in silence'.[40] But notice that even these stronger twentieth-century formulations are not outright dismissals. They acknowledge fundamental obstacles to bringing religious (and other metaphysical) belief inside the valid space mapped out by reason within our phenomenal world; but that is not the same as the positivist position of condemning all metaphysical language to the flames. Even Hume, once this distinction has been grasped, can be seen as very far from the proto-positivist that he is often represented as being. When he insisted on the necessity of deriving claims about 'matters of fact' from some experiential base, he explicitly allows that there may be realities 'behind' the correl-ations we observe: there may be, he pointedly acknowledges, 'ultimate springs and principles of nature'; it is just that they must remain, in his graphic phrase 'totally shut up from human curiosity'.[41] (And perhaps, he suggests elsewhere, they may even be a proper object for faith, if not of reason.[42])

When we reflect further on the kinds of philosophical project found in Hume, or Kant, or the early Wittgenstein, it becomes clear that they do not, and indeed *could not* with any plausibility propose to eliminate the very possibility of a domain of reality lying beyond the phenomenal world. It would be outrageous arrogance to suppose that the limits of our puny human scientific or even conceptual resources must necessarily determine the actual limits of reality. As Hume himself nicely observes (in quite another context) 'what peculiar privilege has this little agitation of

---

40 'Die Grenzen der Sprache . . . die Grenzen meiner Welt bedeuten'; 'Wovon man nicht sprechen kann, darüber muß man schweigen'. *Tractatus Logico-Philosophicus* [1921], propositions 5.62 and 7.

41 '[T]he utmost effort of human reason is to reduce the principles productive of natural phenomena to a greater simplicity and to resolve the many particular effects into a few general causes . . . But as to the causes of these general causes, we should in vain attempt their discovery . . . These ultimate springs and principles are totally shut up from human curiosity and enquiry.' *Enquiry concerning Human Understanding* [1748], §IV, pt. i.

42 The 'best and most solid foundation' for theological belief is 'faith and divine revelation'; Hume, *An Enquiry concerning Human Understanding*, §XII, pt. iii. Here, as often in Hume, it is not easy to read the 'tone' of the passage; there is very probably a certain irony in what may look like a concession to the religious believer, since the 'faith' he allows the believer comes with the implied price tag of admitting that its content is not analysable in terms of either of the two categories (relations of ideas or matters of fact) into which Hume maintains all philosophically sound assertion falls.

the brain which we call *thought*, that we must thus make it the model of the whole universe?'[43] Moreover, not only is it outrageous to deny the possibility of a space of reality beyond the limits of our human epistemic and conceptual resources, but it is an unavoidable aspect of our minds that for any proposed limits on our thinking we will always strive to reach beyond them – though in so doing we may need to stretch language beyond its literal uses, and reach for imaginative and figurative modes of discourse. Compare this extraordinary and widely admired passage from the fourteenth-century mystic Mother Julian of Norwich:

It was at this time that our lord showed me a spiritual vision of how intimately he loves us. I saw that he is to us everything that we know to be good and beneficial. He is our clothing, for love wraps us and enfolds and embraces us; that tender love completely surrounds us, never to leave us. As it became clear to me, he is everything that is good.

And he showed me more, a little thing, the size of a hazelnut, lying on the palm of my hand, round like a ball. I looked at it thoughtfully and wondered, 'What can this be?' And the answer came '*It is all that is made.*' I marvelled that it continued to exist and did not suddenly crumble away; it was so small. And the answer came into my mind: '*It exists, both now and for ever, because God loves it.*' And so everything owes its existence to the love of God.[44]

The vision of holding the entire created universe in the palm of one's hand may seem a paradigm case of trying to adopt a 'sideways on' perspective on reality (in John McDowell's graphic phrase).[45] And of course we could never ourselves attain to such a perspective: our aspirations to knowledge have to operate, as Kant rightly insisted, within the domain of the phenomenal world, and it makes no sense to think of ourselves dualistically set over against reality so as to establish some match between how we see it and how it truly is. But when all that is conceded, Julian's vision presents us with an idea that many have found quite patently intelligible: that there might be a conscious being who stands in relation to the entire created universe in a relation that is analogous to

---

43 From David Hume, *Dialogues concerning Natural Religion* [published posthumously, 1779], pt. II. Compare the following remarks by Tim Williamson (albeit lifted from a rather different context): 'that the conceptual has no outer boundary beyond which lies unconceptualized reality . . . seems to require the premiss that everything (object, property, relation, state of affairs) is thinkable. That premiss is highly contentious. What reason have we to assume that reality does not contain *elusive objects*, incapable of being individually thought of . . . We do not know whether there are elusive objects. It is unclear what would motivate the claim that there are not, if not some form of idealism. We should adopt no conception of philosophy that on methodological grounds excludes elusive objects.' ('Past the Linguistic Turn', in Leiter (ed.), *The Future for Philosophy*, pp. 109–10).

44 *The Revelations of Divine Love* [1373], Short Text, Ch. IV (modernised).

45 McDowell, *Mind and World*, pp. 34–46.

how a human being stands when she holds a hazelnut in the palm of her hand. The model presented construes the entire domain of the phenomenal world as a sphere, and in the ecstatic vision this totality is grasped and viewed as it were from the outside. It is *all that is made* – the world, everything that is the case; yet we can see it, albeit in a figurative and symbolic way, as something that is minute, finite, created, in comparison to an unimaginable Other. We can never bring such a vision within the domain of discursive knowledge; yet it is a vision that we can clearly understand (though not in a literal way).[46]

If the argument just developed is right, then not only are contemporary defenders of religion unwise to attack the 'Enlightenment position' (since the respect it accords to reason and science is a precious part of our human heritage), but they do not even *need* to attack it, since, properly construed, the Enlightenment position allows for an intelligible discourse of faith, albeit the claims it makes do not meet the necessary criteria to qualify as items of knowledge.[47]

Yet it might be objected that to place the object of faith outside the realm of discursive knowledge is to concede that we can say nothing definite about it, or at least nothing there could be any basis for believing, even on 'faith'. That space beyond the domain of evidence and rational argument may be filled by Mother Julian with a loving creator, or may be filled in all sorts of other ways by mystics and poets of various persuasions, but if we are left with no possible way of integrating such visions into the domain of evidence and justification, they will surely remain like Wittgenstein's idle cog wheel – an isolated decoration spinning in the void.[48]

One approach to answering this is by invoking our familiar theme of the importance of praxis. The theistic vision of Julian escapes the charge of being an isolated fantasy because it is integrated into the life of its author: her religious and spiritual practice enables her, day by day, to see

---

46 There are many reasons why such a vision could only be expressible in non-literal modes of discourse. First, the idea that we are dealing with a domain wholly beyond the phenomenal world implies that the relation of creator to created cannot *literally* be like that of someone holding the universe in the palm of the hand – for the transcendent domain will not be spatially related to the phenomenal. For similar reasons, such a domain cannot be temporally related to our universe. There are notorious problems generated by this: how can an eternal, non-physical reality be causally related to a temporal and material world? (Construed in even a very minimally literal way, the 'hazelnut' model does of course imply two-way causal relations – the nut is, for example, seen and touched, both of which experiences involve causality.) For discussion of these problems, see Ch. 7, §4, esp. n. 21.

47 The idea of a 'discourse of faith' is problematic for a number of reasons (not least the spectre of a certain kind of 'fideism' that may seem to license irrationalism). I shall return to this theme in the following chapter.

48 Cf. Wittgenstein, *Philosophical Investigations* (*Philosophische Untersuchungen*, 1953) pt. I, §271.

the world as imbued with value and purpose, to see the whole of existence as a gift, in short to subscribe to the ancient metaphysical maxim of Aquinas (a maxim with even earlier Platonic roots) *omne ens qua ens est bonum:*[49] being and goodness are inter-convertible because, as Julian expresses it, all that is is held in being by the love and benevolence of its creator. One way of putting this would be to say that the praxis of the religious adherent generates a certain mode of receptivity such that the world we experience is seen as carrying *traces* of the transcendent divine world that is its ultimate source. These traces are not to be experimentally verified like the measurable properties of science, nor indeed are they capable of being established in a way that would command the assent of any detached and objective observer.[50] But they are vividly consistent with the experience of the religious adherent, and they connect up with a metaphysical vision that, while not being able in principle to satisfy accepted Humean and Kantian standards of human knowledge, is at least expressible via a certain figurative mode of discourse.

The world in its goodness and its beauty contains traces of its creator. Since that creator is taken to be a transcendent being, we cannot characterize that goodness and beauty in straightforwardly literal terms; but there is little point in throwing up one's hands at this concession, since it is a familiar theme of religious discourse that the nature of the infinite being that is God eludes normal human comprehension.[51] The point is not merely an academic or philosophical one, but finds an echo in many religious writers – in the end it is a variation on Paul's famous assertion that here we see only via reflections in a mirror, dimly.[52] But this does not (as Hume sometimes seemed to suggest) land us up in a morass of mysticism that is little better than saying nothing at all.[53] The faith of

49 'Every entity qua entity is good', or 'Every entity is good by its very nature' (*omne ens est bonum per suam essentiam*): Aquinas, *Summa theologiae* [1266–73], pt. I, qu. 6, art. 3. For discussion of other relevant texts, see Stump, *Aquinas*, pp. 62–5.

50 See above, Ch. 1 and Ch. 5, n. 6.

51 A recurring theme in Descartes, for example, is that 'our soul, being finite, cannot comprehend the Infinite' (letter to Mersenne of 11 November 1640, AT III 234: CSMK 154).

52 βλέπομεν γὰρ ἄρτι δι' ἐσόπτρου ἐν αἰνίγματι (1 Corinthians 13:12). It should perhaps be added that there are many passages in Paul which suggest a more 'robust epistemology' based on the vivid revelatory experience of God through the life of Christ. Compare Ephesians 1:3–14; Philippians 1:9; 1 Corinthians 2:1–4. (I am indebted to Andrew Moore for drawing my attention to this point, and the associated references.) The idea of the incarnation is, however, precisely, the idea of the transcendent becoming immanent in human life (and therefore to that extent no longer wholly transcendent).

53 'How do you mystics, who maintain the absolute incomprehensibility of the Deity, differ from sceptics or atheists, who assert that the first cause of all is unknown and unintelligible?' David Hume, *Dialogues concerning Natural Religion* [c. 1755], pt. IV, first paragraph. For more on the question of the mystical and its relation to religious language, however, see Ch. 8, below.

the religious believer has a thin but discernible content, and it is a content whose significance is activated and energized by the way it is worked out in the lived experience and praxis of the believer.

The suspicion may remain that our argument has conceded too much. By retreating from traditional grand metaphysics, which claimed to be able to support its theistic assertions by compelling rational demonstrations, have we not been left with a somewhat hazy and ill-defined idea of the dependency of our universe on something unknown that is beyond it, something whose nature we cannot rationally grasp, but which is taken to be somehow analogous to that of a good and loving creator? Is such a faith one that we can responsibly adopt? One could, of course, stress how uplifting such a faith may appear in the mouths of ecstatic mystics like Mother Julian, or one could invoke the Kantian suggestion that we have a human need to postulate an ultimate triumphant good as a precondition for the viability of the moral life;[54] but to shift the ground of debate in this way might seem like a retreat from the question of whether such faith is epistemically responsible in the first place. For 'when the chips are down' (to quote a present-day philosopher) 'that a doctrine might give us a boost does not mean we have [reason] to accept it.'[55]

I shall aim to address the question of epistemic responsibility in the next chapter. But to give an initial sketch of that response, let me close the present chapter not by providing more quotations from spiritual and mystical writers (although I suspect that their work of 'opening the heart' is ultimately the only way forward from this epistemic impasse), but rather by citing the work of an analytic philosopher, Alvin Plantinga. Plantinga in his recent philosophy has argued strongly against what he calls 'evidentialism' – the view that a person who accepts a religious belief must have propositional evidence for it. I do not wish to defend or adopt that controversial position here, but I do want to take one leaf from Plantinga's book, namely that there are circumstances in which belief, even though not supported by propositional evidence, may be perfectly responsible. Suppose that in terms of rational argument and evidence there is a standoff – either because, as per the Enlightenment position, we are dealing with a transcendent area which lies outside the domain of discursive knowledge, or because the arguments either side are simply indecisive. In such circumstances, Plantinga argues, the religious adherent may be in the following position:

---

54 Kant, *Critique of Practical Reason* [*Kritik der Praktischen Vernunft*, 1788], pt. I, bk. II, ch. 2, §5.
55 Jonathan Rée, review of J. Cottingham, *On the Meaning of Life*, *Times Literary Supplement*, 5 December 2003, p. 6.

They read the critics but on careful reflection do not find them compelling; likewise, though they are aware of theistic arguments and find some of them not without value, they do not believe on the basis of them. Rather this person has a rich inner spiritual life; it seems to them that they sometimes catch a glimpse of the overwhelming beauty and loveliness of God; they are often aware, as it strongly seems to them, of the work of the Holy Spirit in their heart, comforting, encouraging, teaching, and leading them to accept 'the great things of the gospel', as Jonathan Edwards calls them [*Religious Affections*, 1746]. After long, hard, conscientious reflection, they find all this enormously more convincing than the complaints of the critics. Are they then going contrary to duty in believing as they do? Are they being irresponsible? Clearly not . . . They could be wrong, desperately wrong, pitiably wrong, in thinking these things. But they are not flouting any discernible duty; they are doing their level best to fulfil their epistemic responsibilities.[56]

Would it not be more responsible to remain aloof, to abstain from pronouncing on what may or may not lie beyond the phenomenal world, to follow the Wittgensteinian maxim and 'remain silent'? That will depend on individual experience. For one who 'at a crash' has had a Pauline conversion experience,[57] or for one who has enjoyed an ecstatic vision of the creator's goodness, not to speak out will be inconceivable.[58] But even for one who has merely 'caught a glimpse', in Plantinga's phrase, of the realities towards which religious language reaches, the door to faith may be open, and able to be entered without loss of responsibility.[59] Faith and hope, like the love that inspires both, are not virtues that can be cultivated from a detached perspective.[60] But they have long been seen as genuine virtues – dispositions of character (or gifts of grace, as some would see it) that are constitutive of human fulfilment. Tradition has called them 'theological' virtues; and certainly, if the argument of this chapter has been right, then no thesis derived from the Enlightenment, if properly understood, requires them to be considered as philosophical or epistemic vices.

We may well want to say more: not just to acquit faith from philosophical condemnation but to establish its epistemic, and indeed moral,

---

56 Alvin Plantinga, 'Religion and Epistemology', in E. Craig (ed.), *Routledge Encyclopedia of Philosophy* (London: Routledge, 1998), vol. VIII, p. 214.

57 'Whether at once, as once at a crash Paul, or as Austin lingering-out sweet skill . . .' Gerard Manley Hopkins, 'The Wreck of the Deutschland', stanza 10; in *Poems (1876–1889)*, ed. W. H. Gardner, p. 15. For the conversions referred to see Acts 9:1–9, (for Saul/Paul), and for 'Austin' (Augustine), *Confessions*, e.g. bk. VII.

58 'For we cannot but speak the things which we have seen and heard' (Acts 4:20).

59 The extent to which the Plantinga position slides (if it does) into the domain of faith will be postponed for discussion until the following chapter.

60 See above, Ch. 1, §3.

credentials in more positive ways. For on the *epistemic* front, the advocates of the religious perspective will want to argue that religious faith does not have to be construed as blind or irrational assent, but on the contrary as a commitment that is supported by widely recognised features of our human experience of reality. And on the *moral* front, the religious adherent will want to claim that because of its transformative power, faith, and the spiritual practices that accompany and reinforce it, are capable of supplying a deficit in our fragmented and vulnerable human existence and thus rendering our lives incomparably richer and more meaningful than they would otherwise have been. But these are topics for the next chapter.

CHAPTER 7

Religion and the good life: the epistemic and moral resources of spirituality

Thou art not yit at Jerusalem, but bi smale sodeyn lightnynges that gliteren oute thorugh smale cranés fro the cité schalt thou mowen see it from feer, or thou come therto. ('Thou art not yet at Jerusalem. But by small sudden lightnings that glide out through small crannies from that city, thou shalt be able to see it from afar, before thou come thereto.')

Walter Hilton.[1]

Naturae nostrae infirmitas est agnoscenda.
('We must acknowledge the weakness of our nature'.)

René Descartes.[2]

I WHAT IT MEANS TO BELIEVE

Suppose, as suggested at the end of the last chapter, that one has reached a position of faith in a conscious creative power, independent of the phenomenal universe, a power that stands over against the universe as fundamentally 'other', yet which fills something like the role envisaged in traditional theological metaphysics – the uncaused cause of the cosmos and all its energy, the necessary foundation for the entire series of contingent events studied by science, the perfect source of all value, and the ultimate good towards which all things strive.[3] What would it mean to believe in such a being, the being of which Aquinas said *et hoc dicimus Deum*, 'and this we call God'?[4]

---

1 Walter Hilton, *The Scale of Perfection* [c. 1380], II, 25. The passage evocatively describes what it must have been like to approach a town at night in the middle ages (long before the onset of population growth and light pollution); see the Introduction by A. C. Spearing to another great fourteenth-century religious text, *The Cloud of Unknowing* (Harmondsworth: Penguin, 2001), p. xxxiv.
2 René Descartes, *Meditations* [*Meditationes*, 1641], final sentence.
3 Aquinas, *Summa theologiae* [1266–73], pt. Ia, qu. 59, art. 1; *Summa contra Gentiles* [1259–65], II 47. Cf. Aristotle, *Nicomachean Ethics* [325 BCE], I, 1.
4 Aquinas, *Summa theologiae*, Ia, 2, 3. See further Ch. 5 n. 27, above.

This rather vague question can, I think, be broken down into three sub-questions. One way of inquiring into what it means to be a believer involves asking about the conditions for forming such a belief and the context in which theistic commitment operates. And from one of the principal themes of this book, the idea of the 'primacy of praxis', it should already have emerged that belief in God is something that is characteristically formed not as a result of detached scrutiny of impartially assessed arguments and evidence, but in the context of a dynamic pattern of involvement. As in many other areas of life, we learn to trust by trusting; the theist's commitment is a growing offshoot from the progressive cultivation of the disciplines of spirituality, not the result of an isolated intellectual inquiry that predates any such commitment.[5]

The second way of answering the question 'What does it mean to believe in God?' involves inquiring into the difference such a belief makes in the actual life of the religious adherent. What, for example, is the relationship (if any) between a theistic stance and the cultivation of moral virtue, and what reason (if any) is there to think that a theistic outlook promotes or somehow facilitates either a moral life or (which may not be the same) a fulfilled life? This second group of issues is to be addressed later on in the present chapter.

The third approach to reflecting on what is implied by belief in God (to be explored in the first half of this chapter) focuses in a more abstract and theoretical way on the grounds or warrant for theistic belief – on what *licences* it, as it were. Some will feel this is a matter that has long been overdue for consideration in these pages. For no matter how much stress is put on praxis and involvement, and on practical links with spiritual and moral development, no supporter of theism can indefinitely sidestep the familiar challenge posed by our predominantly secular and sceptical philosophical culture – to show what kind of epistemic credentials, if any, theism is able to produce.

2 FAITH AND EVIDENCE

The argument of the last chapter ended with a reference to Alvin Plantinga's view that theistic belief need not be based on evidence. Plantinga's use of the term 'evidence' relates specifically to a philosophical doctrine he calls 'evidentialism' – the view that a belief is justifiable only if the set of arguments for its truth is stronger than the set of arguments

---

5 See Ch. 1, above, especially the final section.

against. So in the case of religious belief, evidentialism says it is justified only if the arguments for theism (typically the 'big three' – the onto-logical, teleological, and cosmological arguments) outweigh the argu-ments against (notably the problem of evil, either in its logical or probabilistic form, plus assorted philosophical objections having to do with the alleged incoherence of the idea of God, and social or psycho-logical arguments that attempt to explain away belief in God in terms of institutional oppression or some kind of developmental malfunction). Now evidentialism, argues Plantinga, is simply untenable: the view that 'you are justified in believing something only if there is a good argument for it from other propositions you believe' is one he insists there is no reason to accept. Many beliefs – Plantinga cites memory beliefs, belief in other minds, or beliefs such as that gratuitous cruelty is wrong – are just not like that. They are not the conclusions of demonstrative arguments, nor are they hypotheses accepted because of their explanatory powers: they are just 'basic' beliefs – beliefs which we hold without deriving them from other more certain beliefs, but which are no less certain, and no less epistemically respectable, for all that. And for Plantinga, religious belief falls into just this category: 'theistic belief is *properly basic* – that is, such that one can be justified in accepting it without accepting it on the evidential basis of other propositions one believes.'[6]

One may perhaps be sympathetic to Plantinga's account of some supposedly basic beliefs (for example belief in other minds), but the religious case presents special problems of its own, since the object of theistic belief is an infinite being that transcends the ordinary world of space and time. And this brings us straight up against the boundary rules discussed in our previous chapter – the Enlightenment insistence that the scope of rational inquiry which purports to issue in knowledge claims can never transcend the domain of the empirical. In the light of these constraints, it may seem as if those who want with Plantinga to affirm their religious commitments as 'basic' must be abandoning any claim to discursive knowledge (since on Plantinga's own 'anti-evidentialist' terms they are not employing either deductive argumentation or empirical investi-gation of the phenomenal world). So one might conclude that invoking belief in God as 'basic' amounts to a form of fideism: faith takes over where evidence and knowledge peter out. Does the Plantinga position

---

6 Alvin Plantinga, 'Religion and Epistemology', from Craig (ed.), *Routledge Encyclopedia of Philosophy*, vol. VIII, p. 214 (emphasis supplied).

boil down to an advocacy of what in the last chapter we called 'a discourse of faith'?[7]

Here we should note first of all that the spectrum of positions known as 'fideism', despite having attracted many celebrated adherents, is regarded with suspicion in many orthodox religious circles,[8] since in its extreme forms it may seem to propose a blind leap of faith of the kind seemingly advocated by Kierkegaard, or even worse the kind of rank irrationalism conjured up by the slogan (wrongly) attributed to Tertullian, *credo quia absurdum*.[9] Yet in the end, Plantinga's position, when scrutinised, does not look as if it is best interpreted in a fideistic way. For despite his rejection of so-called 'evidentialism', Plantinga's account of the basis for belief in God turns out to be not unrelated to what we might ordinarily call 'supporting evidence'. Thus, after effectively admitting that the traditional arguments for and against may not finally settle the matter, Plantinga himself refers to some typical aspects of the believer's personal experience which at the very least gel powerfully with the commitment to theism: many believers, Plantinga stresses, have 'a rich inner spiritual life' and 'it seems to them they sometimes catch a glimpse of the

7 See above, Ch. 6, §5, p. 122.

8 Though the term 'fideism' was apparently first used by French Protestants in 1870s as a term of approval, it has since widely acquired a pejorative connotation (particularly among Catholic writers), as implying an over-reliance on faith at the expense of reason. For more on this, see Alistair Mason, 'Fideism', in Hastings et al. (eds.), *The Oxford Companion to Christian Thought*, pp. 240–1.

   The classic account of the relationship between reason and faith was given by Thomas Aquinas, who maintained that the two are complementary. Some religious beliefs (for example, the existence of God) can, he argued, be established by 'natural reason', while other beliefs (including the 'revealed truths' of Christianity such as the Incarnation and the doctrine of the Trinity) cannot be reached by reason, but require faith. For Aquinas, there is a harmony between reason and faith, since both types of truth are worthy of our belief. Moreover, he taught that even the truths of natural reason may sometimes be accepted on faith – for example, by those who do not have the time or resources to follow the relevant arguments (*Summa contra Gentiles*, I. 4).

   Aquinas' emphasis on reason and faith as complementary is to some extent anticipated by Augustine and Anselm, though both thinkers may be regarded as a little further along the spectrum towards fideism, since they take it that faith is in some sense prior to reason. The subtitle of Anselm's *Proslogion* is *fides quaerens intellectum* ('faith seeking understanding'). Anselm's starting point is an unquestioned belief in God, which he takes to be a prerequisite for embarking on the meditation that will establish God's existence by rational reflection: *credo ut intelligam* ('I believe in order that I may understand': *Proslogion* [1077–8], ch. 1). The Anselmian approach owes much to Augustine's reflections on the phrase *nisi credideris, non intelliges* 'Unless you have believed you will not understand' (based on the inspired if questionable Septuagint rendering of a verse of Isaiah (7:9): ἐὰν μὴ πιστεύσητε, οὐδὲ μὴ συνῆτε; cf. Augustine, *Contra Faustum Manichaeum* [400 CE], bk. IV. For a critical exposition of the 'faith seeks understanding' programme in Christian philosophical theology, see Paul Helm, *Faith and Understanding* (Edinburgh: Edinburgh University Press, 1997).

9 'I believe because it is absurd'. For the actual words of Tertullian, and for the position of Kierkegaard, see Ch. 2, n. 15.

overwhelming beauty and loveliness of God'; further, it strongly seems to them that 'they are often aware of [a divine presence] comforting, encouraging, teaching and leading.'[10] It is partly in the light of such experiential awareness that Plantinga is able to represent theistic commitment as epistemically responsible, despite the fact that it is not derived as a conclusion from the preponderance of philosophical arguments, or put forward as a scientific hypothesis providing the best explanation for certain empirical data.

Irrespective of what the actual position of Plantinga himself may be, however, in what follows I shall no longer focus on his particular arguments, but simply take my cue from the kinds of experiential awareness of the divine to which he refers. My aim will be to mark out a viable middle ground between the two extremes of rampant fideism on the one hand and traditional argumentative and strictly evidentialist approaches to theism on the other; occupying this middle ground can be thought of as acknowledging the need for a measure of faith, while repudiating the charge that one is jumping outside of the realm of evidence and rational argument altogether. In short, it seems to me we can do justice to the kinds of personal experiential awareness that are often called 'spiritual', and allow that they do indeed provide support of a kind for theistic commitment, while at the same time respecting the Enlightenment strictures against knowledge-claims that float wholly free from their proper sphere of the phenomenal world.

3 TRACES OF THE TRANSCENDENT

Let us first recapitulate some familiar points. Belief in God cannot be a straightforwardly empirical hypothesis, for the good Humean and Kantian reasons explored in the previous chapter: theism posits a reality beyond the phenomenal world, and hence invokes a realm wholly distinct from the empirical domain investigated by science. In this sense, theism is quite unlike a scientific hypothesis of the kind involved when, for example, scientists investigate the causes of hereditable characteristics, or of the refraction of light.

All this is, I think, fairly plain sailing; but before going on to lay down the law about what either science or theology can or cannot do, we should pause to make an elementary but perhaps insufficiently noticed distinction between the *experimental* and the *observational* modes of

---

10 Plantinga, 'Religion and Epistemology', p. 213.

inquiry. Most of modern science is experimental: it aims to vary conditions so as isolate explanatory factors, and thus form hypotheses which
can be tested by repeated experiments over a variety of background
conditions. But there are some phenomena (e.g. in many areas of astron-
omy) where the human observer has only very minimal power to manipulate and vary the relevant conditions. What is more, there are some
cases, as Hume famously pointed out, where we face the very special
difficulty that the phenomenon we are investigating is unique.[11] Thus any
attempt to devise an experimental hypothesis about what kind of cause
produces a universe is doomed to failure: we have nothing to go on except
the single instance.[12]

Does this mean that in this type of case we have to abandon rational
inquiry entirely and leap into the realm of pure faith? Not quite; for
although we are debarred in such cases from experimentation, we are not
debarred from observation. Further consideration of how science tackles
unique phenomena may be helpful here (though the analogy with how
theistic modes of thinking operate is not an exact one). The branch of
scientific inquiry known as cosmology, which looks at the origins of the
material universe, cannot vary the background conditions so as to isolate
the supposed causes of the Big Bang, but it can reflect systematically on
certain observed features now detected within the universe. And famously,
such observations may disclose *traces* – for example traces of background
radiation, which are consistent with a certain account of the 'singularity'
from which it is supposed the cosmos originated.

The singularity which is the initial Big Bang event posited by modern
physics is interesting, since it is *ex hypothesi* supposed to be something
which is not subsumable under the empirical laws governing the observable universe (though the states of affairs minute fractions of a second
after the explosion are); in the words of Stephen Hawking, under conditions when the universe was infinitesimally small and infinitely dense, 'all
the laws of science would break down'.[13] But for all that, the supposition

---

11 There may be other cases – for example cases where we are unable, for reasons of technical
capability, to isolate possible explanatory factors, or to vary conditions. These are cases where it is
impossible in practice to perform the relevant experiments; the 'one-off' case of the origin of the
universe is a case where it is impossible in principle to do so.

12 'When two species of objects have always been observed to be conjoined together, I can infer, by
custom, the existence of one wherever I see the existence of the other; and this I call an argument
from experience. But how this argument can have place where the objects, as in the present case,
are single, individual, without parallel, or specific resemblance, may be difficult to explain.' David
Hume, *Dialogues concerning Natural Religion* [c. 1755], pt. II.

13 Hawking, *A Brief History of Time*, p. 8.

of such a singularity is not simply a matter of blind faith, since although it is not subject to experimental confirmation, we can at least observe traces which are taken to be consistent with its occurrence. Here we have something which is neither blind faith on the one hand, nor experimental science on the other, but which is not wholly unrelated to what we experience. The *trace* remains; and this is precisely what the religious adherent will say of the occasional glimpses he or she has of a world transfigured by overwhelming goodness and beauty, or of the strange spiritual transformations wrought in our lives by prayer and meditation, or in moments of crisis – those 'strange geometrical hinges',[14] when our perspective on reality undergoes a fundamental shift, and we sometimes seem to grasp a significance that had eluded us before. The Godhead, if such there be, is by its very nature beyond the horizon of the phenomenal world (just as, for the cosmologist, the conditions that gave rise to the initial singularity are necessarily beyond the event horizon that forms the boundary of any possible observation). Yet it may still be possible to affirm, in the words of the ancient hymn:

> O Godhead, here untouched, unseen
> All things created bear thy trace!

God's existence may not be the conclusion of a valid argument, or a plausible empirical hypothesis; affirming a transcendent being is thus in this sense a leap into the unknown – a leap beyond the boundaries of discursive knowledge. But for all that, for the believer it is more than a *blind* leap, more than a mere act of will,[15] since the belief resonates in a

---

14 I take this suggestive phrase (somewhat out of its context) from the Jacobean playwright John Webster, *The Duchess of Malfi* [1614], IV. 2. 221.

15 Contrast William James, who famously argued that 'in all important decisions of life we have to take a leap in the dark'. Despite this phrase, however, and the title of his celebrated essay, 'The *Will* to Believe', James's position is perhaps rather closer to the middle ground (neither insistently evidentialist on the one hand, nor rampantly fideist on the other) that is advocated in the present chapter. Religious belief is for James an act of faith, but not a wholly blind one, since, in cases where the intellect cannot decide on the evidence, he maintains that to insist on remaining aloof may close us off to certain kinds of experience that may (eventually) be such as to support the initial act of trust. James instances by way of parallel the kind of trust necessary for entering on a friendship, where 'a fact cannot come at all unless a preliminary faith exists in its coming'. (Compare Nussbaum, discussed at Ch. 1, §3, above.) Hence, for James, 'our passional nature not only lawfully may, but must, decide an option between propositions, whenever it is a genuine option that cannot by its nature be decided on intellectual grounds; for to say, under such circumstances, "Do not decide, but leave the question open", is itself a passional decision – just like deciding yes or no, and is attended with the same risk of losing the truth . . .' All quotations from W. James, *The Will to Believe and Other Essays in Popular Philosophy* (New York: Longmans Green, 1897), ch. 1.

striking way with occasional but powerful intimations, enduring traces
that are manifest in the moral and spiritual fabric of our lives.[16]

4 HORIZONS OF KNOWLEDGE AND INTIMATIONS OF THE BEYOND

At this point in the argument, it may be objected that the analogy just
invoked with physical cosmology is subject to a fundamental flaw. For
although both the theist and the cosmologist postulate unique events or
entities that by their nature take us beyond the normal domain of
empirical science, the physicist still is able to characterize the realities he
posits using the language of mathematics – in other words, in a language
which is continuous with the discourse we know by experience to be
suited to an accurate and predictive account of observable events. The
'event horizon' may shield us from the ultimate nature of the reality
giving rise to the big bang, but at least the theorist's characterization
of that unimaginable singularity is an extrapolation employing the self-
same mathematical reasoning which has been shown time and again in
the last few centuries to be the reliable key to unlocking the secrets of
the empirical world. The entities of the theist, by contrast (so runs the
objection), are of a wholly different kind – a survival from a primitive
anthropomorphic cosmology – and there is no way in which they can
be fitted into a coherent picture of the reality disclosed by modern
science.

It is undeniably true that modern physical cosmology speaks the
language of mathematics, and that the 'traces' it looks for in the cosmos
are themselves characterizable in quantitative terms – they belong to the
language which since the time of Galileo and Descartes has been universally accepted as the reliable code for deciphering the 'great book of

16 A classic scientistic, or positivistic critique of such appeals to experience rests on the principle of
falsification: the religious adherent may appeal to parts of his experience that *support* the faith,
but how far does he seriously attempt to test it *against* possible counter-evidence; indeed, does
the believer allow that anything could conceivably count as counter-evidence? For this line, see the
widely anthologised paper of A. G. N. Flew, 'Theology and Falsification', in Mitchell (ed.), *The
Philosophy of Religion*. Now the main argument of the present chapter readily concedes that what
is at stake in appeals to the experience of 'intimations' or 'traces' of the divine is not evidence in
the scientific sense; so Flew's challenge is not here as troubling as it would be for someone
subscribing to a strictly evidentialist account of religious belief (see §1, above). But, in any case, a
theistic response to the Flew challenge does seem available: a religious faith would indeed be
radically undermined if humans never had any but the most utilitarian and pragmatic responses to
the beauties of nature; if the most devoted spiritual praxis never yielded anything but dryness,
acedia, and weariness; or if suffering and vulnerability never opened the door to new hope.

nature'.[17] But that is not, in the end, a decisive argument for dismissing the quite different types of 'trace' that occur in the context of spiritual experience as irrelevant to the ultimate nature of reality. For these types of 'trace' – the traces which are experienced in that sense of overwhelming beauty and goodness and meaning that is described in countless records of religious experience – are by their very nature not candidates for quantitative description, and hence any attempt to exclude them a priori for this reason would be no more than arbitrary discrimination. This is not to claim a special *ad hoc* privilege for religion that exempts it from the normal demands of scientific inquiry; it is simply to acknowledge the truism that not all discourses are commensurable – and that the language of experiential human response is not reducible to language appropriate for describing the mass and momentum of particles.

But (an objector might counter) is there not good reason to believe that the ultimate nature of reality is of the general kind described by modern mathematical physics, and that religious-style cosmologies are therefore disqualified from being plausible accounts of that reality? It would be easy here to get into an unproductive standoff, with the religious adherent feeling obliged to resist the march of modern science as having taken a wrong turn in adopting the quantitative and mathematicized approach. But such a reactionary stance, like the 'anti-Enlightenment' crowing of the postmodernists we examined in the last chapter, is surely a misguided strategy – there is simply no need for it. When William Blake discerned

> eternity in a grain of sand
> and heaven in a wild flower[18]

the insights he enjoyed do not have to be interpreted as *incompatible* with scientific truth. It may well be (indeed it seems very plausible to suppose) that what Blake experienced was intimately dependent on physico-chemical events in his nervous system and in the environment, and that all these events are accurately describable in the quantitative language of particle interaction: nothing in the present argument, or in the position that defends spiritual experience as revelatory of a divine source, need necessarily take issue with any of these scientific results about the physical basis of conscious experience. But to be supportive of science is not the same as subscribing to *scientism* – the highly implausible view that the

---

17 Cf. Galileo *Il Saggiatore* ('The Assayer') [1623], in *Opere*, ed. A. Favaro (Florence: Barbera, 1889–1901, repr. 1968). vol. VI, p. 232.
18 William Blake 'Auguries of Innocence', from the Pickering manuscript [c. 1803].

language of science exhausts all reality.[19] The things Blake experienced, and whose significance he strove to express in terms of human emotion and insight and reflection, are self-evidently not reducible to quantitative terms – yet that does not eliminate them as important phenomena, important parts of our total human experience of the world, and ones which may therefore reasonably be supposed to have at least some relevance to how that world is ultimately to be understood. The 'traces' which we have been citing as providing some form of support for the theistic interpretation of reality can no more be disqualified from playing such a supporting role than can the traces on an electromagnetic scanner be disqualified as supporting a cosmological theory of the Big Bang just because they are not couched in the language of poetry.

If the argument of the last two sections has been right, then religious adherents have no need to hang their heads in shame when brought to the bar of epistemological scrutiny. Even if we suppose that the traditional arguments for God's existence are flawed (that is an issue that is left entirely open in the present book), and even if we grant that the theistic view is for a variety of reasons ineligible for the status of an empirically testable hypothesis, the faith of the theist is not, for all that, irresponsible or contra-rational. For the theist's position is linked to the claim that one may discern in the world unmistakable traces of that unexperiencable reality that transcends it.

But here a further objection surfaces: can a transcendent reality coherently be said to leave traces? The notion of a trace is fundamentally a *causal* one; yet since the supposed reality invoked by theists *ex hypothesi* transcends the phenomenal world, how can it causally interact with that

19 It is a familiar criticism of postmodernist writers that the early-modern/Enlightenment revolution attempted to construct just such a scientific master-discourse to which all knowledge claims must conform. Thus Richard Rorty calls us to abandon the traditional Enlightenment conception of philosophical knowledge which asserts 'that the universe is made up . . . of simple, clearly and distinctly knowable things, knowledge of whose essence provides the master-vocabulary which permits commensuration of all discourses' (*Philosophy and the Mirror of Nature* (Oxford: Blackwell, 1980), p. 357). It is certainly true that Descartes, for example, like his contemporary Galileo and so many of his successors from Newton to Einstein and beyond, believed that fruitful explanation in physics must be couched in the language of mathematics. But there is no sign anywhere in the Cartesian programme that *all* discourses were supposed to be subsumable under the quantitative models of the mathematician. On the contrary, Descartes himself is famous, indeed notorious, for insisting that the descriptions and explanations applicable to the realm of consciousness were distinct from, and indeed incommensurable with, those applicable to physics – and the later philosophers of the Enlightenment largely followed suit. In short, when thinkers like Rorty cast Enlightenment modernity as the villain, arrogantly laying claim to a discourse of certitude and completeness, they seem to have constructed a straw man. For more on Enlightenment philosophy and its implications, see Ch. 6, above.

world, in such a way as to leave a 'trace'? This type of objection is of a piece with a series of traditional objections to theism: how is a non-spatial and eternal God supposed to interact with his creation – indeed, how can such a being create a temporal universe in the first place?

In responding to such objections the theist has to take care to insist that such notions as that of a 'trace' are not being used in their literal sense – a strategy that is consistent with the long tradition of invoking metaphorical and other non-literal uses of language in attempting to talk about the Deity (see Chapter 5, above). Once literality is abandoned, there seem to be several possible ways in which one might understand the idea of a divine trace in the created cosmos.[20] One is the model of what is done by a creative writer such as a dramatist.[21] A playwright can plausibly be thought of as creating, from another 'dimension', a world (the world composed of the events in the play) which occupies a spatio-temporal framework that is wholly discontinuous with that which the playwright inhabits. For example, the episodes which come 'earlier' or 'later' in the play, have no relation to what is earlier or later in the playwright's life; in this sense, the creator is 'outside' the time that runs through the story of the play. The same is true, *mutatis mutandis*, for the spatial relationships occurring within the play, which exhibit a radical discontinuity with anything in the world of the creator. The idea of radically different 'dimensions' applying to the creator and to his work seems to provide at least the beginning of a handle on how a Creator outside of space and time could create a world structured by a spatio-temporal framework that did not constrain his own existence.

The analogy can be pressed further. While the playwright does not causally impinge on the action of the play in any literal sense, the structure of the play may plausibly be said to exhibit 'traces' of the creative intelligence that composed it (*Macbeth* bears the stamp of its creator, Shakespeare). We are not here thinking of the playwright intervening, like a clumsy *Deus ex machina*, to tinker with the occurrences on the stage;

20 One highly suggestive, if (perhaps appropriately) elusive series of reflections on this idea is found in the work of Emmanuel Levinas; see, for example, his *In the Time of the Nations* [*A l'heure des nations*, 1988], transl. M. B. Smith (London: Athlone Press, 1944); discussed in C. Chalier, 'Levinas and the Talmud', in S. Critchley and R. Bernasconi (eds.), *The Cambridge Companion to Levinas* (Cambridge: Cambridge University Press, 2002), Ch. 5.

21 The analogy goes back to the medieval idea of the 'book' of nature composed by a divine author. In modern times, Dorothy Sayers has argued that '[The] experience of creative imagination in . . . the artist is the only thing we have to go on in entertaining and formulating the concept of creation . . . Although . . . the activity of writing [a] book is a process in space and time, it is known to the writer as *also* a complete and timeless whole.' *The Mind of the Maker* (London: Methuen, 1941), pp. 23, 29.

rather, the conception of the playwright is itself, timelessly, or extra-temporally from the point of view of the events in the play, what gives rise to its very existence – that without which it would have no being, let alone any shape or purpose or significance.[22]

The need to employ analogies of this kind in order to interpret the relationship of a transcendent God with his creation reinforces the point already made that the 'intimations' or 'traces' experienced by the religious adherent cannot be construed as experimental evidence in the scientific sense. But at the same time they do not epistemically count for nothing – any more than they did for Wordsworth when he affirmed a recurring experience that was absolutely central to his life, and the meaning he was able to find there:

> I have felt
> A presence that disturbs me with the sense
> Of elevated thoughts; a sense sublime
> Of something far more deeply interfused
> Whose dwelling is the light of setting suns,
> And the round ocean, and the living air
> And the blue sky, and in the mind of man[23]

To repeat: such experience does not qualify as 'evidence' in the sense that it is available for impartial assessment or repeatable experimentation. As in many areas of human existence, it evades such detached scrutiny, since it is the fruit of a living commitment. But that does not mean it can be dismissed as 'merely subjective'. A lifetime of musical discipline may

22 A final completion of the analogy requires us to note that the play is not like a static sculpture or painting, but is a dynamic process to which the actors, by their own intelligence and sensitivity (or the reverse) contribute; we could even imagine a *pièce de theatre* in which the actors depart from the script, for better or worse, by exercising their own judgment. Or to bring the matter even closer to the human situation, one might suppose that there is no fixed script – that we human agents are here, as the theist might put it, to 'complete the work of creation' by choosing, for better or worse, what decisions to take to advance the action. The results of such free choice might mean that the action of the play went horribly wrong in comparison with how things might have turned out; and one might even suppose that the creator envisages a character appearing on the stage at some point to put things right, a character that only he can play by himself becoming one of the actors. This would be an event which would be at the edges of conceivability from the point of view of the players actually operating within the 'closed' world of the drama; it could only happen at the cost of a radical crossing of boundaries, a kind of leakage from the world of the dramatist to the created world of the play.

23 *Lines Written a Few Miles above Tintern Abbey* [1798], in S. Gill (ed.), *William Wordsworth: A Critical Edition of the Major Works* (Oxford: Oxford University Press, 1984), ll. 89–100. For further discussion of the philosophical significance of this passage, see Cottingham, '"Our Natural Guide . . .": Conscience, 'Nature' and Moral Experience', in Oderberg and Chappell (eds.), *Human Values.*

enable the committed musician to discern profundities and beauties of musical form that are in large part quite literally inaccessible to the novice; but that does not mean that they are mere idiosyncrasies of subjective feeling. On the contrary they are genuine responses to a transpersonal reality – it simply takes a lifetime of the appropriate *askesis* to acquire the capacity to appreciate them.[24] And so it may be with spiritual experience.

One might think there is a circularity here: the *askesis* which surely already presupposes belief in certain realities is supposed to lead to the experience which is then taken to support the existence of those realities. But the circularity is only apparent. The cycle in question is only suspect if one makes the assumption that truth or reality ought to be accessible *irrespective of the character and state of mind of the aspirant to truth.* That is an assumption of modern scientific inquiry – that the truth is simply available for discovery, given sufficient ingenuity and the careful application of the appropriate techniques, and that the dispositions and moral character of the inquirer are entirely irrelevant.[25] But while this assumption may be correct enough in the case of inquiring into truths within meteorology, say, or chemical engineering, there is no reason to accept it when we are dealing with central truths of our human experience – for example truths about how a poem or symphony may be appreciated, or how a loving relationship may be achieved and fostered. In these latter areas, the impartial application of a mechanical technique is precisely the wrong approach: the truth yields itself only to those who are already to some extent in a state of receptivity and trust.[26] And so it may be with regard to spiritual *askesis* and the truths of religion; the truths are made manifest not via impartial interrogation of the data but through an inner transformation of the subject.

---

24 'Transpersonal' is a term which has a certain (deliberate) ambiguity. It would be hard not to concede that beauty of musical form is something that is inter-subjectively accessible (so in this sense is more than merely a idiosyncratic response of the subject); but some would go further (in a 'Platonic' direction) and say that such beauty, like all forms of beauty and goodness, has a certain ontological independence from the contingencies of human activity and preference. My own inclination, as should be clear from Ch. 3, §§4 and 5, above, would be to support the stronger claim as well as the weaker.

25 For more on this theme, see Michel Foucault, Seminar at the Collège de France of 6 January 1982, published as 'Subjectivité et vérité' in *Cités*, ed. Y. C. Zarka (Vendôme: Presses Universitaires de France), vol. II (March 2000), 143ff. See also Cottingham, 'Spirituality, Science and Morality', in Carr and Haldane (eds.), *Essays on Spirituality and Education*, pp. 40–54.

26 Compare Ch. 1, §§3 and 4, above.

5 MORAL PSYCHOLOGY AND THE CULTIVATION OF VIRTUE

Having looked at some of the epistemic credentials of religious faith, and having touched on what may be called the epistemic fruits of spirituality, we are now in a position to return to the question (postponed earlier) about its moral fruits: what difference is theistic belief supposed to make in the actual life of the religious adherent?

Implicit in much advocacy of the path of spirituality is the notion that following such a path is connected with the attainment of moral virtue, and perhaps also of a good life (in the broader sense of a flourishing life, the life that the Greeks called *eudaimon* – happy, worthwhile, fulfilled).[27] But can we really suppose that spirituality is either necessary or sufficient for virtue? And in the second place, can we really suppose that it is either necessary or sufficient for a flourishing life?

It might be suggested that the answer to all four of these questions is obviously 'No'. One might point out, quite correctly, that someone can clearly be a morally virtuous person but entirely lacking a spiritual dimension in her life; conversely he might be devoted to spiritual practice but be morally lax or even transgressive. And similarly, moving to the broader question of a flourishing life, it might appear that someone could have a flourishing life without that life involving any element of spirituality; and conversely that one might lead an unhappy and unflourishing life while resolutely pursuing a spiritual path.

Let me at once concede that there can be no philosophical demonstration of logically necessary connections between spirituality and moral virtue, or spirituality and flourishing; but I want to argue nevertheless that the traditions of spirituality converge on what has served for countless human beings as a highly fruitful solution to addressing certain fundamental obstacles to the attainment of human happiness and virtue. While the path of spirituality may not be the only conceivable way of overcoming such obstacles, a richer understanding of what these obstacles are, and how spiritual praxis is supposed to address them, may at least place the onus on its opponents to indicate what alternatives might be available within an entirely secular and non-spiritual ethical system.

What are these obstacles to our human capacity to attain the good? The first and most obvious is *human weakness*. Notoriously, we may see the good clearly, yet turn away from it, to a lesser good, or to something

---

27 For the notion of *eudaimonia* in Aristotle's ethics, see the Introduction by J. Barnes in *The Ethics of Aristotle*, pp. 33ff. See also Aristotle, *Nicomachean Ethics*, ed. T. Irwin, pp. 407ff.

which is not good at all, except for some speciously glamorous aspect that lures us on. We may rightly desire the good of health, but may be diverted by the allure of the chocolate cake. Diet examples have a faintly jocular ring – but the long-term costs of weakness of will regarding our bodily appetites can be extremely serious, as attested by a long literature of philosophical and theological agonizing over the problem of *akrasia* and the control of the passions.[28] Weakness of will is but one aspect of a more general obstacle to which contemporary philosophical writing on ethics is often surprisingly blind – the problem of the *relative impotence of reason*. Because of a widespread and ingrained hostility to psychoanalytic thought,[29] philosophers often ignore the implications of Freud's famous insight that the Ego is not, as we like to suppose, master in its own house.[30] Good actions, modern ethicists tell us, are those we have reason to perform; right actions are those we have conclusive reason to perform;[31] but implicit in the philosophical literature one often finds a curious kind of Socratic optimism, as if morality consisted in a proper grasp of the relevant array of reasons, and a firm disposition to act on them. Perhaps it does, but until this abstract picture is supplemented with a deeper moral psychology, its relevance to any plausible theory of the good life must remain pretty thin.

One does not have to go all the way with Augustine and the theory of original sin in order to recognize that humans have a massive capacity to rationalize, deceive themselves, excuse themselves, convince themselves they are acting properly and sincerely, when their true motivations are often highly suspect. To take one example, it is all too clear that we constantly rejig our assessments in our own favour: scarcely realizing it, when making decisions we interpret the balance of reasons in a way that is biased towards ourselves. I am not speaking here of the legitimate partiality that allows any sincere person of integrity to assign a certain reasonable

---

28 'For the good that I would I do not, but the evil which I would not, that I do' (Romans 7:19, Authorised Version). For an interesting account of how this familiar human phenomenon continued to preoccupy philosophers of the early-modern period, see Susan James, *Passion and Action: The Emotions in Seventeenth-Century Philosophy* (Oxford: Clarendon Press, 1997).

29 See Ch. 4, §2, above.

30 'But man's craving for grandiosity is now suffering the . . . most bitter blow from present-day psychological research which is endeavouring to prove to the "ego" of each one of us that he is not even master in his own house, but that he must remain content with the veriest scraps of information about what is going on unconsciously in his own mind.' Sigmund Freud, *Introductory Lectures on Psychoanalysis* [*Vorlesungen zur Einführung in die Psychoanalyse*, 1916–17], transl. J. Riviere (London: Routledge, 1922), ch. 18.

31 See for example Philip Stratton-Lake in Stratton-Lake (ed.), *Ethical Intuitionism*, Introduction, p. 15.

weighting to his or her own interests and those of her loved ones,[32] but rather to the distorting shadows cast by pride and vanity and self-importance and fear and embarrassment and self-defensiveness and envy and greed and self-absorption and fantasies of power. Some contemporary moral philosophers, to be sure, write about these topics, and often they may flatter themselves – or indeed quite rightly suppose – that they do so in an acute and insightful way; but one fundamental lesson of psychoana-lytic thought is that the most articulate intellectuals are often the most resistant to self-awareness when it comes to their own case. That self-deception can operate right alongside the clearest intellectual grasp of all the salient features surrounding a decision is something that is not particularly easy to grasp without the kind of personal *askesis* that makes it vivid.

The disciplines of psychoanalysis (as I have argued elsewhere)[33] make available to the subject an understanding – one that is never final, but needs constant practical reinforcement through guided self-examination – of how present objects of choice can become *invested with freight from the past*, so that they take on a special significance which is opaque to the agent himself. The catastrophic errors and bad judgements to which we humans are liable, ones which afterwards we often recognize to our chagrin to have put at risk what is truly precious in our lives, so that like Othello each of us can recognise himself as one who 'like the base Indian, threw a pearl away, richer than all his tribe'[34] – such errors simply cannot be avoided by an earnest resolve to weigh up the reasons for action more carefully. Change and growth require, if the psychoanalytic line is any-thing like correct, a radical vulnerability – a willingness to delve back into those early parts of our lives in which our very ability to value things, our very models of goodness and love and attraction and self-worth, were shaped and formed. That simple maxim, *The child is father to the man*,[35]

---

32 See J. Cottingham, 'Partiality, Favouritism and Morality', *Philosophical Quarterly*, 36 (1986), pp. 357–73.

33 In *Philosophy and the Good Life: Reason and the Passions in Greek, Cartesian and Psychoanalytic Ethics*, ch. 4.

34 William Shakespeare, *Othello* [1604], V.ii.

35 'The Child is father of the Man / And I could wish my days to be / Bound each to each by natural piety.' William Wordsworth, 'Ode, Intimations of Immortality from Recollections of Early Childhood' [1815 version]. Although many have read the phrase 'natural piety' as painting a sentimental picture of idyllic childhood, discerning critics of Wordsworth's project in *The Prelude* (begun 1799) have plausibly seen it as describing the poet's struggle to understand the roots of his psyche – a struggle that in many respects prefigures the psychoanalytic quest for self-awareness. Cf. M. Baron, *Language and Relationship in Wordsworth's Writing* (London: Longman, 1995), ch. 4.

so rarely appreciated in its full significance by intellectualising ethicists, tells us that we cannot overcome the obstacles to moral growth and fulfilment by intellectual analysis alone.

Nor, indeed, by intellect plus will-power. For the other lesson of Freudian theory is that resolute determination very often does not do the job in the way we expect it to. Repression of a desire, determination to 'keep the passions in check', as some of the ancient philosophical pro-grammes recommended, can simply lead to displacements of libido or psychic energy which may break out in different, but possibly even more serious ways. In a sense there is nothing new about this: the lesson is as old as Euripides' *Bacchae*, and Freud's genius was to make explicit what in one way we all knew already. But the lesson remains: we fantasize (and perhaps academics are even more prone to this than most) that we are 'mature', intelligent, rational beings who have our destiny in our own hands; but the child remains within us, and we fail to acknowledge it at our peril.[36]

6 DIMENSIONS OF ASKESIS

What does this excursus into Freudian theory have to do with the question of spirituality and its link with moral virtue? I suggested in an earlier chapter that the spiritual quest and the psychoanalytic quest were in fact much more closely related than is often supposed.[37] What is involved in each case is a systematic programme of *askesis* which is linked to an interior journey – the journey to find the true self with which the smug, superior, intellectualizing, rationalizing ego is so easily confused.

The process of growth and transformation, in order to overcome the cognitive and the conative defects to which the moral deliberator is typically subject,[38] is a crucial part of what it is to become a developed human agent: our moral lives are a *journey* in a much deeper sense than

---

36 For more on these themes, see Cottingham, *Philosophy and the Good Life*, ch. 4.

37 See Ch. 4, §5, above.

38 The distinction between cognitive defects (of perception) and conative defects (of will) is an important one which cannot be explored in detail here. But it is, I believe, insufficiently appreciated that the aim of psychotherapeutic programmes of self-discovery is to produce a kind of self-awareness and integration in which the formerly split-off parts of the psyche no longer appear as alien forces to be subdued by a 'superior' act of will, but instead are perceived in their true colours. The result is that our 'cognitive' and 'conative' incapacities are found to be intimately interrelated; and once the projections of the past are lifted, the healing effects spread to both together (or rather, the defects no longer appear as belonging to entirely separate faculties). For a concrete exploration of this, see the 'Cecil' case in *Philosophy and the Good Life*, Ch. 4, §7.

applies to many parts of our intellectual lives (for example our accumulating knowledge of geography or natural history). Now of course there are many moral philosophers who have acknowledged the importance of *learning* in the moral sphere; Thomas Aquinas, for example, was well aware of the Aristotelian stress on the importance of training and habituation in ethics, and he himself spoke of habits of virtue, and described conscience in terms of habits of will, as well as of practical reasoning.[39] But the human moral journey as described in the works of the great spiritual writers (Augustine is perhaps the paradigm case, though there are many others) is radically different in its outlines – radically different from what one might call the 'classroom' model, a model of careful progressive moulding of habits based on innate capacities of practical intellect and will. All such 'normal' apparatus no doubt has its place, but, if anything like the religious worldview is correct, there is something more dynamic and more dramatic typically at work in the human spirit. As moral beings, we do not just start from a reliable innate deposit, and then accumulate information and get more skilled in processing it; rather, we gradually, laboriously, stimulated by examples, moved by parables, humbled by error, purged by suffering, begin to change. The faculty enabling us to respond in this way may be innate, and in that sense 'natural' (as Aquinas, for example supposed), but it also requires our being open to the possibility of transformation – in Pauline language, to putting off the old nature and taking on the new, or in the language of the fourth Gospel, to the possibility of rebirth.[40]

Such rebirth, for any who are sympathetic to the psychoanalytic model, will involve a guided programme of self-discovery, a long struggle towards greater self-awareness and clearer resolution, whereby we are progressively freed from the shadows and projections inherited from the past. Not all religious thinkers will want to take on board all the Freudian or Jungian apparatus (though it will be very hard for anyone seriously interested in human moral and spiritual development not to acknowledge the need for at least some of it – for example the lessons to be learned concerning the battle against rationalisation and self-deception, the need to recognize the shadow or the darker side of the human psyche, in order to understand and transcend it).[41] But however we work out the details, and the

---

39 Cf. *Summa theologiae* [1266–73], pt. IaIIae, qu. 94, arts. 3 and 6. See also Stump, *Aquinas*, p. 89.
40 Cf. Ephesians 4:20–24; John 3:3.
41 'The psychoanalytic aim is to observe the shadowy presentations – whether in the form of images or of feelings – that are spontaneously evolved in the psyche and appear, *without his bidding*, to the man who looks within. In this way we find once more what we have repressed or forgotten.

structure of the required programme of *askesis*, the central point remains: that the healthy growth of the human spirit requires a therapeutic phase, a way of coming to terms with the obstacles to a balanced and harmonious and integrated life.

So far it may seem as if our argument simply presents the need for what could broadly be called a psychotherapeutic phase in human moral development. That itself would be a fairly ambitious result, taking us way beyond what most of the leading philosophical accounts of the good life (for example those of Aristotle, Spinoza, Bentham, Mill, and even Kant)[42] have been remotely prepared to acknowledge. But even if we grant the need for such a phase, we need to focus on one particular aspect to provide a richer understanding of what is added by a specifically *spiritual* dimension in the programme of *askesis*, and why the full flowering of the moral self may be thought to require it.

7 FROM PSYCHOTHERAPY TO SPIRITUALITY

Consider for the sake of argument someone who has successfully completed a programme of psychotherapeutic analysis (the imagined case is perhaps rather artificial since it is probably a misunderstanding to envisage a final state of 'cure' after which everything is plain sailing, but let that pass for the present). The supposition is of someone who has begun to learn to integrate the disparate and split-off parts of the psyche, who has started to bring to the surface the buried fears and anxieties stemming from early experience, who has begun to master the techniques of self-examination and self-awareness, who has learned something of the

---

Painful though it may be, this is itself a gain – for what is inferior or even worthless belongs to me as my shadow, and gives me substance and mass. How can I be substantial if I fail to cast a shadow? I must have a dark side if I am to be whole; and inasmuch as I become conscious of my own shadow, I also remember that I am a human being like any other.' Jung, 'Problems of Modern Psychotherapy' ch. 2. These reflections perhaps constitute a psychoanalytic analogue of the early Christian idea that the quest for self-perfectioning requires a phase when one goes out into the desert to be tempted.

42 For Aristotle's account of the life of practical wisdom, see *Nicomachean Ethics* [c. 330 BCE], esp. bk. VI. For Benedict Spinoza's intellectualism, see *Ethics* [*Ethica ordine geometrico demonstrata*, c. 1665], esp. pt. IV; for Jeremy Bentham's (rationally determinable) 'felicific calculus', see *Principles of Morals and Legislation* [1789], ch. 4 ; for John Stuart Mill's notion of the assessment of quantities and qualities of utility to be arrived at by the experienced 'competent judges', see *Utilitarianism* [1861], ch. 2; and for the Kantian idea of the moral life as structured by the rational will, see *Groundwork for the Metaphysic of Morals* [*Grundlegung zur Metaphysik der Sitten*, 1785], chs. 1 and 2. Other passages could no doubt be cited from all these authors to support a more nuanced interpretation of their views on the moral life; but it seems to me difficult to find anything that significantly anticipates the far richer account of moral development that becomes available through the resources of psychoanalytic thinking.

dangerous and ever-present propensity to rationalize – the fussy attempts of the controlling intellect to manage life's problems by neatly parcelling them up and thereby concealing all that is most salient to their true meaning. How do we envisage such a person proceeding? After this imaginary 'graduation day', when our subject gets up off the couch and resumes ordinary life, can the *askesis* of spirituality henceforth be ignored? Can our 'cured' patient stride forward into the clear daylight of the moral life, henceforth exercising the sober and self-confident virtue of Aristotle's *phronimos*, the man of 'practical wisdom',[43] liberated from any psychological distortions that might previously have got in the way?

That is certainly one model of the good life. And indeed nothing in the present argument implies any denigration of practical wisdom and its virtues. Without the careful evaluation of evidence, accurate means–ends reasoning, calm consideration of alternatives, reasoned debate and discussion, it would be impossible for human beings to pursue the good in any systematic way. But for all that, to uphold the life of practical reason as, so to speak, the last word on the good life for humankind seems in the end both a naively optimistic position, and at the same time an ultimately pessimistic one. It risks being naïve in so far as it places reliance on the balanced deliberation of the healthy subject to provide a sufficient basis for a fulfilled existence. Freud was more grimly realistic: you have learned to cope with neurotic misery, he said to his patients; now that your treatment is finished, learn to cope with ordinary misery.[44] The fact is that *vulnerability* – to pain, to loss, to fear, ultimately to extinction – is not simply a function of psychological or developmental difficulties, but is part of our very nature as human beings – one of the signs of existence, as the Buddhists have it.[45] And unless the moral life can be lived in a compartmentalized way, in a way that ignores or dangerously blindfolds us to that vulnerability (and this would involve a sacrifice of our wholeness, our integrity), then we are going to need an *askesis* that enables us to come to terms with it.

43　Cf. Aristotle, *Nicomachean Ethics*, bk. 6, chs. 5 and 6.

44　Freud's self-proclaimed aim was to 'turn hysterical misery into ordinary human unhappiness'. See the opening of his 'Studies in Hysteria' ['Die Studien über Hysterie', with J. Breuer, 1896], *PFL* vol. 2.

45　The first of the 'Four Noble Truths' in the Theravada tradition of Buddhism is that the experience of life is *dukkha*, productive of suffering; suffering is one of the fundamental characteristics of everything that comes to pass in the world. See, for example, P. Harvey, *An Introduction to Buddhist Ethics* (Cambridge: Cambridge University Press, 2000), pp. 31ff.

Detachment is of course one strategy: conditions arise and pass away, the self is an illusion, and hence there is nothing to fear (an approach most closely associated with the Buddhist tradition, to which we shall return briefly in our final chapter).[46] But the alternative, the one encapsulated in the Christian traditions of spirituality (and here is the escape from pessimism), is to embrace that vulnerability as ultimately redemptive.[47] To live morally, courageously, generously, while facing the unavoidable fragility of our human lives, we need a continuing programme of spiritual *askesis*, which will replace fear with trust, which will address our vulnerability by transforming it into a receptivity, an openness, a willingness to become like the child that is intimately present deep within the adult life of each of us.

'Unless you become as little children, you shall not enter the kingdom of heaven.'[48] In that saying is implicitly laid down the closest possible link between the religious demand and the moral life. Dependency, vulnerability, the insistence that strength is made perfect in weakness,[49] are the

---

46 See Ch. 8, §2, below.

47 I speak of 'the alternative', but there are, of course, other possible responses to the problem of human vulnerability. One, discussed earlier, is the intellectualistic or rationalistic attempt to rely on practical rationality alone as the key to the good life (cf. §5, above). A second, is the 'heroic' strategy of the Nietzschean (cf. Friedrich Nietzsche, *The Will to Power* [*Der Wille zur Macht*, 1888] transl. W. Kaufmann and R. J. Hollingdale (New York: Random House, 1975), or the 'absurdist' strategy of the existentialist (cf., for example, Albert Camus' account of the myth of Sisyphus [*Le mythe de Sisyphe*, 1942]; some aspects of these strategies are discussed in Cottingham, *On the Meaning of Life*, chs. 1 and 3. There may be other possibilities. A Confucian might take refuge in the ordered structures of a well-run and efficient society where each knows his place. Or, on a more personal level, the kind of equable cheerfulness reportedly achieved by David Hume suggests (if the reports are accurate) that some human beings, including some philosophers, may naturally, or through fortunate upbringing, enjoy the kind of disposition that enables them to 'cope' with life without any recourse whatever to the praxis of spirituality, yet without their happiness being threatened by vulnerability and loss. The strategy of this book is one of advocacy for the spiritual path that is intended to be undogmatic, and to strike a responsive chord in the reader; if no such chord sounds, or if the reader feels able, in good faith, to trust to alternative, purely secular, paths for tackling the human predicament, it is certainly no part of the aim to try to 'refute' or undermine them.

48 Matthew 18:3.

49 See above, ch.2, n. 41. For the relative neglect of human weakness and dependency in most mainstream Western moral philosophy, compare the following: '[Facts] . . . concerning our vulnerabilities and afflictions and those concerning the extent of our dependence on particular others are so evidently of singular importance that it might seem that no account of the human condition whose authors hoped to achieve credibility could avoid giving them a central place. Yet the history of Western moral philosophy suggests otherwise. From Plato to Moore and since there are usually, with some rare exceptions, only passing references to human vulnerability and affliction and to the connections between them and our dependence on others . . . [M]oral agents [are] presented as though they were continuously rational, healthy and untroubled . . . Aristotle [anticipated] a great many . . . in importing into moral philosophy the standpoint of those who

hallmarks of the Judaeo-Christian spiritual tradition (and perhaps the key Islamic notion of *submission* says something not too dissimilar). Our argument has been that the flaws of the human psyche and the fragilities of the human condition are such that, unless we delve deep into ourselves to find that vulnerability, and purify and rebuild ourselves in the light of what we find, we are very unlikely to be equipped for a moral life.

But is it not logically possible that someone could lead a perfectly good life without the underpinning of such a radical programme of *askesis*? Of course. But that weasel-phrase of the philosophers '*logically* possible' is often used in a way that delights in quibbling refutation rather than offering serious alternatives to what is being proposed. It is logically possible, as Hume observed, that the sun will not rise tomorrow.[50] What we are asking is not what is theoretically conceivable but what is likely, in Aristotle's phrase, to be 'true for the most part'.[51] No doubt there could theoretically be a human being who was naturally so clear in intellectual perception, and so steadfast in will, that they needed no painful and exacting voyage in self-discovery, and no supporting discipline of spiritual *askesis* in order to achieve integrity in the moral life. But for most human beings the advice of Descartes referred to in the second epigraph of this chapter is much more sound: we must acknowledge the weakness of our nature.

Mention of integrity brings me to my final point. Our main claim has been that spiritual praxis, something like a continued programme of edification and nourishment for the soul,[52] is for most of us a necessary condition for the moral life; without it the goals of morality are in constant danger of subversion. Is it perhaps not just necessary but also sufficient? Of course not – even for the most advanced adept of the most devout religious order, to claim as much would be a monstrous arrogance. But the hope will be that, the more the moral self is reconstructed and nourished, the more the demands of morality become internalised, so that

have taken themselves to be self-sufficiently superior and of those who take their standards from those who take themselves to be self-sufficiently superior.' Alasdair MacIntyre, *Dependent Rational Animals* (London: Duckworth, 1999), pp. 1–2 and 7.

50 '*That the sun will not rise to-morrow* is no less intelligible a proposition, and implies no more a contradiction, than the affirmation *that it will rise*.' David Hume, *An Enquiry concerning Human Understanding* [1748], §IV, pt. i, second paragraph.

51 *Nicomachean Ethics*, bk. I, ch. 3.

52 There are many questions to be raised about the idea of programmes, or as I put it earlier, 'guided programmes' of this kind, not the least of which is: *which* programmes? I shall aim to pick up this loose end in the final chapter.

they no longer speak with the voice of an alien external power,[53] but call forth so strong an answering resonance that they become an intimate part of our fully realised humanity,[54] then the closer each of us draws to becoming what we are truly meant to be.[55]

53 See above, Ch. 3, esp. §1.

54 It is this kind of transformation that seems to be envisaged by those who claim, with St John Chrysostom [c. 390 CE] that it is 'impossible, utterly impossible, for the man who prays eagerly and invokes God ceaselessly ever to sin.' *De Anna*, 4, 5; in *Patrologia Graeca*, ed. J. P, Migne (Paris, 1844–55), 54, 666.

55 Here our earlier distinction between the moral life and the flourishing or fulfilled life (§1, and the opening of §5, above) begins to lose its point. Contemporary moral theory often presents a somewhat fragmented picture of the good life, in which individual fulfilment is always in potential opposition to the utilitarian goal of maximizing happiness for as many people as possible, while both these consequentialist aims are in turn in potential conflict with the deontic constraints that prohibit certain routes to achieving them. A further hiving off occurs when 'normative' ethics is studied in a way that detaches it from issues of self-development, ethical formation, and moral psychology, sometimes (if they are dealt with at all) assigned to the separate domain of 'virtue theory'. In contrast to these compartmentalized approaches, older ideals of spiritual *askesis* offer a picture in which a moral outlook flows naturally from the integration and healing of the self. There are still, of course, important questions to be asked about how far the 'internal nourishment' of the self will produce a virtue that will 'spill outwards' and be manifest in our relations to others; this issue will be taken up at the end of our final chapter.

CHAPTER 8

Religion and pluralism: which spirituality?

This is not a book of separated philosophy, separated from faith, and separated from concrete life. I believe, on the contrary, that philosophy attains its aims, particularly in practical matters, only when vitally united with every source of light and experience in the human mind. Thus it becomes able, in its own intellectual domain, to ransom the time, and to redeem every human search after truth, however it wanders, in manifold, even opposite ways.

Jacques Maritain.[1]

I RECAPITULATION

In pausing before the final phase of a journey, it may be helpful to reflect briefly on the steps taken so far. I have been underlining in a number of ways the role of the spiritual dimension – the central importance of structured programmes of moral and personal *askesis* – for understanding what it means to adhere to a religion. Spiritual praxis, it has been argued, is prior to metaphysical doctrine in various important respects. In the first place, it is *temporally* prior, because as with any process of acculturation, we characteristically begin the long process of learning and adaptation before we are in a position to scrutinize the theoretical basis of what we are taught.[2] In the second place, it is *heuristically* prior, prior in the order of discovery, because religion is one of many important areas of human experience where personal involvement scores over impersonal detachment in the way it facilitates understanding: just as the detached scrutiny that is appropriate for science will not work in personal relationships, so in the religious domain we can often be blocked from grasping the salient features unless a certain degree of receptivity and openness is already

---

1 Jacques Maritain, *Redeeming the Time*, transl. H. Binsse (London: The Centenary Press, 1943); from the Foreword, first published here. (Though the essays contained in the volume had appeared earlier in French, they had not previously been collected together.)
2 See Ch. 1, §§1 and 2.

present.[3] In the third place, spiritual praxis is *psychologically* (one might almost say 'psychoanalytically') prior to theory: embarking on a path of guided self-transformation cannot wait upon an explicit understanding of what is meant by true self-awareness and spiritual maturity, since these latter goals are the destination of the journey, not its starting point.[4] And in the fourth place, praxis is *morally* prior, since we develop moral understanding and moral virtue not, or not principally, by the intellectual analysis of moral theories, but through disciplined patterns of habituation, which progressively foster our powers of moral and spiritual discernment and resolution until they start to become second nature; it is only at a later stage, if all goes well, that praxis and theory become interfused, and our daily patterns of behaviour become incorporated into an ever fuller and more explicit grasp of the meaning and moral significance of our lives.

These themes, initially broached in Chapter 1, have recurred throughout the subsequent discussion. But this recurring emphasis on the priority of practice does not imply that the religious outlook can dispense with rational argumentation and critical discussion. And hence in addition to the exploration of the various aspects of spiritual praxis just listed, a further crucial part of our task has been concerned with *integration* – the project of making sure that the religious outlook can consistently accommodate basic facts of common human experience that cannot without loss of integrity be denied. Thus, if one's religion is of the traditional theistic kind found in the three great Abrahamic faiths, it must in principle be able to tackle the *problem of evil* – the question of how all the flaws and sorrows found in our world can be seen as not ruling out, or making highly implausible, the claim that it is the work of a benevolent creator (Chapter 2). Next, it is crucial that the ethical system or code of conduct that is integral to the religious outlook of the believer should possess the characteristics of a *genuine moral system*: it must respect our human dignity and hence be such as to allow for the exercise of genuinely free choice based on rational evaluation, rather than blind obedience (Chapter 3). Furthermore, our religious praxis, and the moral awareness that is inseparable from it, should be consistent with our understanding of the *psychology* of human moral development, and the religious quest shown to be in harmony with what we know about the nature of human self-discovery and self-awareness (Chapter 4). In

3 Cf. Ch. 1, §3.
4 Cf. Ch. 4, and Ch. 7, §§5–7, above.

addition, our understanding of the psychology of religious development should be supported by an understanding of how religious *language* operates, and how the complex semantic layering involved resists reduction to the kind of literalistic template suitable for science (Chapter 5). Yet, despite the complexities of religious language (which often need to be understood in figurative and symbolic terms), it remains crucial that the metaphysical, doctrinal, or credal elements inseparable from a religious worldview must be at least *possible candidates for truth* – which means that there must be at least some discernible content to what is believed: the claims of religion must not fall wholly outside the limits of intelligible human discourse (Chapter 6). Moreover, on the *epistemic* front, even if we grant that a religious worldview is for a variety of reasons ineligible for the status of an empirically testable hypothesis, nevertheless the faith of the religious adherent has to be capable of being shown to be *not irresponsible or irrational* (Chapter 7, §§1–4). And finally, returning to the moral front, the religious adherent must in principle be able to show that there is some discernible *link with goodness* – a plausible connection between the cultivation of religion and the attainment or systematic pursuit of a worthwhile life, construed not just as personal fulfilment but also in terms of self-awareness, self-purification and moral growth (Chapter 7, §§5–6).

What is envisaged throughout the argument just summarized is a conception of spirituality that sees spiritual praxis as a catalyst, or enabler for religious belief, rather than the other way round.[5] Typically, it is not as if one waits for a belief in God to somehow form itself in one's mind, and then decides, in the light of that belief, to join a Church or inquire about a possible programme of spiritual *askesis*; rather the spiritual *askesis* is itself what sets the adherent on the long road, the *Itinerarium mentis in Deum*, as St Bonaventure called it seven centuries ago. Significant here is the idea of a search or journey, so that the Latin preposition *in* signals a questing movement *towards* rather than a destination achieved or certified in advance. It is through the disciplines of worship and prayer and meditation, and by using the resulting gifts of self-development and enriched awareness (what the Christian tradition calls 'personal graces'), together with the 'graces of ministry' (the freely bestowed opportunities for those gifts to diffuse outwards in service to others), that progress begins to be made, according to the testimony of some of the great writers on

---

5 Compare Fergus Kerr, *Theology after Wittgenstein* (Oxford; Blackwell, 1986), p. 183: 'Worship is not the result but the precondition of believing in God.'

spirituality.[6] For these enriching patterns of living do not, as might be supposed, *presuppose* a secure and previously established religious conviction; rather it is *by their very means*, we are told, that the seeker starts to grow in knowledge and love of God.

2 WHICH PATH?

The argument just summarised is intended to present a persuasive picture of how religious belief operates, and, on the justificatory front, of the kinds of support available for the adoption of a religious worldview; but it certainly does not pretend to be compelling, in the sense of being apt to secure the assent of any rational inquirer. For it is of the very nature of the argument that it concedes, indeed insists, that there can be no advocacy of the religious outlook that will succeed on the basis of purely philosophical or intellectual methods – by closing every loophole, or by 'giving a final turn of the screw' (to use the alarming phrase of one prominent contemporary religious apologist).[7] In this sort of area, there is, on both sides of the debate, something inherently misguided about the idea of arguments that will constrain the assent, forcing the theist to abandon his belief, or forcing the unbeliever to admit there is no escape but to sign up to a religious form of life; this would be like trying to convince a sceptic by philosophical means that they should get married, or have children, or risk their life in battle. Such 'coercive arguments' are simply not available here (and one may add that even in other contexts they are probably far less appropriate, and far less effective in securing genuine assent, than many philosophers are sometimes apt to suppose).[8]

There is, however, one lacuna that does gape for attention. Throughout the previous chapters we have been referring to 'religion', for the most part in rather general terms, as if there were a single unitary phenomenon called 'the spiritual path' or 'the religious worldview'. Yet the plain fact is, of course, that the world has many religions. And even those sympathetic to the argument about the priority of praxis might reasonably complain

---

6 Within the Christian tradition, see, for example, Thomas Aquinas, *Commentary on I Corinthians* [*Super I ad Corinthios*, c.1260], chs. 13 and 12; see also B. M. Ashley (ed.), *Thomas Aquinas, The Gifts of the Spirit* (New York: New City Press, 1995), pp. 19ff. For some interesting reflections on Aquinas' other writings on the operation of grace, see Stump, *Aquinas*, ch. 15.

7 Alston, *Divine Nature and Human Language*, p. 28. In fairness, it should be noted that the argument that Alston aims to make watertight in this passage is one about the literal nature of religious language, not one aimed at securing belief in God as such.

8 Cf. Kerr, *Theology after Wittgenstein*, p. 163; for 'coercive argument', see R. Nozick, *Philosophical Explanations* (Oxford: Clarendon Press, 1981), pp. 4ff.

that nothing has so far been said about *which* of the many available forms of religious praxis is being advocated.

One could, perhaps, leave this open – on the grounds that it is a matter for personal decision which takes us beyond the methods and scope of the present inquiry, and also perhaps on the grounds that it does not in the end very much matter which path is chosen, provided it leads us progressively towards the good. One might simply suppose that the choice could be left to the contingencies of personal history or geography – perhaps, for example, the motto might be 'when in England, do as the Anglicans'. There would, of course, have to be certain moral constraints: a particular form of spirituality would have to be rejected if it involved unjust or abusive power structures; and the integral connection between religion and morality that we have insisted on would suffice to rule out a form of praxis that entailed personal degradation, or blind obedience instilled merely to enhance the ego or private fortune of the resident guru. But assuming these hurdles to have been overcome (in so far is it is reasonable to expect they could be in any human institution or practice), why not take an '*indifferentist*' stance? Why suppose there *must* be some decisive reason tipping the balance in favour of some one particular faith or denomination among the many that exist?

The indifferentist might draw some support from the recurrence of a number of core ethical values in a whole variety of religious traditions. If one looks not at theological arguments between different denominations, or credal differences between different faiths, but instead at the various frameworks of spiritual praxis found in the major religions, there turns out to be a striking degree of convergence with regard to what one might call the moral psychology of religious practice. Compare the following account by an anthropologist of the practice of 'sermon audition' (via widely available cassette recordings) that has become a notable feature of the Islamic revival in contemporary Egypt:

The effect of sermon speech on the heart is not just one of cleansing. Sermons evoke in the sensitive listener a particular set of ethical responses, foremost among them fear (*khauf*), humility (*kushu*), regret (*nadm*), repentance (*tauba*) and tranquillity (*itmi'nan* or *sakina*) . . . Numerous verses of the Quran depict the impact of godly speech on a rightly-disposed listener, as in the following [from *Al–Anfal*: 2]: 'Believers are only they whose hearts tremble whenever God is mentioned, and whose faith is strengthened whenever his messages are conveyed unto them.'[9]

9 Charles Hirschkind, 'Passional Preaching, Aural Sensibility, and the Islamic Revival', in M. Lambeck (ed.), *A Reader in the Anthropology of Religion* (Oxford: Blackwell, 2002), pp. 540–1. The quotation from the Quran is from Sura 8, *Al-Anfal* ('The Spoils of War'), verse 2.

The various moral concepts invoked here belong to a 'psycho-ethical framework' that would be instantly recognisable to anyone brought up within Judaism or Christianity. The doctrinal beliefs of the followers of Islam may differ markedly from those of the Christian or the Jewish worshipper, but there is a remarkable overlap in the moral objectives of purification and inner transformation, pursued via a structured programme of praxis aimed at achieving psychological changes that facilitate those objectives. Indeed, the framework of humility, moral discipline, inner transformation, and the search for tranquillity seems to be a fairly universal one, wide enough to encompass, for example, many forms of Hinduism and Buddhism as well. So could we not let all the weight rest on the ethical ends, and answer the 'which path?' question by reference to which one could be shown to have the best record in delivering those ends (something presumably that might in principle be assessed by empirical means)? In the case of a tie among the various candidates, the final decision might then turn on personal factors – which of the various forms of praxis ends up proving most suitable for a given individual (and this in turn would probably depend largely on social and cultural background, plus the psychological profile of the individual in question).

Although there may be quite a lot to be said for the indifferentist approach (not least that its adoption might foster considerably more religious tolerance than is now apparent in many parts of the world), it seems unsatisfactory for two reasons. First, it appears to construe the value of religion in purely instrumental terms, since the reason for adopting a given religion will hinge purely on its ability to deliver moral and psychological benefits for the subject; and because of this, it is unlikely to appeal to those searching for the right spiritual path, since it adopts a perspective that in the end does not seem to take the idea of religious allegiance very seriously. It is rather as if one were an indifferentist about sport, or the art of cooking – proposing that it does not matter which sport one takes up provided it generates healthy exercise, or which cuisine one adopts provided it delivers balanced nutrition. There may be nothing whatever wrong with these instrumental aims, but they will not capture what attracts those considering committing themselves to these pursuits, nor will it explain what it is, for the devoted sportsperson or the dedicated chef, that makes these activities central to their lives. The second, and closely related objection to the indifferentist approach can be stated more briefly, and it ties in with more fundamental qualms many people feel about pragmatic criteria for evaluation: to assess spiritual paths in a purely instrumental manner is to examine the reasons for choosing a given religion in a way that seems quite independent of the question of its *truth*.

One way out of these difficulties is suggested by the work of John Hick, in his systematic and widely discussed argument for religious pluralism. This is a complex platform, but its main plank is a Kantian conception of the relation between reality *an sich* (in itself) and the necessarily human concepts and categories in terms of which our experience must be structured:

> the environment is not reflected in our consciousness in a simple and straightforward way, just as it is, independently of our perceiving it . . . Its character as an environment within which we can learn to behave appropriately can be called its *meaning* for us; . . . at the religious level [this] is a consciousness of the ultimate meaning . . . of our situation in relation to the divine reality. This latter consciousness is not however a general consciousness of the divine, but always takes specific forms . . . [The] various specific forms of religious awareness . . . are formed by the presence of the divine Reality, this presence coming to consciousness in terms of the different sets of religious concepts and structures of religious meaning that operate within the different religious traditions of the world.[10]

Although this approach appears hospitable to a wide variety of traditions, it should be noted in passing that not every form of religious awareness counts as authentic for Hick, but only those that can establish themselves by 'soteriological efficacy'[11] – roughly, their ability to generate moral deepening and spiritual growth towards some form of salvation.

Hick's approach has won many converts, amongst whom is the theologian Marcus Borg, who appeals to the 'experience of the sacred across cultures' in arguing that the more traditional 'exclusivistic' religious

---

10 John Hick 'Religious Pluralism' [1985], repr. in Peterson et al. (eds.), *Philosophy of Religion*, pp. 567–8. A more explicitly Kantian account is given elsewhere: 'For Kant, God is postulated, not experienced. In partial agreement with him but also in partial disagreement with him, I want to say that the Real *an sich* is postulated by us as a presupposition . . . of the religious life, whilst the gods, as also the mystically known Brahman, Sunyata and so on, are phenomenal manifestations of the Real occurring within the realm of religious experience. . . [T]he Real is experienced by human beings, but experienced in a manner analogous to that in which, according to Kant, we experience the world: namely by informational input from external reality being interpreted by the mind in terms of its own categorial scheme and thus coming to consciousness as meaningful phenomenal experience. All that we are entitled to say about the noumenal source of this information is that it is the reality whose influence produces, in collaboration with the human mind, the phenomenal world of our experience.' *An Interpretation of Religion: Human Responses to the Transcendent* (Basingstoke: Macmillan Press, 1989), p. 243.
11 'Religious Pluralism', in Peterson et al. (eds.), *Philosophy of Religion*, p. 570.

outlook has 'ceased to be compelling to millions of people'.[12] And describing his stance *vis-à-vis* his own chosen path he writes:

The Bible is a lens, and as a lens it is not the object of belief but a means whereby we see. . . . I do not think being a Christian is primarily about believing. It is not about believing in the lens, but about entering a deepening relationship to that which we see through the lens. It is not about believing in the Bible or the gospel or Christian teachings about Jesus, but about a relationship to the One whom we see through the lens of the Christian tradition as a whole.[13]

Yet despite its attractions, including its apparent suitability for the more global culture in which we now have to operate, the pluralistic position championed by Hick and Borg presents a number of problems. Some (which I shall not discuss here) are theological;[14] but there is a central philosophical difficulty that several critics have been quick to pounce on.[15] If the fundamental defining properties attributed to God in the various religions are not merely diverse but *incompatible* (Christians maintaining he is ultimately triune, Muslims and Jews that he is absolutely and unqualifiedly one, Buddhists that ultimate reality is not personal at all – and indeed on some interpretations that there is nothing ultimate beyond the conditions that arise and pass away), then one begins to wonder what content can be left to the notion of a single 'divine reality' (in Hick's phrase) that is supposedly apprehended under a plurality of different forms.

Thus, to take one example, consider Hick's own characterisation of the picture of reality that comes out of the Zen tradition in Buddhism:

for Zen the Real is immanent in the world process and can be experienced in each present moment of existence by a mind purified of the ego point of view. Zen involves a complete acceptance of the world as a beginningless and endless flow and of ourselves as a part of that flow; and those who have achieved this acceptance report that the world so experienced takes on a new dimension . . . To experience the world in this way, as a moving ocean of reciprocally conditioned change . . . is to see that nothing exists in and of itself but only in dependence upon everything else. This 'not existing in and of itself' is *Sunyata* or emptiness.[16]

---

12 Marcus Borg in N. T. Wright and Marcus Borg, *The Meaning of Jesus: Two Visions* (London: SPCK, 1999), pp. 231–2.
13 *The Meaning of Jesus*, pp. 239–40.
14 For some of these theological objections, see Tom Wright's extended critique of Borg, in Wright and Borg, *The Meaning of Jesus*.
15 See for example M. Peterson et al., *Reason and Religious Belief* (Oxford: Oxford University Press, 1988), pp. 266ff; and W. Rowe, 'Religious Pluralism', in *Religious Studies* 35 (1999), pp. 139–50.
16 Hick, *An Interpretation of Religion*, p. 290.

This seems an attractively concise statement of one very characteristic form of the Buddhist perspective; but what it appears to bring out is precisely the *difference* between such a view – that the flow of conditioned change is all there is – and belief in the transcendent reality we call 'God', an eternal being *beyond* the change and decay of the temporal world. Hick relies on some interpreters of Zen Buddhism who construe *Sunyata* or emptiness as 'the formless self-emptying ground or source of everything . . . the ultimate reality beyond the scope of all concepts, knowable only by its manifestations'[17] – an interpretation that permits him to identify it with the 'Real' that theistic traditions call 'God'. But even if this is a possible interpretation (which I suspect many Buddhists would dispute), it seems doubtful that there are many theists who would be happy with the implication that the *personal* nature of God is merely a phenomenal manifestation, an interpretative category of our culture, not intrinsically any more a part of the nature of God *an sich* than the wholly impersonal characterisations of the Buddhist.[18] What is more, and this is a further worry for the Hick position, divergences in the different conceptions of ultimate reality are often reflected in differences in the praxis and experience characteristic of theistic and atheistic religions respectively. Thus the theologian John Dunne, though very sympathetic to bringing out the links between Christianity and Buddhism, nonetheless underlines a major disparity:

If I compare the Beatitudes with the Four Noble Truths, I can see the apparent difference is in the Buddhist doctrine of 'no self', the thought that selfhood is the root of suffering, and freedom from suffering is in letting go of self. In Christianity the ability to love depends on the willingness to go through suffering. Here . . . there is the combination of willingness and hope. So 'the sense of I' is intact in Christianity, though there is 'the denial of self' in following Christ. Self-denial is simply the willingness to go through suffering.[19]

---

17 Hick, *An Interpretation of Religion*, p. 291, drawing on various Buddhist commentators including D. T. Suzuki and Masao Abe.

18 Hick, consistently with his Kantian stance, argues that the 'non-personal ultimates on which some of the Eastern traditions are focused' are '*impersonae* of the Real', that is to say, different phenomenal manifestations of the same ultimate reality that is experienced in personal terms by the theistic faiths. *An Interpretation of Religion*, pp. 278–9.

19 John S. Dunne, *Reading the Gospel* (Notre Dame, Ind.: University of Notre Dame Press, 2000), p. 93. In fairness, however, it should be noted that the picture is by no means quite as polarised as this contrast might suggest, for Dunne immediately adds: 'All the same, the passage from will to willingness is very close to the letting go of self in Buddhism, for the prime meaning of self is will, as when a little child says "No" and "mine". "No" is will and "mine" is self. So the long spiritual journey from "No" and "mine" to "Yes" and "yours" is a journey through will to willingness. The deeper sense of "I" then is indeed in willingness or indeed in willingness and hope and in the peace at our "center of stillness surrounded by silence".'

3 MYSTICISM AND THE APOPHATIC TRADITION

A possible way round the impasse just described may perhaps be found in recent work on the mystical and apophatic traditions of religious thought and practice. *Apophasis* is a Greek neologism, conveying a collapse or breakdown of language in the face of the Infinite. It is of the very nature of God that, as Descartes put it, he cannot be grasped (*comprehendi*) by a finite mind;[20] and the spiritual outlook that takes this most seriously is the mystical tradition that has aptly been called 'a strategy and practice of unknowing'[21] The 'apophatic' is here contrasted with the 'cataphatic', the 'verbose' element in theology,[22] the attempt to discuss the existence and nature of God though the traditional panoply of philosophical argument, conceptual analysis, scriptural exegesis, and intellectual debate.

Not surprisingly, current analytic philosophy has little time for the concept of the mystical. Most contemporary anglophone philosophers would probably regard it as outside the domain of what can usefully be talked about: 'whereof one cannot speak', as Wittgenstein said, 'thereof one must be silent'.[23] But whether or not we can speak about ultimate mysteries, there clearly remains a genuine and valid philosophical activity of investigating just what are the boundaries of the sayable, and indeed what exactly is meant by notions like 'mystery' and 'mysticism'. Gabriel Marcel's distinction between the *mysterious* and the *problematic* is a useful starting point here:

A problem is something met with which bars my passage. It is before me in its entirely. A mystery, on the other hand, is something in which I find myself caught up, and whose essence is therefore not to be before me in its entirety . . .

---

20 See Third Meditation, *Meditations* [*Meditationes*, 1641], AT VII 46: CSM II 32, and Letter to Mersenne of 27 May 1630 (AT I 152: CSMK 25).

21 '"Apophaticism" is the name of that theology which is done against the background of human ignorance of the nature of God. It is the doing of theology in the light of the statement of Thomas Aquinas . . . that "we do not know what kind of being God is" (*Summa theologiae*, pt. I, qu. 12, art. 13, ad 1). It is the conception of theology not as a naïve pre-critical ignorance of God, but as a kind of acquired ignorance, a *docta ignorantia* as Nicolas of Sues called it in the fifteenth-century. It is the conception of theology as a strategy and practice of unknowing, as the fourteenth-century English mystic called it [in *The Cloud of Unknowing*], who, we might say invented the transitive verb-form 'to unknow' in order to describe theological knowledge in this deconstructive mode. Finally, "apophaticism" is the same as what the Latin tradition of Christian called the *via negativa*, the "negative way". . . . Apophasis is a Greek neologism for the breakdown of speech, which in the face of the unknowability of God falls infinitely short of the mark.' Turner, *The Darkness of God*, p. 19.

22 'The cataphatic is, we might say, the verbose element in theology . . . It is the cataphatic tendencies which account for the sheer heaviness of theological language, its character of being linguistically overburdened.' Turner, *The Darkness of God*, p. 20.

23 See above, Ch. 6, n. 40.

A genuine problem is subject to an appropriate technique by the exercise of which it is defined, whereas a mystery, by definition, transcends every conceivable technique. It is, no doubt, always possible (logically and psychologically) to degrade a mystery so as to turn it into a problem. But this is a fundamentally vicious proceeding, whose springs might perhaps be discovered in a kind of corruption of the intelligence.[24]

In confronting the raw enigma of our human existence, the riddle of the cosmos and its inscrutable source, it is important not to allow our natural wonder to become blunted by familiarity. The controlling intellect will always try to domesticate things, thereby eroding their strangeness; and we look to the mystics, and indeed to the creative artists, poets, and musicians, to reawaken that strangeness for us.

So much, if you like, for the existential dimension. But what the apophatic tradition may provide at the theological level is a possible rescue line for pluralism from the types of difficulty we have just been canvassing. How can it be that there is a single reality towards which quite disparate and apparently incompatible religious traditions are supposed to be groping? A possible answer is suggested in an extremely rich and suggestive study by Denys Turner of what he calls 'negativity' in Christian mysticism, as found, for example in the writings of Denys the Areopagite:

The progress of the mind towards God ascends from complexity of image to simplicity, from many names in potential conflict to abstract and increasingly interchangeable names, from 'dissimilar' to 'similar' similarities, from prolixity to terseness and, ultimately, to silence. As the mind ascends through the hierarchy of language, it moves therefore from that which is most distinct from God to that which is progressively less obviously so, from the more 'unlike' to the more 'like'.[25]

The closer we draw, in short, to the ineffable reality that is God, the more we abstract from the plethora of potentially conflicting accounts in different traditions. Language itself falls silent before the Infinite; but this is not a sign that the earlier differing descriptions need to be re-examined and reconciled – rather it is a recognition that our journey is towards an ultimate reality that necessarily eludes human conceptual resources. One

---

24 Gabriel Marcel, *Being and Having* [*Etre et Avoir*, 1935] (London: Fontana, 1965), pp. 109, 121; cited in Louth, *Discerning the Mystery*, pp. 68–9.
25 Turner, *The Darkness of God*, p. 44. Compare Meister Eckhart: 'The light of the soul which is increate is not satisfied with three Persons, in so far as each subsists in difference . . . but it is determined to know whence this Being comes, to penetrate in the Simple Ground, into the Silent Desert, within which never any difference has lain'. Quoted in Evelyn Underhill, *The Essentials of Mysticism and Other Essays* (Oxford: Oneworld, 1995), p. 10.

could, of course, respond to this by insisting that the earlier contradictions *must* be resolved, that the presence of mystery at the heart of religious belief is a problem that must be overcome on pain of incoherence. But that, perhaps, would be to fail to respect Marcel's distinction between 'problem' and 'mystery'. Or as the theologian Andrew Louth has put it:

[T]he main concern of theology is not so much to elucidate anything, as to prevent us, the Church, from dissolving the mystery that lies at the heart of the faith – dissolving it, or missing it altogether, by failing truly to engage with it . . . The heart of the matter is sharing in the mystery of love which God is.[26]

The theology of mysticism, then, might seem to provide support for Hick-style pluralism: the incompatibilities at the level of particular tradition simply dissolve away as the mind climbs upwards on the path of 'unknowing'. Yet despite the appeal and insightfulness of recent theological work on the mystical tradition, there is, in the context of our present argument, a serious problem, which may be summed up in the challenge to mystical theology posed by David Hume two and a half centuries ago. As Cleanthes, one of the characters in Hume's *Dialogues concerning Natural Religion* acidly puts it: 'How do you mystics, who maintain the absolute incomprehensibility of the Deity, differ from sceptics or atheists, who assert that the first cause of all is unknown and unintelligible?'[27] Indeed, in a typically rhetorical flourish, Hume at one point goes as far as to say that if we examine what the mystics have to say, we ought to conclude that they are 'atheists without knowing it'.[28] Now if the appeal to the path of 'unknowing' is in effect extensionally equivalent to atheism, or (granted that Hume pitched this a little strong) if at the very least there is a philosophical issue about differentiating the propositional content of the mystic's creed from that of the sceptic or agnostic, then one may feel that our putative solution to the problem of the diversity of different religious traditions has been bought at too high a price.

4 FROM MYSTERY TO LITURGY

At this point we seem to have reached a further impasse. Raising the question about which spiritual path should be followed brought us to the idea of the unknowability of ultimate reality; yet it now seems that even if

26 Louth, *Discerning the Mystery*, p. 71.
27 Hume, *Dialogues concerning Natural Religion* [c. 1755], pt. IV, first paragraph (ed. H. D. Aiken (New York: Haffner, 1948), p. 31).
28 *Dialogues concerning Natural Religion*, pt. IV, third paragraph (Aiken edn., p. 32).

we grant the mystics their apophatic route, there must, if theism is to retain any distinctive character whatsoever, be some road back, some way for religious faith to return from the darkness of unknowing and locate itself within the domain of workable human language. Such a return might in any case be desirable for other reasons. For the world of the mystic is a rarefied world, perhaps like the heights of Machu Pichu suited for habitation only by those whose blood has become specially adapted for such altitudes. If religion is not to be confined to a spiritual elite, it must be able to speak a language suitable for ordinary humanity – indeed, to close off that possibility would be a denial of the compassion and universalism that is the hallmark of the great religions.

Talk of the need for the 'word' of religion to find a way to locate itself within the ordinary human world immediately evokes, for the Christian reader, the central concept of the Incarnation: the idea that the 'inaccessible light' of the divinity (1 Timothy 6:16) becomes visible in the person of one human being who is the 'icon of the invisible God' (Colossians 1:15).[29] And this suggests a possible reconciliation between the apophatic and cataphatic traditions. Here is Denys Turner again, this time discussing the theology of St Bonaventure:

> For Bonaventure . . . Christ is the meeting point of all our language about God. But Christ is also the point of juncture of the cataphatic with the apophatic. For if Christ is, on the one hand, the only perfect image of God, he is, on the other, our only access to the unknowability of God. If in Christ is concentrated all our language about God, then in Christ is concentrated all the contradictoriness of that language. But if in Christ is found the unity of our language's multiplication, the reconciliation of its impossible contradictoriness, it is found there only because in Christ is found the *transitus* from affirmation to negation, from the work of the six days of creation to the silence and rest of the seventh, from the knowability of the incarnate Son to the unknowability of the Father.[30]

If we are to respect the otherness, the transcendence of God yet at the same time avoid becoming lost in a silence that risks being elided into agnosticism, we need a transition, a way of understanding God in human terms. And the life of Christ provides (according to Christianity) just such a transition, an intersection point between the vertical and the horizontal, which, as has often been observed, is symbolised in a unique way by the central image of the Cross. Contained here in this sign, for the Christian,

---

29 God dwells in 'light inaccessible' (φῶς ἀπρόσιτον) 'whom no man hath seen nor can see' (1 Timothy 6:16); Christ, who has 'delivered us from the power of darkness' is the image (εἰκὼν) of the invisible God' (Colossians 1:15).

30 Turner, *The Darkness of God*, p. 132.

is the secret 'hid for long ages' of our human redemption, of our access to God, of the mystery that is 'Emmanuel' – God with us.[31]

The transition from the transcendent to the human dimension has immediately led us towards employing a degree of symbolization; this is no accident. I argued in an earlier chapter that symbolic and figurative discourse was the key to understanding the way religious truth can be disclosed; precisely because of its multiple resonances and interfolded layers of meaning, such discourse has the power to echo deep within our minds, often far below the conscious stratum of explicit cognitive awareness. So far from being a 'second best', such symbolic thinking is precisely what one might reasonably expect to be the most fruitful way of approaching the deepest layers of meaning within our lives, and the most likely avenue to glimpsing the ineffable source of such meaning.[32] What I now want to add to this is a further reference to our recurring theme of the importance of praxis. For a striking characteristic of the great religions is that their life blood, their very continued existence in the lives of their adherents, derives not principally from the visionary and ecstatic discoveries of the mystics on the one hand, nor from the cataphatic disquisitions of the theologians on the other,[33] but from repeated practices of prayer and worship, which find an articulate voice in traditional language that contains a very large measure of symbolic and figurative discourse. From the darkness and holy silence of the mystical vision on the one hand, and from the verbosity and prolixity of theological debate on the other, we

---

31 The mystery 'hid for long ages', Colossians 1:26; 'God with us', Isaiah 7:14, Matthew 1:18.
32 See Ch. 5, above.
33 Mark McIntosh (following von Balthazar) has recently drawn attention to the increasingly wide split between spirituality and theology – and the kind of 'enervation and desiccation' that results when theological inquiry is cut off from its sources in lived religious experience: 'theology cut off from spirituality may not only lose contact with important sources of religious reflection but may also lose the proper skills for speaking of the doctrines of Christianity – doctrines conceived not simply as propositions for analysis but as living mysteries to be encountered. This is not a call for theology to cloak its bafflements with an unctuous tone of voice, or as Paul Tillich once warned against, "to fill in logical gaps with devotional material". Quite the opposite, spirituality calls theology to an honesty about the difficulty of understanding what is unfathomable . . . an openness to what is never a puzzle to be solved but always a mystery to be lived.' Mark A. McIntosh, *Mystical Theology* (Oxford: Blackwell, 1998), p. 15. Compare also Denys Turner on the essential unity of theory and practice in the work of Augustine: 'The metaphors [of inwardness and ascent] embody . . . the unity and coherence of Augustine's theory of knowledge with his "spirituality". For the metaphors . . . both explain something and make personal demands; they call upon the Christian to embark on a journey whose course they illuminate; they tell us what and how we can know and elicit the desire to know it. Augustine could not have envisaged a case of doing the one which was not to be doing the other, any more than a flame can shed light without heat or heat without light. And the metaphors of interiority and ascent perfectly embody his conviction of the unity of theory and practice.' *The Darkness of God*, p. 100.

move instead to the daily and seasonal rhythms of worship, to the
vocabulary of expressive symbol and sacramental enactment – in short
to liturgy. Liturgy, to quote Andrew Louth,

is not something we 'make up', nor is it something that can be simply
'understood': it is something we participate in, not just as minds, but with all
that we are – body and soul. Hence the importance in the liturgy of gestures and
movement, of the sequence of the seasons, through which time itself is sanctified.
The liturgy unfolds the varied significance of the mystery of Christ, and the fact
that it cannot all be explained, the fact that much that we do, we do simply
because we have always done it, conveys a rich sense of the unfathomableness of
the Christian mystery.[34]

The place our argument has now reached, after a somewhat circuitous
route, perhaps offers at least a general characterisation of the kind of shape
that a plausible spiritual programme might take when embodied in a
framework of human praxis. Of course the features cited by Louth
(organized ritual, seasonal rhythms, continuity with tradition) may be
found in various faiths, and one may wonder about the move from an
argument for the importance of liturgy in general to the choice of a
specifically Christian mode of worship (I shall return to this issue in the
next section). But if we remain at the level of generality for the moment,
those who accept Louth's broad appeal to the importance of liturgy will
see strong reason to want their religious praxis to involve a number of
elements, notably structures of organized ritual, that are capable of
expressing the mysteries of faith in a dignified and resonant way. And
this in turn will require continuity with a tradition which preserves that
faith through the generations; for just as moral maturity cannot be
achieved as a 'private trip', but only through a systematic accommodation
between one's own self-development and the self-development of the
fellow human beings who are part of the fabric of our lives, so spiritual
maturity cannot be an egocentric journey focused entirely on the individual, but must necessarily, sooner or later, involve integration into that
tradition and community without which one's spiritual impulses could
not have form or expression in the first place.

---

34 Louth, *Discerning the Mystery*, p. 89. Cf. Turner, *The Darkness of God*, where there is mention of
'liturgical and sacramental action . . . music . . . architecture . . . dance and gesture' (p. 20). The
elements are included by Turner under the 'cataphatic' heading, as forming part of a 'discourse of
theological articulation', whereas I would prefer to consider them under a separate category, since
they do not seem to me to be properly *theological* in character (though they are of course a proper
subject for theologians to analyse); perhaps however nothing much turns on this classificatory
issue.

5 DISTINCTIVE CULTURE AND COMMON HUMANITY

Even for those who accept the conclusions just reached, there may be a worry that the argument that produced them is circular. For the emphasis we have just been placing on the importance of liturgy did not, as it were, emerge out of the blue; the sentiments quoted from Andrew Louth, for example, clearly come from someone with a specific religious, and indeed denominational allegiance, and the positive features he invokes, and the specific mode of their expression, will of course be likely to appeal most to those from a similar religious and cultural background. What we get in all this, it might be objected, is an essentially partisan commitment to a particular form of sacramentally based Christianity – and this still leaves entirely open the question of whether quite distinct denominational stances, not to mention entirely different faith systems, might not have equal or even superior status.

Part of the point being made here can be conceded without fuss, but without accepting any vicious circularity. There is indeed a problem with any philosophical attempt to provide 'neutral' evaluations of any belief system from a supposed Olympian standpoint detached from cultural and historical particularities. We can never achieve a 'sideways on' perspective on reality,[35] from which we could pick out a certain set of practices or beliefs as somehow 'objectively' superior to others; for any human evaluation necessarily bears the stamp of the culturally and historically structured conceptual scheme of which it is a part. To use the metaphor of Otto Neurath, which has become a dominant image of contemporary philosophy, our culture and language is the boat on which we sail across the uncharted ocean of human experience: since there is no other vehicle for the voyage, we cannot abandon ship or scrap the boat and rebuild it from scratch; the best we can do is to continue the slow process of improvement, repairing or refashioning individual planks as the occasion arises.[36]

The Neurath metaphor does not, as is sometimes supposed, entail a cautious conservatism – the view that we are stuck willy nilly with our present belief system. Planks may certainly be replaced – but only if others

---

35 Cf. John McDowell, *Mind and World* (Cambridge, Mass.: Harvard University Press, 1994), Lecture II.

36 'We are like sailors who must rebuild their ship on the open sea, never able to dismantle it in dry-dock and to reconstruct it there out of the best materials.' Otto Neurath, 'Protokol Sentences' ['*Protokolsatze*', 1932], transl. G. Schick, in A. J. Ayer (ed.), *Logical Positivism* (New York: Free Press, 1959), p. 201.

are left undisturbed; so critical discussion and rationally supported change are possible, albeit necessarily from within the context of a certain cultural and historical perspective. It follows that the arguments just canvassed in favour of a specific type of spiritual praxis, although they unavoidably have some element of the partisan, since they cannot be mounted from some wholly neutral and Olympian standpoint, should not therefore be regarded as viciously circular. They do, within the limits of our necessary involvement in a particular phase of human history, nevertheless amount to reasons for making a certain sort of choice. A sailor may offer a valid and rational defence of the structure and design of the rudder he has built, even though he was born on ship and recognizes that his view of how things should be done is itself conditioned by the traditions of life aboard this particular vessel.

The upshot of all this is that, despite the prevalence of pluralism and increasing awareness of cultural diversity, the adherent of the Christian spiritual tradition should not need to make any bones about defending that particular tradition wholeheartedly, and indeed trying to persuade others of its validity. Does that lead us back to 'exclusivism' – or worse, to the kind of religious imperialism that we now associate for example with the arrogant proselytising of some Victorian explorers?[37] It need not; and certainly should not. For anyone who subscribes to the authentic moral principles inherent in Christianity can hardly suppose that a surpassingly benevolent and loving creator could attach his favour to adherents purely in virtue of their doctrinal choices. Pauline theology, or at least some of the ways Paul expressed himself, have perhaps encouraged a distorted conception here, as if 'belief' in a certain doctrine could be sufficient for salvation, that belief then being construed in terms of a purely cognitive assent to some proposition (for example about the status of Jesus of Nazareth). Construed dogmatically and literalistically, this could result in an absurd and morally repugnant picture of divine judgement separating out those who have 'backed the right horse' – as in an episode from

---

37 One possible *via media* between pluralism and exclusivism is the 'inclusivist' position of Karl Rahner, which treats sincere adherents of other morally sound faiths as 'anonymous Christians' – those who are in fact saved by the redeeming work of Christ, even though they lack explicit knowledge of the way God's grace has been manifested. See K. Rahner, 'Christianity and the Non-Christian Religions' [notes of a lecture delivered on 28 April 1961] in J. Hick and B. Hebblethwaite (eds.), *Christianity and Other Religions* (Philadelphia: Fortress Press, 1981), ch. 3, esp. p. 75; repr. in Peterson et al., *Philosophy of Religion*, pp. 549ff. This is a theologically ingenious position, though because it is so explicitly *parti pris* I suspect it is unlikely to achieve much mileage in philosophical debate about the relationship between Christianity and other faiths.

the subversive cartoon series 'South Park', which shows a group of recently departed souls gathering anxiously in a large hotel anteroom until an angel marches up to the podium with a golden envelope and says: 'Thank you for your patience folks, I know you're all waiting to know who is going to heaven. And the right answer was . . . The Mormons!'[38]

What one believes does, of course, make a difference; but Paul's stress on *pistis* ('belief') is surely best construed as underlining the importance he attached to trust in the saving power of Christ – something manifested in the actual life and action of the convert. So in this sense the imperatives of morality always take precedence over doctrinal and metaphysical disputes, and the validity of salvific action is always measured by a change of heart and resulting moral growth rather than merely conformity to the tenets of an established religion. Paul's own journey is a striking illustration of this point, since he sacrificed the framework that had hitherto made sense of his life. For someone of his background to accept that the Torah was superseded must have been as wrenching as it would now be for a devout Christian to abandon the idea of the unique role of Christ, or for a Muslim the prophetic primacy of Mohammed. Such doctrinal shifts will always seem monstrous blasphemies for the religious zealot – their mere contemplation deserving of the direst penalties. But if a religious stance is to preserve its vital moral core, zeal for dogma must always be tempered by openness to the possibility of learning from others, and above all respect and compassion for all humankind.

History, of course, has gone otherwise. Christianity, for example, has often fought under the banners of '*Nullo alio nomine*' and '*Salus extra ecclesiam non est*': under no name but that of Christ can we be saved, and outside his Church there is no salvation;[39] and in the name of those slogans it has sometimes forgotten the moral heart of the Gospel it is zealous to promote. But let me end this section by quoting one theologian who takes these Christo-centric and ecclesiocentric slogans very seriously, but at the same time underlines the core message of the Church in terms of which the slogans should be interpreted, namely that the basis of the fellowship of believers 'is not of the order of the intellect and of ideas, but

---

38 Or one may substitute the name of any favourite, or least favourite, group. I hope it is clear that in recalling this piece of satirical television, I mean no disrespect to any particular religious sect or denomination; the point of the anecdote is simply to highlight the dubiousness of any conception of the deity that conceives him as bestowing rewards *simply and solely* on the basis of sectarian membership.

39 'No other name', Acts 4:12; 'no salvation outside the Church', Augustine *On Baptism* [*De Baptismo contra Donatistas*, 400], IV, xvii, 24.

of the heart and of love.' Love and friendship, Jacques Maritain insists, 'does not go out to essences nor to qualities nor to ideas, but to persons', and he adds this heartfelt peroration:

In the common experience of human misery, in the common sorrow of great catastrophes, in humiliation and distress, under the blows of the executioner or the bombs of total war, in concentration camps, in the hovels of starving people in great cities, in any common *necessity*, the doors of solitude open and man recognizes man. Man also recognizes man when the sweetness of a great joy or of a great love for an instant clears his eyes. Whenever he does a service to his fellow men or is helped by them, whenever he shares the same elementary actions and the same elementary emotions, whenever he truly considers his neighbour, the simplest action discovers for him, both in others and in himself, the common resources and the common goodness – primitive, rudimentary, wounded, unconscious and repressed, of human nature. At once the realness of equality and community in nature is revealed to him as a very precious thing, an unknown marvel, a fundamental basis of existence, more important than all the differences and inequalities superimposed upon it. When he returns to his routine pleasures, he will have forgotten this discovery.[40]

Here we find not simply a recognition of the primacy of moral action over theory and doctrine, but a deeper understanding of how the two domains are interfused: theology is linked to a certain set of moral commitments, which in turn feed back into the theology, enriching and invigorating it. The need for awareness of our common humanity, and the ever-present imperative to reach out to others, are not extraneous demands on Christian theology but its life and soul.

6 IMAGES OF INTEGRATION

Heaven doth with us, as we with torches do,
Not light them for themselves. For if our virtues
Did not go forth of us, t'were all alike
As if we had them not. Shakespeare, *Measure for Measure.*[41]

Consideration of the problem posed by various differing traditions of spirituality has brought us round to the integral and absolutely indispensable connections between religious, theological, and moral thought which in one way or another have informed so much of the discussion throughout this book. In drawing to a close, it is worth focusing on how well that

40 Maritain, *Redeeming the Time*, pp. 15f.
41 William Shakespeare, *Measure for Measure* [c. 1604], I. i.

link is illustrated in some reflections by Simone Weil on the mystery of the Trinity, which have recently been developed further by the contemporary theologian Mark McIntosh. Weil writes that 'Pure friendship is an image of the original and perfect friendship that belong to the Trinity and is the very essence of God. It is impossible for two human beings to be one while scrupulously respecting the distance that separates them, unless God is present in each of them'.[42] And McIntosh adds to this model of friendship as image of the Trinity the idea of *selfhood as constituted by its relationship to the other*. Despite the language of 'self-giving', what is involved, argues McIntosh, is not a 'displacement of the self in favour of the other', but rather

a complete freedom from self-preoccupation – an extreme attentiveness to the other which is actually the vitalizing of the self and its empowering beyond its 'ordinary' self-conception . . . The divine activity of being God, namely the infinite self-bestowal of the Trinitarian persons one to another, is the eternal mutual activity of 'selving' which alone sustains particular identity. It is this activity that evokes human identity in the first place, and it is by ever-less-obstructed participation in this activity that human identity flourishes. So the reality we call human selfhood is constituted by its basis in the infinite self-giving of trinitarian life.[43]

On the mundane or secular level, what is envisaged here broadly corresponds, I think, to the Aristotelian triadic conception of virtue, as flanked by two corresponding and opposite vices: the achievement of true human selfhood is a normative state which lies between a vice of excess (self preoccupation, self-aggrandisement, the desire to occupy all available space), and a vice of deficiency (lack of self-esteem, masochistic self-abasement). In the middle lies what Aristotle called *philautia* – that legitimate love of self that is grounded in authentic esteem of oneself as one who loves and is loved.[44]

The Aristotelian idea has a psychoanalytic analogue. To be able to confront the other respectfully, making room, allowing their nature to flourish, yet without a subordination, without seeing oneself as merely

---

42 Simone Weil, *Waiting for God* [*L'attente de Dieu*, c. 1942, first pub. 1950] transl. E. Craufurd (New York: Harper and Row, 1973), p. 208. Cited in McIntosh, *Mystical Theology*, p. 236.
43 McIntosh, *Mystical Theology*, p. 238.
44 For Aristotle's triadic structure, with each virtue being flanked by a vice of excess on one side, and a vice of deficiency on the other, see *Nicomachean Ethics* [c. 325 BCE], bk. II, chs. iv-vii. For his account of the vice of *pleonexia* (the Greek term for the tendency to grab more than your fair share), and his contrast between this and *philautia*, legitimate self-esteem, see *Nicomachean Ethics*, bk. IX, chs. iv-viii. See also Cottingham. 'Partiality and the Virtues', in Crisp (ed.), *How Should One Live*, p. 64.

instrumental – this, as the psychologist Melanie Klein has insightfully argued, is the paradigm of what happens in a truly mature human relationship. The growth to human maturity involves leaving behind the childish desire to control and dominate, a relic of the infant's rage against a world it cannot control. As these dark images are replaced by the healthier models of concern and affection, of mutual trust and letting be, there remains, to be sure, a vulnerability: but it loses its character of abjectness and abandonment as we realize that being caringly responsive to the genuine otherness of the other, and (which is perhaps harder still) allowing them reciprocally to be responsive to us as we open our hearts in trust, are integral to one's very constitution as a self.[45]

What the Trinitarian images of Christianity add to this, at one level, is a *vehicle* for focused understanding: the figure of Christ the Son becomes (in a way not dissimilar to that envisaged in the writings of Carl Jung)[46] a kind of icon of the self, and is related in just this mutually trustful way to the Father; while the Spirit is an icon of the vivifying power that flows from this perfect balance. So one could say that here the secular morality of Aristotle, the psychotherapeutic ideas of Klein and Jung, and the religious iconography of Christianity all converge: a philosophical model of the true friendship that is the key to virtuous and fulfilled existence is supported by a psychological model of what it means to achieve a healthy interior life; and both receive enduring expression in the ancient trinitarian formula, which is in turn incorporated into daily spiritual praxis that reinforces the relevant insights in such a way as to promote further moral and psychological growth.

Talking of the religious language as a 'vehicle' may suggest a kind of optional extra – rather as if the thematic insights provided by thinkers like Aristotle, or by the psychoanalytic writers, were set to music, or expressed in some other vivid art form, which captured the imagination but did not add to the content. But our earlier discussion of the dimensions of meaning conveyed by figurative and symbolic modes of discourse[47]

---

45 Compare Melanie Klein: 'If love has not been smothered under resentment . . . but has been firmly established in the mind, trust in other people and belief in one's own goodness are like a rock which withstands the blow of circumstance . . . Then a man can distribute to others the help and love of which he himself is in need.' 'Love, Guilt and Reparation', in Melanie Klein, *Love, Guilt and Reparation and Other Works 1921-1945* (New York: Free Press, 1975), p. 341. For some insightful reflections on this passage, see Edward Harcourt, 'Psychological Maturation and Learning to be Good', typescript.

46 For the idea of Christ as an icon of the self as it appears in the psychoanalytic theories of Carl Jung, see above Ch. 4, n. 29.

47 See Ch. 5, above.

should have put paid to the notion that the narratives and symbols, or the praxis and liturgy, of Christianity can be construed as a merely decorative flourish, superimposed on human insights that can survive perfectly well if the decoration is stripped away. The language and liturgy of a living religion are not simply 'vehicles' for the underlying insights they convey – like the talc that is used in tablets to make them apt for carrying the active ingredients; rather, they are themselves the potentizing elements that heal and enrich and transform the life of the believer; for without such incorporation into a sustaining form of life, the results of moral philosophy or psychotherapeutic theory would remain simply formulae, of no more power to enact a change in the subject than the mere chemical formula of a tablet could do its work without being instantiated and incorporated into the actual manufacture of the medicine.

But even if all this is true, is a religious form of life something that can be embraced by those who are committed to the ideals of intellectual integrity and philosophical vigour? In an earlier age of faith, the goals of religion and of philosophy were regarded as being in harmony. In our modern culture, they have often been taken to be in discord. But that sense of dissonance has been artificially sustained, I believe, by the effects of the fragmented and compartmentalized environment in which so much academic debate now operates. Religion has been isolated as an object for dissection, scrutinized as a set of abstract doctrines, abstracted from the ethical commitment that makes it truly meaningful. It has been cut off from the spiritual praxis that makes it live, from the psychological and developmental story that links it to our human quest for self-understanding, from the linguistic domain of symbolic understanding and the multiple layers of significance that are its natural means of expression, and from the liturgical and sacramental tradition that sustains it. So lopped and trimmed, it is hardly surprising that a formerly flourishing plant appears to many as a sickly specimen, fit only to be disposed of as quickly as possible.

But once these branches are grafted back on, it becomes possible to have a different image of religion: one that reveals it not as a set of quasi-scientific hypotheses, but as nevertheless compatible with the results of science; not as a weird, irrational activity separated from the rest of our lives, but as an embodiment of the human quest for meaning which we all share. For we human beings were never meant to live fragmented lives, splitting off the intellect from the emotions, or keeping our theoretical beliefs neatly separated from our deepest commitments and responses. Rather, our inner and outer lives, our personal confrontation with the mystery of existence and our need to join with others in exploring the meaning of that mystery, call out to be integrated into a living structure that can sustain our energies and keep alive our hopes. Although all the specific secular disciplines and activities may be involved as contributors, no other form of human life – not philosophy, not psychoanalysis, not science, not politics, not even great art – is equipped for this quest in the way that religion, at its rare best, aspires to be: in a way that is truly unifying, and nurturing of our most precious human potential, the potential for wholeness or integrity. By incorporating into our lives, through the discipline of spiritual praxis, the deep need for a religious dimension in our human existence, we can reach towards that integrity, and perhaps, if the message of faith is true, begin to learn how to be grafted onto the true vine that is the image of the best that humanity can become.[48]

48 John, Ch. 15.

Bibliography

ACKRILL, J., *Aristotle the Philosopher* (Oxford: Oxford University Press, 1981).

ADAMS, D., *The Restaurant at the End of the Universe* (London: Pan Books, 1984).

ADAMS, R. M., 'A Modified Divine Command Theory of Ethical Wrongness', in G. Outka and J. P. Reeder (eds.), *Religion and Morality* (Garden City: Anchor, 1973), pp. 318–47.

ALSTON, W. P., *Divine Nature and Human Language* (Ithaca: Cornell University Press, 1989).

'Realism and Antirealism' in A. Hastings et al. (eds.), *The Oxford Companion to Christian Thought*.

ANON., *Catechism of the Catholic Church* (New York: Doubleday, 1995, rev. 1997).

ANSELM OF CANTERBURY, *Proslogion* [1077–8].

AQUINAS, THOMAS, *Catena Aurea* [1262–67], English transl. J. H. Newman [1841] (repr. London: The Saint Austin Press, 1997).

Summa contra Gentiles [1259–65], transl. A. C. Pegis (Notre Dame, Ill.: Notre Dame University Press, 1975).

Summa theologiae [1266–73], transl. Fathers of the English Dominican Province (London: Burns, Oates, and Washbourne, 1911).

ARISTOTLE, *Nicomachean Ethics* [c. 325 BCE], ed. T. Irwin (Indianapolis, Ind.: Hackett, 1985). Also in *The Ethics of Aristotle*, transl. J. Thomson, rev. H. Tredennick (Harmondsworth: Penguin, 1976).

ARMSTRONG, K., *A History of God* [1993] (London: Vintage, 1999).

ASHLEY, B. M. (ed.), *Thomas Aquinas, The Gifts of the Spirit* (New York: New City Press, 1995).

AUGUSTINE OF HIPPO, *Against Faustus the Manichean* [*Contra Faustum Manichaeum*, 400 CE], in P. Schaff (ed.), *A Select Library of the Nicene and Post-Nicene Fathers* (Oxford: Parker, 1899).

The City of God [*De civitate Dei*, 413–26 CE] transl. M. Dodds (Edinburgh: T. and T. Clark, 1871).

Confessions [*Confessiones*, c. 398 CE], transl. W. Watts (Cambridge, Mass.: Harvard University Press, 1912).

AYERS, M., *Locke* (London: Routledge, 1991).

BACON, FRANCIS, *Novum Organum* [1620], in *The Works of Francis Bacon,* ed. J. Spedding and R. E. Ellis, abr. J. M. Robinson (London: Routledge, 1905).

BARON, M., *Language and Relationship in Wordsworth's Writing* (London: Longman, 1995).

BARON, M. W., *Kantian Ethics Almost Without Apology* (Ithaca, N. Y.: Cornell University Press, 1995).

BENNETT, J., 'Descartes' Theory of Modality', *Philosophical Review* 88 (1979), pp. 639–67, repr. in J. Cottingham (ed.), *Descartes* (Oxford: Oxford University Press, 1998).

BENTHAM, JEREMY, *Principles of Morals and Legislation* [1789], ed. J. Burns and H. Hart (New York: Methuen, 1982).

BLACKBURN, S., *Think* (Oxford: Oxford University Press, 1999).

BLAKE, WILLIAM, 'Auguries of Innocence' [c. 1803], in *Complete Poems* ed. A. Ostriker (Harmondsworth: Penguin, 1978).

BLOOMFIELD, P., *Moral Reality* (Oxford: Oxford University Press, 2001).

BONAVENTURE, *Commentarii Sententiarum Petri Lombardi* [1248–55], in *Opera Omnia* (Collegium S. Bonaventurae: Quarachhi, 1891).

BORG, E., 'An Expedition Abroad: Metaphor, Thought and Reporting', in *Midwest Studies in Philosophy* XXV (2001), ed. P. French and H. Wettstein (Oxford: Blackwell, 2001).

BROWN, S. (ed.), *Reason and Religion* (Cornell: Cornell University Press, 1977).

CALVIN, JOHN, *Institutes of the Christian Religion* [*Institutio Christianae religionis*, 1536], transl. H. Beveridge (London: Hatfield, 1599).

CAMUS, ALBERT, *The Myth of Sisyphus* [*Le Mythe de Sisyphe*, 1943], transl. J. O'Brian (Harmondsworth: Penguin, 1955).

CAPUTO, J., *Religion* (London: Routledge, 2001).

CAPUTO, J. D. AND SCANLON, M. J. (eds.), *God, the Gift, and Postmodernism* (Bloomington: Indiana University Press, 1999).

CICERO, *De Finibus* [45 BCE], in M. R. Wright, *Cicero on Stoic Good and Evil* (Warminster: Aris and Phillips, 1991).

COMTE-SPONVILLE, A., *A Short Treatise of the Great Virtues* [*Petit Traité des Grandes Vertus*, 1996] (London: Heinemann, 2002).

COOPER, D. E., *Metaphor* (Oxford: Blackwell, 1986).

COPLESTON, F., *A History of Philosophy* [1950] (New York: Doubleday 1962).

CORNFORD, F. M., *Plato's Cosmology* (London: Routledge, 1937),

CORNWALL, J., 'Hawking's Quest: A Search without End', *The Tablet*, 27 March 2004.

COTTINGHAM, J., *On the Meaning of Life* (London: Routledge, 2003).

   Philosophy and the Good Life: Reason and the Passions in Greek, Cartesian and Psychoanalytic Ethics (Cambridge: Cambridge University Press, 1998).

COTTINGHAM, J. (ed.), *Western Philosophy* (Oxford: Blackwell, 1996).

COTTINGHAM, J., 'Descartes and the Voluntariness of Belief', *Monist* 85:3 (October 2002), pp. 343–60.

'Our Natural Guide: Conscience, "Nature" and Moral Experience', in D. S. Oderberg and T. Chappell (eds.), *Human Values* (London: Palgrave, 2004), pp. 11–31.

'Partiality and the Virtues', in R. Crisp (ed.), *How Should One Live? Essays on the Philosophy of Virtue* (Oxford: Oxford University Press, 1996), pp. 57–76.

'Partiality, Favouritism and Morality', *Philosophical Quarterly* 36 (1986), pp. 357–73.

'Spirituality, Science and Morality', in D. Carr and J. Haldane (eds.), *Essays on Spirituality and Education* (London: Routledge, 2003), pp. 40–54.

CRITCHLEY, S. AND BERNASCONI, R. (eds.), *The Cambridge Companion to Levinas* (Cambridge: Cambridge University Press, 2002).

DANTE ALIGHIERI, *The Divine Comedy* [*La Divina Comedia*, c. 1300–10], ed. and transl. G. Bickersteth (Oxford: Blackwell, 1981).

DARWALL, S., *The British Moralists and the Internal 'Ought'* (Cambridge: Cambridge University Press, 1995).

DAVIES, B., *Aquinas* (London: Continuum, 2002).

DAWKINS, R., *The Selfish Gene* (Oxford: Oxford University Press, 1976).

DERRIDA, J., *Margins of Philosophy* [*Marges de la philosophie*, 1972], transl. A. Bass (Brighton: Harvester, 1982).

DESCARTES, RENÉ, *Œuvres de Descartes*, ed. C. Adam and P. Tannery (12 vols., rev. edn., Paris: Vrin/CNRS, 1964–76) [The standard Franco-Latin edition, referred to as 'AT'].

The Philosophical Writings of Descartes, transl. J. Cottingham, R. Stoothoff, and D. Murdoch, vols. I and II (Cambridge: Cambridge University Press, 1985); vol. III, *The Correspondence*, by the same translators plus A. Kenny (Cambridge University Press, 1991) [The standard English edition, referred to as 'CSM' and 'CSMK'].

DUMMETT, M., 'The Intelligibility of Eucharistic Doctrine', in W. J. Abraham and S. W. Holtzer (eds.), *The Rationality of Religious Belief* (Oxford: Clarendon Press, 1987).

DUNNE, J. S., *Reading the Gospel* (Notre Dame, Ind.: University of Notre Dame Press, 2000).

EMPSON, W., *Seven Types of Ambiguity* [1930] (Harmondsworth: Penguin, 1995).

EPICTETUS, *Discourses* [*Diatribae*, c. 100 CE], transl. W. A. Oldfather (Cambridge, Mass.: Harvard University Press, 1928).

FLEW, A., 'Theology and Falsification', in B. Mitchell (ed.), *The Philosophy of Religion* (London: Methuen, 1971).

FOUCAULT, M., 'Subjectivité et vérité', in *Cités*, ed. Y. C. Zarka (Vendôme: Presses Universitaires de France), vol. II (March 2000).

FREGE, GOTTLOB, *The Basic Laws of Arithmetic* [*Die Grundgesetze der Arithmetik*, vol. I, 1893], transl. M. Furth (Berkeley: University of California Press, 1964).

FREUD, SIGMUND, *Introductory Lectures on Psychoanalysis* [*Vorlesungen zur Einführung in die Psychoanalyse*, 1916–17], transl. J. Riviere (London: Routledge, 1922).

The Penguin Freud Library, ed. A. Richards and A. Dickson, 15 vols. (London: Penguin Books, 1985) [cited as *PFL*].

Standard Edition of the Complete Psychological Works of Sigmund Freud, ed. J. Strachey (London: Hogarth, 1953–74).

FROMM, E., *Psychoanalysis and Religion* (New Haven: Yale University Press, 1950).

GALILEO GALILEI, *Il Saggiatore* ('The Assayer') [1623], in *Opere*, ed. A. Favaro (Florence: Barbera, 1889–1901, repr. 1968).

GARDNER, S., *Irrationality and the Philosophy of Psychoanalysis* (Cambridge: Cambridge University Press, 1993).

Kant and the Critique of Pure Reason (London: Routledge, 1999).

GELLNER, E., *The Psychoanalytic Movement* (London: Granada, 1985).

GEUSS, R., 'Poetry and Knowledge', *Arion* 11:1 (Spring/Summer 2003), pp. 1–31.

GLENDINNING, S. (ed.), *Edinburgh Encyclopedia of Continental Philosophy* (Edinburgh: Edinburgh University Press, 1999).

GLOCK, H.-J., *A Wittgenstein Dictionary* (Oxford: Blackwell, 1996).

GOLDIE, P., *The Emotions* (Oxford: Clarendon Press, 2000).

HABERMAS, J., *Postmetaphysical Thinking* [*Nachmetaphysisches Denken*, 1988], transl. Hohengarten (Cambridge: Polity Press, 1992).

Texte und Contexte [1991], transl. in J. Habermas, *Religion and Rationality* (Cambridge: Polity Press, 2002).

HACKER, P. S. M., *Insight and Illusion: Themes in the Philosophy of Wittgenstein* (Oxford: Oxford University Press, rev. edn. 1988).

HADOT, P., *Philosophy as a Way of Life* (Cambridge, Mass.: Blackwell, 1995). Originally published as *Exercises spirituels et philosophie antique* (Paris: Etudes Augustiniennes, 1987).

HALDANE J. (ed.), *Mind, Metaphysics and Value in the Thomistic and Analytical Traditions* (Notre Dame, Ind.: University of Notre Dame Press, 2002).

HAMPSON, D., *After Christianity* (London: SCM Press 1996; 2nd edn. 2002).

HARE J. E., *The Moral Gap: Kantian Ethics, Human Limits and God's Assistance* (Oxford: Clarendon Press, 1996).

HARVEY, P., *An Introduction to Buddhist Ethics* (Cambridge: Cambridge University Press, 2000).

HASTINGS, A., MASON, A., AND PYPER, H. (eds.), *The Oxford Companion to Christian Thought* (Oxford: Oxford University Press, 2000).

HAWKING, S., *A Brief History of Time* (London: Bantam Press, 1988).

'Gödel and the End of Physics', at http://www.damtp.cam.ac.uk/strtst/dirac.hawking/.

HEGEL, GEORG FRIEDRICH, *Phenomenology of Mind* [*Phänomenologie des Geistes*, 1807], transl. A. V. Miller (Oxford: Oxford University Press, 1977).

HELM, P., *Faith and Understanding* (Edinburgh: Edinburgh University Press, 1997).

HICK, J., *Evil and the God of Love* [1966] (London: Macmillan, 1985).

An *Interpretation of Religion: Human Responses to the Transcendent* (Basingstoke: Macmillan Press, 1989).

'Religious Pluralism' [1985], repr. in M. Peterson et al., *Philosophy of Religion: Selected Readings*, pp. 567–8.

HICK J. AND B. HEBBLETHWAITE (eds.), *Christianity and Other Religions* (Philadelphia: Fortress Press, 1981).

HOPKINS, GERARD MANLEY, *Poems (1876–1889)*, ed. W. H. Gardner, *The Poems and Prose of Gerard Manley Hopkins* (Harmondsworth: Penguin, 1953).

HUME, DAVID, *Dialogues concerning Natural Religion* [c. 1755, first published posthumously 1779], ed. H. Aiken (New York: Hafner, 1948).

An *Enquiry concerning Human Understanding* [1748], ed. L. A. Selby-Bigge, rev. P. H. Nidditch (Oxford: Clarendon Press, 1975). Also available in Oxford Philosophical Texts series, ed. T. L. Beauchamp (Oxford: Oxford University Press, 2000).

A *Treatise of Human Nature* [1739–40], ed. L. A. Selby-Bigge, rev. P. H. Nidditch (Oxford: Clarendon Press, 1978). Also available in Oxford Philosophical Texts series, ed. D. F. and M. J. Norton (Oxford: Oxford University Press, 2000).

INWAGEN, P. VAN, 'Metaphysics', in Hastings et al. (eds.), *The Oxford Companion to Christian Thought*, pp. 426–9.

JACKSON, F., *From Metaphysics to Ethics* (Oxford: Clarendon Press, 1998).

JAMES, S., *Passion and Action: The Emotions in Seventeenth-Century Philosophy* (Oxford: Clarendon Press, 1997).

JAMES, WILLIAM, *The Will to Believe and Other Essays in Popular Philosophy* (New York: Longmans Green, 1897).

JONES, W., 'Self-Deception, Religious Conversion, and Pascal's Wager', *Journal of the History of Philosophy* 36:2 (April 1998), pp. 167–88.

JULIAN OF NORWICH, *The Revelations of Divine Love* [1373] (London: Hodder and Stoughton, 1999).

JUNG, CARL G., *Collected Works*, ed. H. Read et al. (London: Routledge, 1953–79) [cited as *CW*].

Modern Man in Search of a Soul. Essays from the 1920s and 1930s, transl. C. F. Baynes (London: Routledge, 1933).

KANT, IMMANUEL, *Critique of Practical Reason* [*Kritik der Praktischen Vernunft*, 1788], transl. T. K. Abbott (London: Longmans, 1873, 6th edn. 1909).

Critique of Pure Reason [*Kritik der Reinen Vernunft*, 1781/1787], transl. N. Kemp Smith (New York: Macmillan, 1929).

Groundwork for the Metaphysic of Morals [*Grundlegung zur Metaphysik der Sitten*, 1785], transl. H. J. Paton (London: Hutchinson, 1948). Also available in Oxford Philosophical Texts series, ed. T. E. Hill Jr and A. Zweig (Oxford: Oxford University Press, 2003).

Kant's gesammelte Schriften (Akademie edition Berlin: Reimer/De Gruyter, 1900–).

Prolegomena to any Future Metaphysic that will be able to present itself as a Science [*Prolegomena zu einer jeden künftigen Metaphysik die als Wissenschaft wird auftreten können*, 1783], transl. P. G. Lucas (Manchester: Manchester University Press, 1953). Also available in Oxford Philosophical Texts series, ed. G. Zöller (Oxford: Oxford University Press, 2004).

KEKES, J., *Pluralism in Philosophy: Changing the* Subject (Ithaca: Cornell University Press, 2000).

KERR, FERGUS, *Theology after Wittgenstein* (Oxford: Blackwell, 1986).

KIERKEGAARD, SØREN, *Concluding Unscientific Postscript* [*Afsluttende Uvidenskabelig Efterskrift*], transl. D. F. Swensen (Princeton, N. J.: Princeton University Press, 1941).

Fear and Trembling [*Frygt og Bæven*, 1843], transl. in J. Chamberlain and J. Rée (eds.), *The Kierkegaard Reader* (Oxford: Blackwell, 2001).

KIRWAN, C., *Augustine* (London: Routledge, 1989).

KOLAKOWSKI, L., *Religion* (South Bend: St Augustine's Press, 2001).

KRETZMANN, N. AND STUMP, E. (eds.), *The Cambridge Companion to Aquinas* (Cambridge: Cambridge University Press, 1993).

KRIPKE, S., *Naming and Necessity* (Oxford: Oxford University Press, 1980).

KUHN, T., *The Structure of Scientific Revolutions* (Chicago: University of Chicago Press, 1962).

LAMBECK, M. (ed.), *A Reader in the Anthropology of Religion* (Oxford: Blackwell, 2002).

LEAR, J., *Happiness, Death, and the Remainder of Life* (Cambridge, Mass.: Harvard University Press, 2000).

LEIBNIZ, GOTTFRIED WILHELM, *Theodicy* [*Essais de théodicée*, 1710], transl. E. M. Huggard (New York: Bobbs Merrill, 1966).

LEITER, B., (ed.), *The Future for Philosophy* (Oxford: Clarendon Press, 2004).

LEVINAS, EMMANUEL, *In the Time of the Nations* [*A l'heure des nations*, 1988], transl. M. B. Smith (London: Athlone Press, 1944).

LEWIS, C. DAY, *The Gate and Other Poems* (London: Jonathan Cape, 1962).

LEWIS, C. S., 'Priestesses in the Church' [1948], in *Faith, Christianity and the Church* (London: Harper Collins, 2000).

LOCKE, JOHN, *An Essay concerning Human Understanding* [1690], ed. P. H. Nidditch (Oxford: Clarendon Press, 1975; repr. 1984).

LONG, A. A. AND SEDLEY, D. N., *The Hellenistic Philosophers* (Cambridge: Cambridge University Press, 1987).

LOUTH, A., *Discerning the Mystery* (Oxford: Clarendon Press, 1983).

LOUX, M. J. AND ZIMMERMAN, D. W. (eds.), *Oxford Handbook of Metaphysics* (Oxford: Oxford University Press, 2003).

LOVIBOND, S., *Ethical Formation* (Cambridge, Mass.: Harvard University Press, 2002).

LOWE, J., *A Survey of Metaphysics* (Oxford: Oxford University Press, 2002).

LOYOLA, IGNATIUS, *Spiritual Exercises* [*Ejercicios espirituales*, c. 1522–41], transl. J. Munitz and P. Endean (Harmondsworth: Penguin, 1996).

LYOTARD, J.-F., *The Postmodern Condition* [*La condition postmoderne*, 1979], transl. G. Bennington and G. Massumi (Manchester: Manchester University Press, 1984).

MACINTYRE, A., *Dependent Rational Animals* (London: Duckworth, 1999).

MACKIE, J., *The Miracle of* Theism (Oxford: Clarendon Press, 1982).

MAGEE, B., *Schopenhauer* (Oxford: Clarendon Press, 1983).

MARCEL, GABRIEL, *Being and Having* [*Etre et Avoir*, 1935] (London: Fontana, 1965).

MARITAIN, J. *Redeeming the Time*, transl. H. Binsse (London: The Centenary Press, 1943).

MARTIN, T., *Oppression and the Human Condition* (Lanham, Md.: Rowman and Littlefield, 2002).

MATTHEWS, G. (ed.), *The Augustinian Tradition* (Berkeley: University of California Press, 1999).

McDOWELL, J., *Mind and World* (Cambridge, Mass.: Harvard University Press, 1994).

Mind, Value and Reality (Cambridge, Mass.: Harvard University Press, 1998).

'Values and Secondary Properties', in T. Honderich (ed.), *Morality and Objectivity* (London: Routledge, 1985), pp. 110–29.

McINTOSH, M. A., *Mystical Theology* (Oxford: Blackwell, 1998).

MEISSNER, W., *Psychoanalysis and Religious Experience* (New Haven: Yale University Press, 1984).

MERTON, T., *Contemplative Prayer* (London: Darton, Longman and Todd, 1969).

Seeds of Contemplation [1961] (Wheathamstead: Anthony Clarke, 1972),

MIGNE, J. P. (ed.), *Patrologia Graeca* (Paris, 1844–55).

Patrologia Latina (Paris, 1857–66).

MILL, JOHN STUART, *Utilitarianism* [1861], ed. M. Warnock (Glasgow: Collins, 1962).

MOORE, A., *Reason and Christian Faith* (Cambridge: Cambridge University Press, 2003).

MULHALL, S., *Inheritance and Originality: Wittgenstein, Heidegger, Kierkegaard* (Oxford: Clarendon Press, 2001).

MURDOCH, IRIS, *The Sovereignty of the Good* (London: Routledge, 1970).

NAGEL, T., *Mortal Questions* (Cambridge: Cambridge University Press, 1979).

NEURATH, OTTO, 'Protokol Sentences' ['Protokolsatze', 1932], transl. G. Schick, in A. J. Ayer (ed.), *Logical Positivism* (New York: Free Press, 1959), pp. 199–208.

NIETZSCHE, FRIEDRICH, *The Will to Power* [*Der Wille zur Macht*, 1888], transl. W. Kaufmann and R. J. Hollingdale (New York: Random House, 1975).

NOZICK, R. *Philosophical Explanations* (Oxford: Clarendon Press, 1981).

NUSSBAUM, M., *The Fragility of Goodness* (Cambridge University Press, 1986).

Love's Knowledge (Oxford: Oxford University Press, 1990).

NUSSBAUM, M. (ed.), *The Poetics of Therapy*, Apeiron XXIII, no. 4 (December 1990).

ODERBERG, D. S., 'How to Win Essence Back from Essentialists', *Philosophical Writings* (Autumn, 2001), pp. 27–45.

ODERBERG D. S. AND CHAPPELL, T. (eds.), *Human Values; New Essays on Ethics and Natural Law* (London: Palgrave, 2005).

O'NEILL, O., *Constructions of Reason* (Cambridge: Cambridge University Press, 1989).

PALMER, M., *Freud and Jung on Religion* (London: Routledge, 1977).

PASCAL, BLAISE, *Pensées* [1670], ed. L. Lafuma (Paris: Seuil, 1962).

PEIRCE, CHARLES SANDERS, *Collected Papers* (Cambridge, Mass.: Harvard University Press, 1958).

PETERSON, M., et al. (eds.), *Philosophy of Religion: Selected Readings* (Oxford: Oxford University Press, 1996, 2nd edn. 2001).

Reason and Religious Belief (Oxford: Oxford University Press, 1988).

PLANTINGA, A., 'Religion and Epistemology', in E. Craig (ed.), *Routledge Encyclopedia of Philosophy* (London: Routledge, 1998). vol. 8, pp. 209–18.

PLATO, *Euthyphro* [c. 390 BCE], transl. F. Church (New York: Prentice Hall, 1956).

Meno [c. 380 BCE], transl. W. C. K. Guthrie (Harmondsworth: Penguin, 1956).

Timaeus [c. 360 BCE] in Plato's Cosmology, ed. and transl. H. Cornford (London: Routledge, 1937).

PLOTINUS, *Enneads* [c. 250 CE], transl. A. H. Armstrong, 7 vols. (Cambridge, MA: Loeb Classical Library, 1967–88).

POPPER, KARL, *Conjectures and Refutations* (London: Routledge, 1963).

PROUST, MARCEL, *A la recherche du temps perdu* [1913–27], transl. L. Scott Moncrieff (London: Chatto and Windus, 1967).

PUTNAM, H., *Philosophical Papers, Vol. 2: Mind, Language and Reality* (Cambridge: Cambridge University Press. 1985),

QUINE, W. V. O., *From a Logical Point of View* (Cambridge, Mass.: Harvard University Press, 1951; rev. edn., New York: Harper and Row, 1963).

RAHNER, K., *Foundations of Christian Faith* [*Grundkurs des Glaubens*, 1976] (London: Darton, Longman and Todd, 1978).

The Practice of Faith: A Handbook of Contemporary Spirituality [*Praxis des Glaubens: Geistliches Lesebuch*, 1982] (London: SCM Press, 1985).

RAPHAEL, D. D. (ed.), *British Moralists* (Oxford: Clarendon Press, 1969).

RATZINGER, J., *God and The World* [*Gott und die Welt*, 2000] (San Francisco: Ignatius Press, 2002)

RICE, P. AND WAUGH, P. (eds.), *Modern Literary Theory* (New York: Oxford University Press, 1989; 4th edn. 2001).

RILKE, RAINER MARIA, *Duineser Elegien* [1922], ed. and transl. in J. B. Leishman and S. Spender (eds.), *Rainer Maria Rilke: Duino Elegies* (London: Hogarth Press, 1939; 4th edn. 1968).

ROBINSON, D. M., 'How Religious Experience "Works"', *Review of Metaphysics* 224 (June 2003), pp. 763–78.

RORTY, R., *Philosophy and the Mirror of Nature* (Oxford: Blackwell, 1980).

ROWE, W., 'Religious Pluralism', in *Religious Studies* 35 (1999), pp. 139–50.

RUNZO, J. (ed.), *Is God Real?* (New York: St Martin's Press, 1993).

RUSSELL, BERTRAND, *The Problems of Philosophy* [1912] (Oxford: Oxford University Press, 1967).

'Why I am Not a Christian' [1927], in *Why I am Not a Christian, and Other Essays* (London: George Allen and Unwin, 1957), pp. 1–17.

SARTRE, JEAN-PAUL, *The Emotions: Outline of a Theory* [*Esquisse d'une théorie des emotions*, 1939], transl. B. Frechtmann (Secaucus, N. J.: Citadel Press, 1975).

SAYERS, DOROTHY, *The Mind of the Maker* (London: Methuen, 1941).

SCANLON, T., *What we Owe to Each Other* (Cambridge, Mass.: Belknap, 1998).

SCHOPENHAUER, ARTHUR, *The World as Will and Representation* [*Die Welt als Wille und Vorstellung*, 1818], transl. E. F. J. Payne (New York: Dover, 1966).

SCOTUS, JOHN DUNS, *Quaestiones in libros metaphysicos*, in *Opera Omnia* (Paris: Vives, 1891–5).

SENECA, *Epistulae Morales* ['Moral Letters', c.64 CE], ed. R. M. Gummere (London: Heineman, 1925).

SHAFER-LANDAU, R., *Moral Realism* (Oxford: Oxford University Press, 2003).

SHAKESPEARE, WILLIAM, *Measure for Measure* [c. 1604], in *Complete Works*, ed. C. J. Sisson (London: Odhams, 1953).

Othello [1604] in *Complete Works* ed. C. J. Sisson (London: Odhams, 1953).

SINGER, P., 'Famine, Affluence and Morality', *Philosophy and Public Affairs* (1972), pp. 229–43.

SOSKICE, J. M., 'Theological Realism', in W. Abraham and S. Holtzer, *The Rationality of Religious Belief* (Oxford: Clarendon Press, 1987) pp. 105–19.

SPERBER, D. AND WILSON, D., 'Loose Talk', *Proceedings of the Aristotelian Society* LXXXVI (1986).

SPINOZA, *Ethics* [*Ethica ordine geometrico demonstrata*, c. 1665], in *Opera*, ed. C. Gebhardt, 3 vols. (Heidelberg: Winters, 1925, repr. 1972). Transl. in *The Collected Works of Spinoza*, ed. E. Curley, vol. I (Princeton: Princeton University Press, 1985).

STOCKER R., with E. Hegeman, *Valuing Emotions* (Cambridge: Cambridge University Press, 1996).

STRATTON-LAKE, P. (ed.), *Ethical Intuitionism* (Oxford: Clarendon Press, 2002).

STRAWSON, P., *Individuals* (London: Methuen, 1959).

STUMP, E., *Aquinas* (London: Routledge, 2002).

SWINBURNE, R., *The Existence of God* (Oxford: Clarendon, 1979, 2nd edn. 2004).

Revelation: From Metaphor to Analogy (Oxford: Clarendon Press, 1992).

TAYLOR, C., *Sources of the Self* (Cambridge: Cambridge University Press, 1989).

TERTULLIAN, *De carne Christi* ('On the Incarnation of Christ') [c. 200 CE], ed. and transl. E. Evans (London: SPCK, 1956).

TURNER, D., *The Darkness of God* (Cambridge: Cambridge University Press, 1995).

UNDERHILL, E., *The Essentials of Mysticism and Other Essays* (Oxford: Oneworld, 1995).

VERMES, G., *Jesus the Jew* [1973] (London: SCM, 1983).

VOLTAIRE, *Philosophical Letters* [*Lettres philosophiques*, 1733], ed. E. Dilworth (New York: Macmillan, 1961).

WAINWRIGHT, W., *Reason and the Heart* (Ithaca, N. Y.: Cornell University Press, 1995).

WARD, G. (ed.), *The Postmodern God: A Theological Reader* (Oxford: Blackwell, 1997).

WAUGH, EVELYN, *Unconditional Surrender* (London: Chapman and Hall, 1961).

WEBSTER, JOHN, *The Duchess of Malfi* [1614] (Oxford: Oxford Paperbacks, 1996).

WEIL, SIMONE, *Waiting for God* [*L'attente de Dieu*, 1950], transl. E. Craufurd (New York: Harper and Row, 1973).

WHITE, V., *God and the Unconscious* [1952] (London: Collins, 1960).

WILLIAMS, B., *Problems of the Self* (Cambridge: Cambridge University Press, 1973).

    Truth and Truthfulness (Princeton: Princeton University Press, 2002).

WILLIAMS, R., 'Belief, Unbelief and Religious Education' (London: Lambeth Palace Press Office, 8 March 2004).

WINNICOT, D., *Playing and Reality* (London: Tavistock, 1971).

WITTGENSTEIN, LUDWIG, *Culture and Value: A Selection from the Posthumous Remains* [*Vermischte Bemerkungen: Eine Auswahl aus dem Nachlass*, 1994], ed. G. H. von Wright, transl. P. Winch (Oxford: Blackwell, rev. edn. 1998).

    Philosophical Investigations [*Philosophische Untersuchungen*, 1953], transl. G. E. M. Anscombe (New York: Macmillan, 1958).

    Tractatus Logico-Philosophicus [1921], transl. D. F. Pears and B. F. McGuinness (London: Routledge, 1961).

WOLLHEIM, R., *The Thread of Life* (Cambridge, Mass.: Harvard University Press, 1984).

WORDSWORTH, WILLIAM, *Lines written a few miles above Tintern Abbey* [1798], and 'Ode, Intimations of Immortality from Recollections of Early Childhood' [1815 version], in S. Gill (ed.), *William Wordsworth: A Critical Edition of the Major Works* (Oxford: Oxford University Press, 1984).

WRIGHT, J., *The Sceptical Realism of David Hume* (Cambridge: Cambridge University Press, 1983).

WRIGHT, N. T., *The Resurrection of the Son of God* (Minneapolis: Fortress Press, 2003).

WRIGHT, N. T. AND BORG, M., *The Meaning of Jesus: Two Visions* (London: SPCK, 1999).

WYNN, M., *Emotional Experience and Religious Understanding: Integrating Perception Conception, and Feeling* (Cambridge: Cambridge University Press, 2005).

    'The Relationship of Religion and Ethics: A Comparison of Newman and Contemporary Philosophy of Religion', *Heythrop Journal*, 2005.

Index